Apocalyptic Paul

Apocalyptic Paul
Cosmos and Anthropos in Romans 5–8

Beverly Roberts Gaventa
Editor

BAYLOR UNIVERSITY PRESS

© 2013 by Baylor University Press
Waco, Texas 76798

All Rights Reserved. No part of this publication may be reproduced, stored in a retrieval system, or transmitted, in any form or by any means, electronic, mechanical, photocopying, recording or otherwise, without the prior permission in writing of Baylor University Press.

Cover design by Cynthia Dunne, Blue Farm Graphics
Cover image: Eighth-century mosaic of St. Paul the Apostle; a feature of the papal Lateran Palace, now on display in the Vatican Museum, Rome.

First issued in paperback in July 2019 under ISBN 978-1-60258-970-4

The Library of Congress has cataloged the hardcover edition as follows:

Library of Congress Cataloging-in-Publication Data

Apocalyptic Paul : cosmos and anthropos in Romans 5–8 / Beverly Roberts Gaventa, editor.
 207 pages cm
 Includes bibliographical references and index.
 ISBN 978-1-60258-969-8 (hardback : alk. paper)
 1. Bible. Romans V–VIII—Criticism, interpretation, etc. I. Gaventa, Beverly Roberts, editor of compilation.
 BS2665.52.A66 2013
 227'.106--dc23
                       2013012373

Contents

Preface *Beverly Roberts Gaventa*		vii
1	Paul's Mythologizing Program in Romans 5–8 *Martinus C. de Boer*	1
2	Righteousness, Cosmic and Microcosmic *Stephen Westerholm*	21
3	A Tale of Two Gardens: Augustine's Narrative Interpretation of Romans 5 *Benjamin Myers*	39
4	Under Grace: The Christ-Gift and the Construction of a Christian *Habitus* *John M. G. Barclay*	59
5	The Shape of the "I": The Psalter, the Gospel, and the Speaker in Romans 7 *Beverly Roberts Gaventa*	77
6	Double Participation and the Responsible Self in Romans 5–8 *Susan Eastman*	93
7	The Love of God Is a Sovereign Thing: The Witness of Romans 8:31-39 and the Royal Office of Jesus Christ *Philip G. Ziegler*	111
8	Creation, Cosmos, and Conflict in Romans 8–9 *Neil Elliott*	131

Afterword: The Human Moral Drama *J. Louis Martyn*	157
Works Cited	167
List of Contributors	181
Index of Ancient Sources	183
Index of Authors	191
Subject Index	194

Preface

No syllable in Paul's letter to the Romans could be termed "neglected," but recent decades have witnessed something of a shift in scholarly interest away from chapters 5–8. Chapters 1–4 have generated debate regarding Paul's use of the diatribe and speech-in-character, not to mention heated discussion of the "faith of Christ" and the place of justification in Paul's thought. The long history of treating chapters 9–11 as an afterthought or an illustration has given way to intense industry in an effort to account more adequately both for the content of Paul's argument and for its place in the letter as a whole. Chapters 12–16 have come to the foreground as well, particularly as scholars labor to catch a glimpse of the composition of the Roman congregations and the character of Paul's mission.

This volume invites readers of Paul to consider again the large questions raised by Romans 5–8, questions of the gospel's implications both cosmological and anthropological. The approaches and conclusions are by no means monochrome, but they converge around the effort to understand the relationship between divine activity and its human reception in a cosmos that remains contested territory.

Martinus C. de Boer opens the volume exploring Paul's argument about the Law in relationship to the mythologizing language of chapters 5–8. In "Righteousness, Cosmic and Microcosmic," Stephen Westerholm takes up 5:1 as evidence of the ethical and 5:19 as evidence of cosmic interpretations of righteousness. Questions about the individual come to the fore also in Benjamin Myers' study of Romans 5 in Augustine's interpretation of the self's existence within the intersecting narratives of Christ and Adam. John M. G. Barclay explores the relationship between grace and obedience, focusing particularly on Romans 6 and in conversation with Pierre Bourdieu's notion of the *habitus*.

Drawing on linguistic theory about the peculiarities of personal pronouns, Beverly Gaventa considers how the "I" of Romans 7 both reflects and distorts important features of the "I" of the lament psalms. Susan Eastman also looks at the singular "I" in Romans 7, here with a view to undermining the conventional scholarly dichotomy between the individual and corporate identities.

The liberating role of Jesus Christ is brought to bear also in Philip G. Ziegler's exploration of Romans 8 and the royal office of Jesus Christ in "The Love of God Is a Sovereign Thing." And Neil Elliott, in "Creation, Cosmos, and Conflict in Romans 8–9," resists any suggestion that what Paul has to say about creation in Romans 8 can be understood apart from what is said about Israel in Romans 9–11. He finds in the larger argument of Romans important claims contrary to Roman imperial ideology.

In the afterword, J. Louis Martyn takes Raphael's painting of Paul preaching at Athens as a starting point for reflection on the human moral drama in conversation with other contributions to the volume. His image of the circle of discussion aptly draws the volume to a close, but it also rightly anticipates further conversation about anthropology and cosmology in Paul's apocalyptic interpretation of the gospel.

Initial versions of these chapters were given as plenary papers at a conference held at Princeton Theological Seminary in May 2012 as part of the seminary's bicentennial celebration. I am indebted to then-President Iain Torrance for the invitation to host that conference, where participants included a lively international array of systematicians, biblical scholars, pastors, and students. I am also indebted to Professors Shane Berg, Jacqueline E. Lapsley, Katharine Doob Sakenfeld, and J. Ross Wagner for their advice, suggestions, and support throughout the planning of the conference. Able administrators Mary Marcus and Amy Ehlin not only thought of a thousand details but dispatched each and every one with grace.

From a conference—even a highly successful conference—to a book, the journey is arduous. Taking valuable time and attention away from her own dissertation, Mary K. Schmitt worked meticulously to bring the essays into stylistic conformity, and I deeply appreciate her careful labor. Last and far from least, I am grateful to Dr. Carey C. Newman for his enthusiastic acceptance of this book and his patient (well, nearly patient) endurance even to the end.

Benjamin Myers observes that Augustine began a commentary on Romans but worked only as far as 1:7 before giving it up, "discouraged by the vastness and difficulty of the project" (see chapter 3). All of us who work to understand Paul's Romans know that discouragement, but we also know the joy of discovery and the rich rewards of the conversation. My hope is that readers of this volume will find much here that stimulates their own conversation with and about the letter.

Beverly Roberts Gaventa

1
Paul's Mythologizing Program in Romans 5–8

Martinus C. de Boer

My title contains an obvious allusion to Rudolf Bultmann's well-known program of demythologization.[1] I want to argue in this paper that Paul's concern in Romans 5–8 is not *demythologization* but *mythologization*, if the word can be allowed. One of the main reasons Paul programmatically mythologizes in these chapters is to explain why the Law is not, or no longer, a viable option for those who have come to believe in Christ.

Paul's concern with the Law is evident throughout the first eight chapters, indeed the first ten chapters (e.g., esp. 2:12-17; 3:19-31; 4:1-25; 5:13, 20; 6:14-15; 7:1–8:4; 9:31–10:5; 13:8-10). This focus on the Law in Romans reflects its unique occasion. Briefly, the letter appears to have a triple occasion: (1) Paul has received information about differences, even conflicts, among believers in Rome (evident especially in chapters 14–15); (2) as Christ's apostle to the Gentiles, Paul has made plans to go on to new missionary territory in Spain by way of Rome (15:20, 24-25, 28); and (3) before going to Rome, he plans to go to Jerusalem with a collection of funds from the Gentile churches he had founded (15:23-33). Paul hopes that this collection will be accepted by "the saints" (15:31) in Jerusalem, and he fears that he will receive a hostile reception there from those he calls "the unbelievers

---

[1] See Rudolf Bultmann, "New Testament and Mythology: The Problem of Demythologizing the New Testament Proclamation," in *New Testament and Mythology and Other Basic Writings* (ed. S. M. Ogden; Philadelphia: Fortress, 1984), 1–43. The essay was first published in 1941 in Germany during World War II!

in Judea" (15:31). At issue for Paul on all three fronts are the status and the role of the Law now that Christ has come on the human scene. Closely related to the issue of the Law is the question of "the righteousness of God" and justification. Again, this theme pervades much of Romans (cf. 1:17; 2:12; 3:4-30; 4:1-25; 5:1-21; 6:7, 13-20; 8:10, 30, 33; 9:30–10:10; 14:17), especially the first four chapters, but also chapter 5 (and chapters 9–10).

In my view, one of Paul's major aims in this letter is to remind the believers in Rome that they are not "under the Law" (ὑπὸ νόμον)[2] but "under grace" (ὑπὸ χάριν), as he puts it in 6:14 (cf. 6:15). "The Law" and "grace" constitute the overarching polarity in Romans 5–8. The other major polarities in these chapters—sin and righteousness, death and life, flesh and spirit—are largely brought into the service of explaining the fundamental polarity of the Law and grace. Paul wants to bring out the implications and advantages of being under grace rather than being under the Law. One of these implications is to see the world as it really is now that Christ has appeared on the human scene, and another is to redefine the status and the role of the Law in the light of this event.

It will also be relevant to take note here of the broader context of chapters 5–8. In chapters 9–11, Paul's concern is explicitly with unbelieving Israel—put otherwise, with a form of Judaism in which Christ has no place, whether that be in Jerusalem or in Rome. In these chapters Paul returns to the issues of justification and the Law (especially in chapters 9 and 10) that were prominent in the first four chapters, using similar terminology and formulations. In that light, it seems to me probable that in chapters 1–4 Paul also has unbelieving Israel in view. That is to say, Paul is here in dialogue with a form of contemporary Judaism embracing a certain understanding of sin and justification and the Law, one in which Christ has no place. It will be my working assumption that the apocalypses of 4 *Ezra* and 2 *Baruch* are representative of the views with which Paul is in dialogue in the opening chapters of Romans, including chapter 5.[3] Both works stem from the late first or early second century, it is true, but scholars also maintain that they mediate traditions that go back to the early and middle of

---

[2] Literally, "under Law," but the absence of the article after prepositions is common in Paul and appears to be a matter of style. Cf. BDF #258.2. All translations from the New Testament are my own unless indicated otherwise.

[3] The analysis below will indicate whether this working assumption is indeed sound.

the first century, when Paul was active.[4] Paul is in dialogue with these views in his Letter to the Romans evidently because, so Paul assumes, the believers in Rome will hear and read his letter with these views in the backs of their minds.[5]

Bultmann's Proposal and Käsemann's Reaction

Bultmann argued that one must attempt to understand "the mythical world picture" of the NT[6] "in terms of its real intention," and that is to give expression to "how we human beings understand ourselves in our world. Thus," he claimed, "myth does not want to be understood in *cosmological* terms but in *anthropological* terms."[7] The point is to get "to the understanding of [human] existence" contained in the mythological or cosmological language.[8]

---

[4] For translation and discussion, see B. M. Metzger, "The Fourth Book of Ezra," 516–59; and A. F. J. Klijn, "2 (Syriac Apocalypse of) Baruch," 615–52, in *Apocalyptic Literature and Testaments* (vol. 1 of *The Old Testament Pseudepigrapha*; ed. J. H. Charlesworth; Garden City, N.Y.: Doubleday, 1983). Both *4 Ezra* and *2 Baruch* were written in Hebrew in Palestine. Both were subsequently translated into Greek and then a third language (Latin in the case of *4 Ezra*, Syriac in the case of *2 Baruch*), which have provided the basis for the existing English translations (the original Hebrew versions as well as the Greek translations of both have unfortunately been lost). *4 Ezra* comprises chapters 3–14 of the work known as 2 Esdras in the Apocrypha of English Bibles such as KJV, RSV, and NRSV.

[5] In earlier work I suggested that Paul may also be in dialogue with Jewish-Christian views on sin, justification, and the Law, which (apart from the Christology) were similar to those of Paul's presumed Jewish conversation partners. See Martinus C. de Boer, *The Defeat of Death: Apocalyptic Eschatology in 1 Corinthians 15 and Romans 5* (JSNTSup 22; Sheffield: Sheffield Academic, 1988), 154; idem, "Paul and Jewish Apocalyptic Eschatology," in *Apocalyptic and the New Testament: Essays in Honor of J. Louis Martyn* (ed. Joel Marcus and Marion L. Soards; JSNTSup 24; Sheffield: Sheffield Academic, 1989), 169–90, esp. 183. I leave that issue aside here. I await further clarification on this matter from the forthcoming commentary on Romans by Beverly Roberts Gaventa.

[6] Bultmann, "New Testament and Mythology," 1–3.

[7] Bultmann, "New Testament and Mythology," 9 (emphasis added). Bultmann problematically added here: "or, better in *existentialist* terms" (emphasis added). His proposal can be evaluated, however, apart from the existentialist hermeneutic, which he derived from Heidegger. If we leave the Heideggerian turn aside, the point is that cosmological statements give expression to anthropological realities and thus may be interpreted, and appropriated, in that light.

[8] Bultmann, "New Testament and Mythology," 10.

In his demythologizing program, Bultmann saw himself as following in the footsteps of John and Paul. For our purposes what Bultmann says about Jewish apocalyptic eschatology with respect to Paul is particularly pertinent. Jewish apocalyptic eschatology is defined by Bultmann as a "basic dualistic view according to which the present world and the people living in it are under the dominion of demonic, satanic powers and in need of redemption, a redemption that they themselves cannot provide and that can be given them only through divine intervention."[9] For Jewish apocalyptic eschatology, that divine intervention is an imminently future event whereby God "puts an end to this old age and ushers in the new one through God's sending of the Messiah."[10] Paul has demythologized this Jewish apocalyptic eschatology in at least two ways according to Bultmann:

1. Jewish apocalyptic eschatology is "demythologized insofar as the day of salvation has already dawned for believers and the life of the future has already become present."[11] In other words: present eschatology.
2. Paul emphasizes individual responsibility and "decision" (*Entscheidung*). Talk of cosmic powers lording it over human beings serves to indicate that "we can in no way free ourselves from our factual fallenness in the world, but are freed from it only by an act of God."[12] That point is crucial for Bultmann because it distinguishes faith from philosophy, which can pose the problem of inauthentic existence but cannot provide the needed solution.[13] Nevertheless, for Bultmann, there is "never any doubt about our responsibility and guilt" or that "God is also the Judge before whom we are responsible."[14]

---

[9] Bultmann, "New Testament and Mythology," 14.

[10] Bultmann, "New Testament and Mythology," 14.

[11] Bultmann, "New Testament and Mythology," 18.

[12] Bultmann, "New Testament and Mythology," 26. On this page and elsewhere, Bultmann refers frequently to what "the New Testament" says, but he supports his claims exclusively with references to Paul's letters.

[13] Bultmann, "New Testament and Mythology," 27. See also his follow-up essay, "On the Problem of Demythologizing," in *New Testament and Mythology*, 95–130, esp. 110–23.

[14] Bultmann, "New Testament and Mythology," 15. Bultmann observes that "the New Testament" contains "a peculiar contradiction: on the one hand, human beings are cosmically determined, and, on the other hand, they are summoned to decision (Entscheidung); on the one hand, sin is fate, and, on the other hand, it is guilt. . . . In

With respect to Paul, then, Bultmann's demythologization of Paul came down to a deapocalypticized Paul, a Paul with no future eschatology and no cosmological powers.[15] In response to Bultmann, his former student, Ernst Käsemann, argued for the following two points:

1. Despite the new emphasis on the present reality of salvation in Paul's thought, "Paul remained an apocalyptist" in that a "future eschatology" remained a crucial element of his thinking.[16]
2. Bultmann's interpretation of Paul's cosmology in terms of an individualistic anthropology is untenable. Paul's use of the Greek term σῶμα ("body") belies Bultmann's claims. Bultmann rightly saw that Paul used this term to designate the whole person,[17] but he failed to see that the body signifies for Paul the creaturely solidarity of human beings with one another and with the rest of creation. The Pauline understanding of σῶμα, Käsemann argued, signifies that the individual cannot isolate herself from the world to which she belongs and that the human being is subject to "the rule of outside forces" that determine his existence, identity, and destiny.[18] So for Käsemann, "The world is not neutral ground; it is a battlefield, and everyone is a combatant. Anthropology must

---

short, human beings are understood, on the one hand, as cosmic human beings and, on the other hand, as independent persons who can win or lose themselves by their own decisions" (11). Bultmann gives the preference to the second of these alternatives, allowing this second alternative to provide the clue for interpreting the first: "the issue," he writes, "is whether the New Testament offers us an understanding of ourselves that constitutes for us a genuine question of decision" (15).

[15] Congruent with this is Bultmann's understanding of the Spirit: the Spirit is not "a natural force" for Paul but represents "the possibility of life," one that a human being "must take hold of by resolve (*Entschluss*)" ("New Testament and Mythology," 20). "We are not relieved of decision," Bultmann emphasizes when he cites such passages as Gal 5:16 with its imperative: "Walk by the Spirit" (RSV). The decision for faith, for authentic existence, must be taken every day anew: "So it is," Bultmann concludes, "that the concept of the 'Spirit' is demythologized."

[16] Ernst Käsemann, "'The Righteousness of God' in Paul," in *New Testament Questions of Today* (Philadelphia: Fortress, 1969), 168–82, here 181; see further, in the same volume, "On the Subject of Primitive Christian Apocalyptic," 108–37, esp. 131–33.

[17] Cf. Rudolf Bultmann, *Theology of the New Testament* (vol. 1; New York: Scribner, 1951), 192–95.

[18] Käsemann, "On the Subject of Primitive Christian Apocalyptic," 135–36; "On Paul's Anthropology," in *Perspectives on Paul* (Philadelphia: Fortress, 1969), 1–31, esp. 19–22; idem, *Commentary on Romans* (Grand Rapids: Eerdmans, 1980), 176.

then *eo ipso* be cosmology."[19] Or, as he puts it elsewhere: since a human being's life is "from the beginning a stake in the confrontation between God and the principalities and the world," it "can only be understood apocalyptically."[20]

Käsemann thus offered what we may call a "cosmological-apocalyptic" reading of Paul.[21]

The difference between Bultmann and Käsemann was also evident in their different interpretations of Paul's theology of justification. For Bultmann, "the righteousness of God," ἡ δικαιοσύνη τοῦ θεοῦ (Rom 1:17; 3:5, 21, 22; cf. 2 Cor 5:21), is a gift for the individual, the "favorable standing" a believer has in God's court.[22] The righteousness of God is "God-given, God-adjudicated righteousness."[23] For Käsemann, the formulation "the righteousness of God" actually refers to God's own righteousness and concerns God's reestablishing his sovereignty over the world. Thus, "the righteousness of God does not, in Paul's understanding, refer primarily to the individual and is not to be understood exclusively" as anthropology.[24] Because "the righteousness of God" refers first and foremost to God's own saving action, effective

---

[19] Käsemann, "On Paul's Anthropology," 23.

[20] Käsemann, "On the Subject of Primitive Christian Apocalyptic," 136. From the previous discussion, it will have become evident that for Käsemann the term "apocalyptic" can be used for both Paul's future eschatology and his cosmology (the suprahuman forces that determine human existence, identity, and destiny). This is so despite Käsemann's occasional formal definition of apocalyptic as the expectation of the Parousia and the like. For discussion of this issue, see de Boer, *Defeat of Death*, 15–16, 29–30.

[21] Congruent with these two points is Käsemann's understanding of the Spirit in Paul. The Spirit is not, as it is for Bultmann, the "possibility of life," to be "taken hold of by resolve" (see n. 15 above), but God's eschatological power already present in the world (cf. Käsemann, "On Paul's Anthropology," 28): When Paul talks about the spiritual warfare between the Spirit and the Flesh, as he does in Romans 8 (as also in Gal 5), he does not refer to the individual but to realities, "which, as the power either of the heavenly or the earthly, determines him from outside, takes possession of him and thereby decides into which of the two dualistically opposed spheres he is to be integrated" (Käsemann, "On the Subject of Primitive Christian Apocalyptic," 136). The dialectic between indicative and imperative reflects this situation in the present. The powers remain an ongoing threat, and that explains the need for the imperative: the struggle is not yet over.

[22] Bultmann, *Theology*, 1:273.

[23] Bultmann, *Theology*, 1:295.

[24] Käsemann, "'Righteousness of God,'" 180.

in the lordship of the crucified Christ, the justifying action on behalf of the ungodly not only "declares righteous" (is not simply a forensic-eschatological pronouncement, as it is for Bultmann) but also actually "makes righteous."[25] It does so by coming on the human scene to liberate human beings from cosmological forces and powers that have enslaved them.

Now, it is interesting to observe that Bultmann predicated his forensic-eschatological understanding of justification and God's righteousness largely on Romans 1–4, whereas Käsemann based his cosmological-apocalyptic reading of Paul largely on Romans 6–8.[26] Romans 5 is contested territory in that the views of both Bultmann and Käsemann can find support in this passage (see below). The Bultmann-Käsemann exchange allows us to see, or at least to suspect, that Romans 5 marks a shift from predominantly forensic-eschatological categories (focused on the individual) to predominantly cosmological-apocalyptic ones in Paul's argument in Romans. The question this phenomenon of course raises is: why is this the case and what does it signify?

The Cosmic Context of the Gospel

Paul begins chapter 5 with the following words: "Since, then, we have been justified on the basis of faith [rather than on the basis of the Law—a summary of the preceding argument] we [now] have peace with God through our Lord Jesus Christ, through whom we have obtained access into this grace in which we [now] stand" (5:1-2a). This emphasis on the present (cf. Bultmann), on what has been attained, is certainly retained throughout the first eleven verses. The opening paragraph concludes in verse 11 with the words, "We rejoice in God through our Lord Jesus Christ through whom we have *now* received reconciliation." The result of justification is peace or reconciliation with God.

At the same time, another note may be heard—one that points to the future (cf. Käsemann): because "we" have been justified and thereby obtained peace with God and access to the grace in which "we" now stand, "we" can also "boast in the *hope* of the glory of God" (5:1-2). Or as Paul expresses it later in the passage: "having been justified, how much more *shall* we be saved through him from wrath" (5:9), and "having been reconciled how much more *shall* we be saved in his

---

[25] Käsemann, "'Righteousness of God,'" 176.
[26] Cf. Käsemann, *Commentary on Romans*, 163.

life" (5:10). Hope indeed "does not disappoint, since the love of God *has been* poured into our hearts through the holy spirit that *has been* given to us" (5:5). God's love becomes manifest in the justifying and reconciling death of Christ (5:8-10), and this fact of faith provides the basis for hope—hope for the future, not only for the long term (the Parousia) but also for the lives of believers from now on.

These new accents are continued in the second paragraph of chapter 5, verses 12-21, but Paul now also places Christ's work within an explicitly cosmic framework. By "cosmic" I mean simply "pertaining to the whole human world"; Paul uses the term κόσμος in verse 12 to refer to "the whole human world"—not the universe or the earth, two possible other meanings of the term (cf. 1:8 ["the whole world"]; 3:19 ["the whole world"]; 4:13; 2 Cor 5:19). If in verses 1-11 he repeatedly uses the first person plural "we" ("*we* have peace with God," "*we* boast," and so forth), limiting his discussion to believers, he now uses a third-person construction (until the very end of v. 21, when he reverts back to the first-person plural as a transition to chapter 6). Paul widens the scope as it were, from the new situation in which believers find themselves, the realm of God's grace, to the whole human cosmos:

> Just as through one human being [i.e., Adam] sin came into the world and through sin death [came into the world] . . . [Rom 5:12a] so also grace might reign through justification[27] for eternal life, through Jesus Christ our Lord. [Rom 5:21b]

Romans 5:12a and 5:21b stand at the beginning and at the end of the paragraph. Just as sin came into the world through one human being, along with death, so also grace came to reign through justification for life, through Jesus Christ "our Lord." That is the literary frame of the second paragraph and the intervening verses may be regarded as annotations and explications of this central claim.[28]

---

[27] From this point on I consistently translate all words from the stem δικαι- (δικαιοσύνη, δικαιόω, δίκαιος, δικαίωμα, δικαίωσις) with words from the stem "just-" (justify, justification, just). I do this to preserve as much as possible the visual, aural, and semantic relationship between them, evident in the Greek. I leave aside here the issue of whether so translating the Greek sufficiently reflects the meanings Paul attaches to these words. By translating the instance of δικαιοσύνη in 5:21b not with "righteousness" but with "justification," the *inclusio* with 5:1 ("having been *justified* on the basis of faith") becomes immediately evident.

[28] See de Boer, *Defeat of Death*, 162–63.

Romans 5:12-21 is not the first time Paul has used a cosmic frame of reference in Romans, particularly in connection with the human condition before and apart from Christ. From 1:18 onward there is an account of human wrongdoing that is universal in scope as is the account of God's wrath against this wrongdoing. We may refer in particular to 3:23: "for all have sinned and fall short of the glory of God," which contains an allusion to Adam's lost glory (cf. *Apoc. Mos.* 20:2; 21:6; 39:2-3; *4 Ezra* 7:122-25; *2 Bar.* 51:3; 54:15, 21; 1QS IV, 23; 1QH XVII,15; CD III, 20). Romans 5:12-21, however, is the first time Paul refers explicitly to Adam, whereby the cosmic context of Paul's understanding of Christ's work also becomes explicit. Adam is here called "the type" of "the coming one," that is to say, of Christ (v. 14). Christ is thus Adam's antitype. As Adam's antitype, Christ is "the one human being" (vv. 15, 19) who stands over against the other "one human being," Adam, undoing what Adam brought about. And Christ does so on a correspondingly cosmic scale, as verses 18-19 make plain: "So then, as through one trespass there was for *all people* condemnation, so also through one act of justification (δικαίωμα) there is for *all people* justification (δικαίωσις) of life. For just as through the disobedience of the one human being *the many* [= all] were made sinful (ἁμαρτωλοί),[29] so also through the obedience of the one [human being] *the many* [= all] will be made just (δίκαιοι)."[30]

Paul, then, places Christ and his saving work in a cosmic context, and he does so by contrasting Christ with the figure of Adam. Paul has made this move earlier, in 1 Corinthians 15, where the resurrection of Christ is placed in a cosmic context against some believers in the Corinthian church who were denying the resurrection of the dead:

> Through a human being, death,
> Also through a human being, resurrection of the dead.
> For just as in Adam, *all* die
> So also in Christ, *all* will be made alive. (1 Cor 15:21-22)

Just as Adam stands at the head of the old world or age *for all*, so Christ stands at the head of the new world or age *for all*. This cosmic frame of reference is one of the distinguishing marks of an apocalyptic perspective, as is the implicit notion of two world ages. Again, by placing Christ over against Adam, Paul makes plain that Christ's work is

---

[29] Or "sinners."
[30] Or "just ones."

as cosmic (= pertaining to all human beings) in its implications and consequences as Adam's initial trespass or disobedience. If all died because of Adam, all will be made alive because of Christ. Verse 22 makes explicit the universal implications of verse 21—for both Adam and Christ.

In 1 Corinthians 15, then, Paul's interest in Adam is limited to two things: (1) his agency in causing death to come into the world (through a human being = in Adam); and (2) the cosmic consequences of this agency (death = all die). Furthermore, Paul's appeal to Adam functions primarily as a foil for Christ. Just as Adam determined universal human destiny, so also Christ does. Christ's saving role is analogous to, even as it also surpasses, Adam's destructive role, particularly in terms of its (1) agency (through a human being = in Christ); and (2) the cosmic consequences of this agency (resurrection of the dead = all will be made alive).[31]

Much the same may be said about Paul's recycling of the Adam-Christ typology in Romans 5; it is a matter of agency and of the cosmic consequences of this agency. But there are some differences.

Adam and Christ, Death and Life

In Romans 5, the issue is not the resurrection of the dead but "life," ζωή (vv. 17, 18) or "eternal life," ζωὴ αἰώνιος (v. 21). Those "who receive the abundance of grace, i.e., the free gift of justification, will reign in *life*" (v. 17). The "one act of justification for all people is for justification of *life*" (v. 18). Grace "more than abounded" (v. 20) so that it "might reign through justification for *eternal life*" (v. 21). The mention of grace in v. 21 indicates that the issue in Romans is the status and the function of the Law, which Jewish sources refer to as "the Law of life" (4 *Ezra* 14:30; 2 *Bar.* 38:1: "Your Law is life"; cf. Sir 17:11; 45:5). Grace is for Paul the antithetical correlate of the Law, as 6:14 shows (see Introduction). That explains why Paul explicitly mentions the Law in verses 13 and 20 of chapter 5. Christ and his saving work—"life"—are, then, placed not only in opposition to Adam and his trespass but *also* to the Law as the presumed remedy for the trespass, a point to which I return below in the section titled "The Status and the Role of the Law."

Because the issue here is "(eternal) life" rather than the resurrection of the (physically) dead as in 1 Corinthians 15, the primary

---

[31] De Boer, *Defeat of Death*, 109–12.

referential meaning of the term "death" (θάνατος) in Romans 5 is not physical death, as it is in 1 Corinthians 15. Paul works with at least three referential meanings for "death" as an anthropological reality of the present world: physical death (bodily demise), moral death or spiritual death (sinful behavior as a form of death), and eternal death (perdition, damnation). The close association of death with sin and the dualistic contrast of death with (eternal) life in Romans 5 as well as the chapters that follow indicate that the last two meanings are at the forefront. What binds these various referential meanings to one another is the notion of separation from God and from life before God. That, for Paul, truly is death.

In Romans 5, in contrast to 1 Corinthians 15, sin is explicitly brought into the equation (though it may be implicit in 1 Corinthians 15 as well; cf. 15:3, 17). And that brings me to the much-discussed verse 12.

Corporate Destiny or Individual Culpability?

Many interpreters have noted the evident tension between the first half of the verse (12a) and the second half (12b):

> Just as through one human being sin came into the world and through sin death, [12a]
> and so death spread to all human beings, since all sinned. [12b]

The tension between the two halves of the verse has usually been described in terms of the contrast between corporate destiny in the first half (Adam caused the fatality of death to come upon all people) and personal responsibility in the second (since all sinned, all are also responsible for their own deaths). A frequent argument is that Paul in effect corrects the former motif with the latter.[32] The Adam motifs to which Paul is here indebted have of course ultimately been derived from Genesis 3, but then as interpreted in a certain strain of Jewish apocalyptic eschatology, as witnessed to by the apocalypses of 4 *Ezra* and 2 *Baruch*. These books, though written some decades after Paul wrote Romans, clearly make use of earlier and commonly available traditions and do so independently of each other.[33] In both works, the

---

[32] So Rudolf Bultmann, "Adam and Christ According to Romans 5," in *Current Issues in New Testament Interpretation: Essays in Honor of Otto A. Piper* (ed. W. Klassen and G. F. Snyder; New York: Harper & Brothers, 1962), 143–65, here 153.

[33] For a recent treatment, see Matthias Henze, "4 *Ezra* and 2 *Baruch*: Literary

destruction of Jerusalem in 70 C.E. and the gift of the Law are placed against the cosmic backdrop of Adam's transgression and its disastrous consequences for the world, for all humanity.

In *2 Baruch*, we read: "Adam sinned and death was decreed against those who were to be born" (23:4) and "when he [Adam] transgressed, untimely death came into being" (56:6; cf. Gen 2:17; 3:19). It is also said, however: "Adam is . . . not the cause, except for himself, but each of us has become our own Adam" (54:19). Adam may have "sinned first" (54:15), but he was not the last! The death that Adam brought into the world is justifiably imposed on those who are descended from him. In *4 Ezra*, there is a very similar tale. God "laid one commandment" upon Adam, we read in 3:7, "but he transgressed it, and immediately you [God] appointed death for him and his descendants." But we also read: "O Adam, what have you done? For though it was you who sinned, the fall was not yours alone, but ours also who are your descendants. For what good is it to us, if an eternal age has been promised to us, but we have done deeds that bring death?" (7:118-20)

The figure of Adam thus has a double function in both works: to give expression to the all-embracing reality of death in the present world and to assign responsibility for the reality of death to the willful and thus accountable repudiation of God by human beings. The logically irreconcilable tension between corporate destiny and personal culpability discernible between the two halves of Romans 5:12 is thus part and parcel of the Adam tradition as it occurs in these Jewish apocalyptic texts. The figure of Adam functions as both a corporate personality who determines all subsequent human destiny and as the paradigmatic human being who sets the pattern for his descendants. It thus seems unlikely that the motif of personal culpability in the second half of verse 12 is to be construed as Paul's "correction" of the motif of corporate destiny in the first half. They belong together in the tradition about Adam in Jewish thought of the period.

It may also be noted here that in both *4 Ezra* and *2 Baruch* the fundamental sin of Adam and his descendants is the refusal to acknowledge and to worship God the Creator (cf. *4 Ezra* 7:118; 8:60). As *2 Baruch* puts it: God "knew the number of those who are born from him [Adam] and how they sinned before you [God], those who existed and who did not recognize you as their Creator" (48:46; cf. 14:15-19;

Composition and Oral Performance in First-Century Apocalyptic Literature," *JBL* 131 (2012): 181–200, esp. 197–98.

54:18). Paul shows his deep familiarity with such conceptions in chapters 1–3 of Romans. To cite an example, Romans 1:28-32:

> And since they did not see fit to acknowledge God, God gave them up to a base mind and to improper conduct. They were filled with all manner of wickedness, evil, covetousness, malice. Full of envy, murder, strife, deceit, malignity, they are gossips, slanderers, haters of God, insolent, haughty, boastful, inventors of evil, disobedient to parents, foolish, faithless, heartless, ruthless. Though they know God's decree that those who do such things deserve to die [lit. are worthy of death, ἄξιοι θανάτου] they not only do them but approve those who practice them. (RSV)

We would not blink an eye or raise an eyebrow if we had come across this passage in either *4 Ezra* or *2 Baruch*. Paul is in dialogue with such views in the early chapters of Romans. But that then raises the question of Paul's distinctiveness.

Paul's Distinctiveness

What is distinctive in Paul's use and application of the story of Adam in 5:12-21 is his characterization of sin and death as cosmological forces that have invaded the human cosmos as alien intruders: "Sin [capital S] came into the world, and through Sin, Death [capital D] [came into the world]." In short, Paul personifies and thereby "mythologizes" the notions of sin and death, which is to say, he talks about them as he elsewhere does about Satan (cf. Rom 16:20; 1 Cor 5:5; 7:5; 2 Cor 2:11; 11:14; 12:7; 1 Thess 2:18; cf. 2 Cor 4:4; 6:14; 1 Thess 3:5), evil angels (cf. Rom 8:38; 1 Cor 4:9; 6:3; 2 Cor 11:14; 12:7), or demons (cf. 1 Cor 10:20-21), i.e., as inimical powers or beings that victimize and enslave human beings,[34] and that do so contrary to God's intention for the world.[35] Paul is not interested in cosmological speculation for its own sake, but in giving an account of the *human* condition or plight. Put otherwise, Paul's cosmological language about Sin and Death as malevolent powers represents an attempt to account

---

[34] On Sin as a power in Romans, see Beverly Roberts Gaventa, "The Cosmic Power of Sin in Paul's Letter to the Romans," in *Our Mother Saint Paul* (Louisville: Westminster John Knox, 2007), 125–36.

[35] For parallels in Jewish apocalyptic literature, see the useful survey on angels and demons provided by D. S. Russell, *The Method and Message of Jewish Apocalyptic* (OTL; Philadelphia: Westminster, 1964), 235–62.

for anthropological realities and experiences. Behind *human* sinning and *human* dying, Paul discerns cosmological powers at work which he calls Sin and Death. He thus mythologizes with what Käsemann called "anthropological relevance."[36]

In Paul's mythologization of death, death is not thought of as the punishment for sin (as in 1:32, cited above),[37] but as the ineluctable result or outcome of sin (6:16b; 6:21b; 6:23a; 7:5b). Sin came into the world with Adam, and the ineluctable result was Death. And that means, then, that where the one is, the other also is. Paul's appropriation of the Adam tradition places the motif of personal accountability or culpability in a new context, a cosmological-apocalyptic one (cf. Käsemann). For Paul, the fact that "all sinned" (5:12d; 3:23) signifies that all human beings since Adam have been and are, as he has already asserted in 3:9, "under (the power of) Sin." The second half of verse 12 ("And so Death spread to all people, since all sinned") is to be interpreted accordingly. The power of Death came upon all people, since all, by being under the power of Sin, sinned. Sinning is not the result of a bad choice made by an autonomous individual; it is the result and the mark of a cosmological force that has come into the world and has reigned over human beings since the time of Adam, bringing Death in its wake (v. 21a; cf. 7:17).

Paul's mythologization of Sin and Death has particular pertinence for what he says about the Law, or the observance of the Law.

The Status and the Role of the Law

As I have noted, grace, which is mentioned several times in 5:12-21, is the antithetical correlate of the Law (cf. 6:14-15). Paul's mention of the Law in verses 13 and 20 is therefore no accident. Before we look at what precisely he says and why, it will be useful to return here briefly to *2 Baruch* and *4 Ezra* to see how they regard the Law as the divinely given solution to the human condition since Adam. According to *2 Baruch*, God has graciously given the Law as the remedy for the world determined by the sentence of death imposed on Adam and

---

[36] Cf. Käsemann, "On Paul's Anthropology," 27. See further de Boer, *Defeat of Death*, 179.

[37] Rom 1:32 contains the only instance of the noun θάνατος ("death") before 5:12-21 (apart from the instance in 5:10 referring to the death of Jesus). In contrast to the five instances in 5:12-21, the instance in 1:32 has a forensic-eschatological meaning (death as punishment) and is equivalent to "wrath" (ὀργή), a term Paul uses seven times before 5:12-21 (1:18; 2:5 [twice]; 2:8; 3:15; 4:15; 5:9).

his progeny. By giving the Law, God also allows each person to determine her or his ultimate destiny. In 19:1, God tells the seer that he had made a covenant with the people in the time of Moses and confronted them with a choice: "Behold, I appoint for you life and death" (cf. 44:3; 84:2), a partial citation of Deuteronomy 30:19: "I have set before you life and death, blessing and curse; therefore, choose life that you and your descendants may live." In 2 *Baruch*, the terms "life" and "death" from Deuteronomy 30:19 have not only moral connotations as they do in Deuteronomy itself, but also eschatological ones (cf. also 46:3). Observance of the Law in the present determines whether the sentence of death passed on Adam and all his descendants will be the ultimate rather than the penultimate destiny of Adam's offspring, i.e. whether this death will in fact be eternal or overcome with the gift of "life" in the world to come (cf. 42:7-8; 44:7-15; 51:3, 7-8). Each person can freely choose to obey the Law (51:16), whereby the claim of the Creator is acknowledged (48:47), and thus inherit "that world which has no end" (48:50). "For the Judge will come and will not hesitate. For *each* of the inhabitants *of the earth* [note the cosmic framework and the individualism here!] knew when he acted unrighteously, and they did not know my Law because of their pride" (48:40). "For although Adam sinned first and has brought death upon all who were not in his own time, yet *each of them* who has been born from him [again, note the individualism and the cosmic framework] has prepared for himself the coming torment. And further each of them has chosen for himself the coming glory" (54:15-16). Your destiny is in your own hands now that God has given the Law (cf. 48:38-40)! For those destined to be "saved because of their works," "the Law is now a hope" (51:7). The present is a time of *decision*—for or against the Law, which is a decision for or against life.

In 4 *Ezra*, a primary concern is what is called "the evil heart" (*cor malignum* in 3:21, 26; 4:4; or *cor malum* in 7:48) and the ability of the Law to counter its effects. The seer, called Ezra, wonders whether the Law is sufficient to overcome the problem: "For the first Adam, burdened with an evil heart, transgressed and was overcome, as were also all who were descended from him. Thus the disease became permanent." He then adds the following interesting observation: "the Law was in the people's heart along with the evil root, but what was good departed, and the evil remained" (3:21-22). Thus Ezra complains that when God gave the Law to Israel he did "not take away from them the evil heart, so that your Law might bring forth fruit in them" (3:20;

cf. 7:48; 9:36). This sounds almost Pauline! The angel (Uriël) sent to converse with Ezra about such matters, who speaks for God and thus probably represents the views of the author of the book,[38] responds that though the number of those saved will indeed be few, those who have kept the Law "perfectly" (7:89) will receive the award of "immortality" (7:13, 97, 113). It is "for this reason, [that] the Most High has made not one world but two" (7:50), to give people the opportunity to prove themselves in this age and to receive their proper reward in the age to come: "This is the meaning of the contest which *every human being* who is born on earth [again, note the cosmic framework and individualism] shall wage, that if he is defeated he shall suffer what you [Ezra] have said, but if he is victorious he shall receive what I [the angel] have said" (cf. *2 Bar* 15:8). The angel then goes on to cite from Deuteronomy 30:19: "For this is the way of which Moses, while he was alive, spoke to the people saying, 'Choose for yourself life, that you may live!'" (7:127-29). The angel thereby affirms that the Law is indeed the remedy for the "disease of the evil heart," the observance of which is the condition for participation in the coming age (cf. 7:17, 21, 45, 92). The Law is after all "the Law of life" (14:30). Those with "a treasure of good works laid up with the Most High" (7:77; cf. 8:33, 36) will be saved. For the author of *4 Ezra* it is possible to "choose life" in the midst of the present evil age of death.

Again, in the first part of Romans, Paul exhibits his deep familiarity with this theology of the Law. Take 2:5-8:

> But by your hard and impenitent *heart* you are storing up wrath for yourself on the day of wrath when God's righteous judgment will be revealed. For he will render to every one according to their works: to those who by patience in well-doing seek for glory and honor and immortality, he will give eternal life; but for those who are factious and do not obey the truth, but obey wickedness, there will be wrath and fury. (RSV)

Or 2:13: "For it is not the hearers of the Law who are righteous before God, but the doers of the Law who will be justified!" Or 3:19: "We know that whatever the Law says it speaks to those in the Law, that

---

[38] Cf. Wolfgang Harnisch, *Verhängnis und Verheissung der Geschichte. Untersuchung zum Zeit- und Geschichtsverständnis im 4. Buch Esra und syr. Baruchapokalypse* (FRLANT 97; Göttingen: Vandenhoeck & Ruprecht, 1969), 48–50, 60–67.

every mouth [individualism!] may be stopped and the whole world [cosmic scope!] may become accountable to God." In the first three chapters, through 3:19, Paul adopts this perspective in order to undermine it, concluding in 3:20: "Therefore, no one shall be justified before Him as a result of works of the Law, for through the Law comes [only] knowledge of Sin."

In 3:21, he then goes on to maintain that in any case the Law has been overtaken by events, or rather by an event, that of Jesus Christ, whereby "the righteousness of God" has become manifest "apart from the Law." But Paul's argument is not simply that believers in Christ are now justified on the basis of faith rather than as a result of "works of the Law" (3:20, 28). In 5:12-21, Paul goes on to place the Law within a cosmological-apocalyptic context: "For [the power of] Sin was in the world prior to the Law," i.e., before the Law could "register" it (v. 13). If Sin was in the world prior to the Law, so of course was Death: "Death reigned from Adam to Moses," just as Sin did. Death reigned "also over those who did not commit sin in the likeness of the transgression (παράβασις) of Adam" (v. 14). No, those who lived prior to the Law did not transgress a specific divine commandment as did Adam. There was no Law to transgress, since "where there is no Law there is no transgression" either (4:15)! Nevertheless, those who lived prior to the coming of the Law did sin, did all commit the fundamental "trespass" (παράπτωμα; five instances in vv. 15, 17, 18, 20; cf. Wis 10:1) of Adam in that they repudiated the Creator (cf. 1:28). Paul seems to use the word παράπτωμα to mean a "falling away" from God, a repudiation or rejection of God (cf. 4:25; 11:11, 22). It is for this reason that Death "reigned" (5:14) from Adam onward, also before the Law came on the scene, when of course Sin also reigned (5:21), even if there was no Law to transgress. The significance of these claims about a bygone period of human history becomes evident in verse 20, where Paul writes that "the Law came in alongside (παρεισῆλθεν)," that is to say, came into a situation already fully determined by these twin powers. In other words, the Law has been—and still is—no match for the power of Sin and its partner Death (cf. 8:3). "The Law came in alongside, so that the trespass might increase," and that means for Paul that "[the power of] Sin increased" (v. 20b), intensified and solidified its death-dealing grip over human beings, so that "Sin reigned in Death," which is to say, in the realm of separation from God and life.

But now it is interesting to observe that *2 Baruch* and *4 Ezra*, which James D. G. Dunn has labeled "the two classic Jewish apocalypses,"[39] do not support Paul's cosmological-apocalyptic construal of Sin and Death. The absence of cosmological powers from these two works is striking.[40] *2 Baruch* and *4 Ezra* represent a Jewish apocalyptic worldview in which such malevolent forces play no role.[41] The emphasis falls on choice and on personal accountability and culpability (cf. Bultmann's interpretation of Paul). *Paul*, I have argued, has introduced the cosmological understanding of sin and death into the Jewish Adam traditions—and he has done so to show that the Law, instead of being the solution for sin and thus death as in *2 Baruch* and *4 Ezra*, only solidified the hold of Sin and thus Death on human beings: Alas, the Law has nothing to do with obtaining the requisite righteousness, nor with justification, nor, then, with (eternal) life. Nothing.

Paul's appraisal of the Law's status and the role of the Law in the light of Christ hinges in part on his understanding of Sin and Death as cosmological powers. The Law is their plaything and tool. It is no more than "the Law of Sin and Death," as he writes in 8:2. The Law itself may be holy, good, and spiritual (7:12-14), but Christ's death has unmasked the terrible fact that the (observance of the) Law is not—in fact, cannot be—the remedy for sin and does not—in fact, cannot—bridge the yawning chasm of death that, because of Sin, separates human beings from God and life. In the face of the powers of Sin and Death, those who predicate their hopes on Law observance live under an illusion. The Law does not and cannot, in Paul's view, liberate human beings from the deadly orb in which Sin rules, cannot rectify their broken relationship with God, cannot grant or assure

---

[39] James D. G. Dunn, *Theology of Paul the Apostle* (Edinburgh: T&T Clark, 1998), 88.

[40] *4 Ezra* and *2 Baruch* show, therefore, that not all apocalyptic eschatology is necessarily cosmological, even though both Bultmann and Käsemann appear to work with that assumption (see the section of this article titled "Bultmann's Proposal and Käsemann's Reaction," above). For the two patterns (or "tracks") of Jewish apocalyptic eschatology, see de Boer, "Paul and Jewish Apocalyptic Eschatology" and *Defeat of Death*, 85–88. For a summary and restatement of my views, see de Boer, *Galatians* (Louisville: Westminster John Knox, 2011), 31–35, 79–82.

[41] In a recent survey article, "Paul in Current Anglophone Scholarship," *ExpTim* 123 (2012): 367–81, N. T. Wright has asked for "evidence of the split between two types of 'apocalyptic' theology" for which I have argued. The evidence is available in my earlier publications (see previous note) as well as in this chapter.

eternal life (cf. Gal 2:21; 3:21). The Law only "came in alongside" the powers of Sin and Death, and, as the crucifixion of Christ has revealed, increased Sin's lethal hold on human beings (cf. 7:7-8:8).[42]

Paul's Aim

Paul's mythologizing agenda in Romans 5:12-21 and beyond seems, then, to mark a major shift in Paul's argument in Romans. However, that shift finds its anticipation in 1:16-17 and 3:9. In 1:16-17 Paul personifies "the righteousness of God" as God's saving power (if Käsemann is right, and I think he is), and in 3:9 he personifies sin as a cosmological, subjugating power, anticipating the material extending from 5:12–8:3, where he speaks of sin as a cosmological power some forty times. These two texts—1:16-17 and 3:9—occur at crucial junctures in Paul's argument in the first three chapters. The first arguably states the fundamental theme of the epistle, while the second summarizes the multifarious sins of both Jews and Gentiles, catalogued in the preceding discussion, as proof that they are all "under (the power of) Sin." His mythologizing program, therefore, is anticipated in the earlier chapters.

Now, one can regard Paul's mythologizing of Sin and Death merely as a rhetorical ploy, determined by the need to exclude the Law, or "works of the Law," as the solution to the problem of the human condition among the Roman Christians.[43] However, Paul has made similar moves in earlier letters. In 1 Corinthians 15, he ranges the death that came into the world through Adam with the principalities and powers that Christ must put under his feet; Death is "the last enemy" (15:24-26). In Galatians, he has argued that "the Scripture shut all things [including even the Law] under [the power of] Sin (ὑπὸ ἁμαρτίαν)" (3:21), using the same expression that he uses in Romans 3:9: "all people, both Jews and Greeks, are under [the power of] sin (ὑφ' ἁμαρτίαν)."[44] Paul's mythological / cosmological understanding of Sin

---

[42] As Gaventa writes, Sin is "a cosmic terrorist. Sin not only entered the cosmos with Adam; it also enslaved, it unleashed Death itself, it even managed to take the law of God captive to its power" ("Cosmic Power," 130–31; emphasis removed).

[43] For other possible objections—Paul's personification of Sin is a mere metaphorical device; modern people cannot share Paul's worldview—see the instructive discussion of Gaventa, "Cosmic Power," 133–35.

[44] The slight difference in the spelling of the preposition is not significant. More important is the fact that this is first time Paul uses the word ἁμαρτία in Romans, and he uses it to personify Sin as a cosmic power.

and Death appears to belong to his primary convictions as an apostle of the crucified and risen Christ. As the coming of Christ has shown, the human predicament is much worse than it appears before or apart from that event.

Paul is not a preacher of bad news, however. His focus is finally not the terror of the human predicament, but the miracle of God's grace that has invaded the human cosmos in the "justifying work" (δικαίωμα) of the one human being, Jesus Christ. Just as Paul thinks of sin and death as cosmological powers, so also, in Romans 5:20-21, does he characterize God's grace as tantamount to a cosmological power in the world. If Sin and Death are said to reign, so also does Grace (hence the capital G) in 5:21. Grace is not simply the divine favor, it is also the divine saving activity, and as such, the sphere within which believers are repeatedly granted life (5:1-2).[45] "Where Sin increased, Grace more than abounded" was more than sufficient to meet the challenge.[46] In Christ, God himself has entered the human cosmos, and God's powerful Grace, in contrast to the weak and ineffectual Law, is more than equal to the task of putting an end to the reigns of Sin and Death.

---

[45] See Michael Winger, "From Grace to Sin: Names and Abstractions in Paul's Letter," *NovT* 41 (1999): 145–75, esp. 154–55.

[46] Cf. Gaventa, "Cosmic Power," 131–32, 134.

2
Righteousness, Cosmic and Microcosmic

Stephen Westerholm

According to the Gospel of Mark, Jesus began his public activities by proclaiming a pending cosmic transformation: "The time has come. The kingdom of God has drawn near." The announcement of God's cosmic plan did not, as one might imagine, render the response of individual human beings vain or irrelevant. Rather, it lent that response urgency: "Repent and believe the gospel" (Mark 1:14-15). And the first thing Jesus did, with the dawn of God's kingdom on the horizon, was to summon local fishermen to help get the word out quickly and sign up subjects for the kingdom (Mark 1:16-20).

In a variety of forms, from direct pronouncements to parables and everything in between, and with a variety of pictures, from wedding banquets to harvests to the growth of a mustard seed, the indicative element in Jesus' message throughout the Synoptic Gospels amounts to the announcement of the dawning rule of God and the simultaneous overthrow of the powers of evil. To illustrate the point, Jesus drove out demons, healed the sick, fed the hungry, raised the dead (Matt 11:2-6; 12:28). But *with* the proclamation of the inaugurated cosmic transformation, brought about—be it noted—entirely by divine initiative, came the summons to human beings to get on board with what God was doing. In the Synoptic Gospels, equal billing with the indicative announcement of God's rule was given to imperatives outlining what it would take to "enter the kingdom" and to warnings of exclusion.[1] Response of one kind or another was not only essential

---

[1] E.g., Mark 9:43-48; 10:15, 23-27; Matt 5:20; 7:13-14, 21.

but inevitable—those not with Christ were in fact against him (Matt 12:30). And response was called for from everyone. As individuals responded, one way or the other, sons were divided against fathers, daughters against mothers, daughters-in-law against mothers-in-law (Matt 10:34-35). The individual who would find life—and everything Jesus said indicated that this *should* be a pressing concern—was told of sacrifices that must be made, loyalties that must be paramount, temptations that must be avoided (e.g., Matt 10:37-39; 16:24-25; 19:16-26). The required faith, the necessary sacrifices, the inevitable temptations to be overcome may be viewed globally as the lot of all who would enter the kingdom, but they could only be experienced individually. The road to destruction is broad; the narrow gate that leads to life admits one person at a time (Matt 7:13-14; Luke 13:23-24). If we wanted to combine in a single sentence language in vogue in different generations of New Testament scholarship, we could say that, in the message and activity of Jesus, *apocalyptic* pronouncements and developments were inseparably combined with summons to *existential* decisions.

The focus here is on Paul, but it is important to remember the rootedness of his mission and message in the mission and message of the Lord whose apostle, slave, and ambassador he was. In Paul, as in Jesus, we find the same combination of cosmic events announced and individual responses demanded: here, too, the marriage of the apocalyptic and the existential permits no divorce. In the face of the imminent cosmic outpouring of God's wrath, the Thessalonian believers distinguished themselves from their compatriots by believing in the apostolic message, receiving it as the very word of God (1 Thess 2:13), thus proving to be among those destined not for wrath but for obtaining salvation through the Lord Jesus Christ (5:9). The announcement to the Corinthians that God was at work in Christ reconciling the world to himself is followed immediately by the appeal, "We beg you, for Christ's sake, be reconciled to God" (2 Cor 5:19-20). Examples from throughout Paul's letters could easily be multiplied; but here I want to focus on two verses from Romans 5, both involving the language of righteousness, one making claims of cosmic divine activity, the other implying the requisite individual response. Romans 5:1 reminds us of the latter: "Therefore, having been declared righteous by faith, we have peace with God through our Lord Jesus Christ." Romans 5:19 proclaims the former: "As by the disobedience of one man the many were rendered sinners, so also by the obedience of one the many will be rendered righteous." The remainder of this paper will be devoted to the interpretation of these two texts and to reflections on the relationship between them.

Justified by Faith

First, then, Romans 5:1: "Therefore, having been declared righteous by faith, we have peace with God through our Lord Jesus Christ." The verse may, of course, be said to sum up the argument of the preceding chapters in general; but it follows immediately the closing verses of chapter 4, according to which Genesis 15:6 was written not only on account of believing Abraham, to whom righteousness was credited, but also on "our" account, we who likewise believe and to whom, likewise, righteousness is to be credited (Rom 4:23-24). Paul then goes on: "*Therefore*, since we have been declared righteous by faith, we have peace with God." Recalling the progression of thought in these verses is useful because it means that doubts raised in recent literature whether Paul's πίστις χριστοῦ formulas speak of the faith of the believer in Christ or of Christ's faithfulness are not an issue here. Here the faith spoken of, as in the immediately preceding verses, and as throughout Romans 4, is determined by the controlling example of Abraham: it is that of the one to whom righteousness is credited. So Romans 4:3: "Abraham believed God, and it was credited to him for righteousness." In 4:5, it is explicitly "*their* faith" (i.e., the faith of everyone who does not work but believes) that is credited to them as righteousness. Paul can thus speak of "the righteousness of faith" (4:11; the phrase is repeated in 4:13) and of Abraham as the father of all who believe, to whom righteousness is therefore credited (4:11-12).

Righteousness language will occupy us shortly, but I want us to pause first over the existential reality of faith as Paul portrays it in this context. The analogy between Abraham's faith and that of the Christian believer goes beyond the mere fact that both involve a trust in God. In Galatians, Paul is content to use Abraham's faith and Genesis 15:6 to establish the principle that righteousness is by faith (Gal 3:6-7). In Romans 4, by way of contrast, the whole story of Abraham engages him. As a prelude to his references in chapter 5 to the character-building, hope-creating sufferings that necessarily attend Christian faith, Paul develops at some length the trials that beset believing Abraham: his was a faith rooted in hope—in a situation that was beyond all hope (Rom 4:18). The century-old patriarch was to be a father of many nations at a time when his body was as good as dead, and when the womb of his wife, the designated mother-to-be, was itself dead. The textual tradition at this point (4:19) leaves us uncertain whether Paul wants to say that Abraham *considered* all this but nonetheless did not waver in his confidence in God's promise, or whether his point is that Abraham blithely *disregarded*—he did *not even* consider—all that made fulfillment of God's promise impossible from a human perspective. Curiously, in this case the presence or absence of a negative makes no difference to the thrust of Paul's argument; despite all appearances that would throw the object of his faith into question, Abraham persevered, believing that what God had promised, he was able to do. Abraham's faith was credited to him as righteousness. And he is the father of all who believe.

Two aspects of the analogy Paul draws merit mention here. First, faith is the common factor that unites Abraham with the believers of Paul's day. Second, the faith shared by all is necessarily the existential experience of individuals, demanding sacrifices, beset by temptations, accompanied by sufferings that are unique to each believer.

First, the commonality. If Jesus came to bring not peace but a sword, dividing all who encountered him into those *for* and those *against* him, the same can be said of Paul. His was a scented message, an odor of life for some, of death for others (2 Cor 2:15-16); what determined the outcome was the submissive, obedient response of faith, on the one hand (cf. Rom 1:5), or the "disobedient," *unsubmissive* response of unbelief, on the other (cf. 2 Thess 1:8). Paul's communities were made up, both exhaustively and exclusively, of οἱ πιστεύοντες, "those who believe," a term that required no further definition (1 Cor 14:22; 1 Thess 1:7; 2:10, 13). Theirs is the "righteousness of faith" (Rom 10:6), inasmuch as they *believe* with their heart and are *justified* (Rom 10:10). Outsiders are οἱ ἄπιστοι, "the unbelievers" (1 Cor 6:6; 10:27; 14:22-24). Since it belonged to the essence of Paul's message to call for faith, and since that message then became the object of faith, Paul can sum up what he proclaimed simply as "the faith," again without further definition (Gal 1:23). And faith, as we have seen, is the common and necessary possession of all those whom God finds righteous, before as well as after Christ, Gentile as well as Jew—beginning with Abraham (Rom 3:29; 4:9-12).

If all this seems too anthropological in its focus, the reminder is very much in order that the human faith credited as righteousness is not a virtue inherent in the individual who believes, nor even a self-generated response to the proclamation of the gospel, and certainly not the calculated decision of rational human beings. Faith, in Abraham's case as in that of the Christian believer, is a response called into being by the word of God. The faith of which Paul speaks comes by hearing the word of Christ (Rom 10:17). Believers have faith because the word of God proclaimed to them is effective within them (1 Thess 2:13). The word of God "bears fruit" in those who believe (Col 1:5-6; cf. 2 Thess 3:1). If Paul's communities are made up of οἱ πιστεύοντες, those who believe, they can also be said to be made up of οἱ κλητοί, the called ones, and the designations are not unrelated.[2] Believers are those who hear the effective *call* of God in the gospel and respond with faith (2 Thess 2:14). Their faith is thus itself a gift of God (Phil 1:29).

But the call of God, though resulting in a collective—the community of believers—must be heard as individually addressed if it is to result in a faith like Abraham's. Though Christ died "for all" (2 Cor 5:14-15), his self-sacrificing love must be experienced, as Paul put it and Luther was wont to repeat,[3] as a love "for me," a giving of himself "for me" (Gal 2:20), if it is to evoke in "me" the trust that does not waver in the face of suffering and temptations. Faith, in this sense, is an existential reality for the individual—or it is no reality at all. The call of Christ divided son from father, daughter from mother. Paul's communities, too, included husbands whose wives were ἄπιστοι, wives whose husbands were ἄπιστοι (1 Cor 7:12-13), servants whose masters were unbelievers (1 Cor 7:21), and masters whose servants were unbelievers (Phlm 10-11). A believer could well be opposed by those of his or her own household (cf. Matt 10:36). And the division was brought

---

[2] Note, e.g., how those who are being saved through the kerygma in 1 Cor 1:21 are "those who believe"; the same people are referred to three verses later as "those who are called."

[3] Note, e.g., his comments on Gal 2:20 in the 1535 *Lectures on Galatians*: "Read these words 'me' and 'for me' with great emphasis, and accustom yourself to accepting this 'me' with a sure faith and applying it to yourself. Do not doubt that you belong to the number of those who speak this 'me.' Christ did not love only Peter and Paul and give Himself for them, but the same grace belongs and comes to us as to them; therefore we are included in this 'me.'" Martin Luther, *Luther's Works* 26 (ed. Jaroslav Pelikan; Saint Louis: Concordia, 1963), 179. Also Luther's *Treatise on Good Works* in *Luther's Works* 44 (ed. Jaroslav Pelikan; Philadelphia: Fortress, 1966), 38: "Faith must spring up and flow from the blood and wounds and death of Christ. If you see in these that God is so kindly disposed toward you that he even gives his own Son for you, then your heart in turn must grow sweet and disposed toward God. And in this way your confidence must grow out of pure good will and love—God's toward you, and yours toward God."

about, as we have seen, by the proclamation of the gospel. That all who heard God's call and believed were then exposed to temptation, liable to suffering, and summoned to a life of love, joy, thanksgiving, and patience meant that all could be the object of common exhortations. It remains true that the temptations, the suffering, and the disciplines of faith were necessarily peculiar to each individual.

Justified by Faith

Abraham heard the word of God, believed, and was credited with righteousness. Paul writes to those who likewise had heard the word of God in the gospel message, believed, and were declared righteous. As everyone notes who writes on the subject, the language of justification is only one of a number of ways in which Paul can speak of the salvation offered in Christ. It becomes significant first in Galatians, where Paul finds in Genesis 15:6 a godsend for refuting opponents who invoked the story of Abraham for a different purpose: in *their* view, messianic redemption functions within the framework of a covenant that includes circumcision and the laws of Moses; that Abraham and all who belonged to his household were circumcised proved their point. In Paul's terms, such people seek righteousness on the basis of the law, where it cannot be found (Gal 2:21; 5:4); Abraham, who was declared righteous on the basis of his faith in the word of God, shows the path that God has ordained (Gal 3:6-9). This usage of righteousness language, developed as Paul dealt with the Galatian controversy, had become part of his repertoire when he wrote Romans and Philippians, though the contrast remained with a righteousness purportedly based on law (3:11-12; Rom 10:5-10; Phil 3:9).

Nearly a century has passed since Albert Schweitzer famously labeled justification by faith a "subsidiary crater" in Paul's thought;[4] curiously, among those inclined to dispute traditional understandings of the doctrine, the temptation remains strong to exaggerate its significance by including as part of its meaning all manner of other convictions important to Paul.[5] One should not, perhaps, be too upset when

---

[4] Albert Schweitzer, *The Mysticism of Paul the Apostle* (New York: Seabury, 1931), 225.

[5] The argument that follows presents, in summary form, the main points made in Stephen Westerholm, *Perspectives Old and New on Paul: The "Lutheran" Paul and His Critics* (Grand Rapids: Eerdmans, 2004), 261–96, with bibliographical references. See now also David J. Southall, *Rediscovering Righteousness in Romans* (Tübingen: Mohr Siebeck, 2008), 9–20.

attention is drawn to crucial Pauline themes like the uniting of Jew and Gentile in one family of faith, the gift of the Spirit to the believer, or the deliverance Christ brings about from captivity to sin and death; but to stretch Paul's language of justification to make *it* include these latter themes has the inevitable result of distracting from or distorting the more limited but still essential truth of justification itself.[6] As background to Paul's claims about righteousness in both Romans 5:1 and 5:19, let me begin with a few observations about the terminology. I speak in the first place of the Hebrew terms *tzaddiq*, "righteous," *tzedeqah*, "righteousness," and the verb in the hiphil stem, *hitzdiq*, which I will render "find" or "declare righteous" rather than "justify" in order to underline its relation with the cognate adjective and noun.

The first thing to be said about these words is that they are perhaps the most basic terms in the ethical vocabulary of the Hebrew language. The *tzaddiq* is the person who does what he or she is morally bound to do, and what they do is *tzedeqah*. Parallel to the *tzaddiq* are the "blameless" (Gen 6:9; Job 12:4), the "innocent" (Job 22:19; Ps 94:21), the "upright in heart" (Ps 32:11; 64:10 [M.T. 64:11]; 97:11). Opposite are the "wicked" (Gen 18:25; Ps 1:6). It is of course important to add that Hebrew understandings of *what* things are the right things to do—and even more basically, of what *makes them* the right things to do—differ in varying degrees from the moral convictions of most if not all moderns. When Ezekiel describes the *tzaddiq*, the righteous person, as one who "does not eat upon the mountains or lift up his eyes to the idols of the house of Israel, does not defile his neighbor's wife or approach a woman in her time of impurity, does not oppress anyone, but restores to the debtor his pledge, commits no robbery, gives his bread to the hungry and covers the naked with a garment, does not lend at interest," and so on (Ezek 18:5-9), it is clear *both* that Ezekiel means by the *tzaddiq* the person who does what he or she ought to do *and* that Ezekiel's notion of what one ought to do overlaps but does not completely coincide with the notions of people today. When Proverbs tells

---

[6] N. T. Wright has recently lamented the plethora of articles on justification in theological and biblical dictionaries that make no mention of "Abraham and the promises God made to him, incorporation into Christ, resurrection and new creation, the coming together of Jews and Gentiles, eschatology in the sense of God's purpose-driven plan through history, and, not least, the Holy Spirit and the formation of Christian character." *Justification: God's Plan and Paul's Vision* (Downers Grove, Ill.: IVP Academic, 2009), 31–32. For my part, I lament that, in such esteemed company, what Paul, more specifically, means by justification is liable to go unnoticed.

us that the righteous person has regard for the well-being of animals (12:10), hates lying (13:5), is generous (21:26), and shows concern for the poor (29:7), we could well imagine its world to be our own. But we are drawn up short when it becomes clear that Proverbs sees no difference between the righteous person and the one who is wise, or between the wicked and the fool; and we are left dumbfounded by the apparently facile expectation of Proverbs that the righteous will get on well in this world—have full stomachs, full barns, good health, and long life—whereas the wicked are doomed to terrestrial trouble (e.g., 10:3, 24, 27; 11:8, 31; 12:21; 13:25).

For Proverbs, as for all the writers of Hebrew scripture and for Paul as well, we live in a world ordered by the wisdom of God. In *such* a world, the right thing to do is also the wise thing to do: that is, to refrain from doing what is wise or right *in one's own eyes* (Prov 3:7; 12:15; 16:2; 21:2; 30:12), and to seek out the course of action that is in keeping with the wisdom that formed the world in the beginning and that makes it go round to this day (3:19; 8:12-36). It is only natural, then, to expect that those who live in harmony with the order of the cosmos will get on well within it. To be sure, even Proverbs is aware that does not always happen; it is still better, it is more in keeping with the way things ought to be, to be poor and maintain one's integrity than rich and crooked in one's dealings (28:6; cf. 19:22). To do so, to do what is right, is to be righteous and wise. And it all begins with the fear of the Lord (1:7).

As the divine order pervades the whole universe, so expectations of right behavior are universal. The language of righteousness is by no means confined to the covenant people of God, nor does it denote belonging to their number. It pervades the book of Proverbs, where there is no talk of ethnicity or covenant. Throughout the Hebrew scriptures, nothing prevents a non-Israelite (i.e., one outside God's covenant with Israel) from being found "righteous."[7] "Noah was a righteous man" (Gen 6:9), and the announcement that he should enter the ark because God found him righteous in his generation (Gen 7:1) implies that he, not others, is being delivered from divine judgment because he is righteous and they are not—though they should have

---

[7] Conversely, the people of Israel were rebellious, not righteous, before and after they entered the covenant at Sinai (Deut 9:4-7). Clearly, they were expected to be righteous (though they were not) even before they entered the covenant—and entering the covenant did not make them righteous.

been no less than he. There was, moreover, nothing in principle unreasonable in the minimal expectation that there would be fifty *tzaddiqim*, fifty righteous people, in a Canaanite city like Sodom (Gen 18:24), though the city was later destroyed for lack of ten. Human beings are by nature moral beings; inside or outside God's covenant people, they are expected to do what is right; and they are righteous only if they do so. And implicitly from the beginning, though first explicitly later, the laws given to Israel were understood, at least in part, as the articulation of what is in keeping with the divine order of the world in which we live, and thus right for all human beings to do: even the nations, Deuteronomy observes, must acknowledge the righteousness of the statutes and ordinances in Moses' law (Deut 4:6-8).[8]

Three other observations should be made before we turn to Paul. First, as human righteousness amounts to living in conformity with the order imposed by divine wisdom on the cosmos, so God's righteousness consists in his readiness to uphold or restore that order when it is violated: by vindicating those who are innocent though wronged, delivering the oppressed, or keeping faith with his people.[9] Second, on the human level, perfection was neither expected nor a prerequisite for being righteous. Among the marks of those who live as they ought in Proverbs is their willingness to listen to rebuke (12:1; 13:18; 15:5). Their righteousness thus consists in their basic orientation toward what is right, not in their success in never doing otherwise. Admittedly, a few Old Testament texts use the terminology in a stricter sense: the point then is that no human being, rigorously appraised, can be righteous before God. One such text, the prayer of Psalms 143:2, was a favorite of Paul's: "Enter not into judgment with your servant, for no one living is found righteous before you" (cf. also Job 4:17-19; 15:14-16; 25:4-6; Ps 130:3-4). That is a point worth making, but the texts that make it are few. Most are content to ascribe righteousness to imperfect human beings whose basic mindset is right.

My third observation expands on the fundamental point that the language of "right" and "righteousness" is simple moral vocabulary;

---

[8] That a *commandment* can be "righteous" is itself evidence that the term does not refer to covenant membership; note also "*paths* of righteousness" in Ps 23:3, and the "righteous" weights and measures of Lev 19:35-36! Things as well as people can be "righteous" if in harmony with a rightly ordered universe.

[9] Cf. Mark A. Seifrid, "Righteousness Language in the Hebrew Scriptures and Early Judaism," in *Justification and Variegated Nomism* (ed. D. A. Carson, Peter T. O'Brien, and Mark A. Seifrid; Tübingen: Mohr Siebeck, 2001), 415–42.

namely, it need not imply or presuppose a legal setting. To be sure, the verb, by which pronouncements are made about whether or not one is in the right in a particular and contested situation, is largely confined to legal or quasi-legal contexts. Two crucial remarks need to be made about this usage. First, the connection of righteousness language with doing what one ought to do is not lost when the cognate verb is employed in a legal or quasi-legal setting. It is true that such judgments pertain, not to one's overall ethical character as righteous or sinner, but only to the specific issue or action under review. Still, the pronouncement pertains precisely to whether or not one is in the right, whether or not one has acted as one ought, in that particular instance. Ethical behavior, as the Israelites understood ethical behavior, is still at stake. Second, it is emphatically *not* the case that the verdict of the judge is what *makes* a person righteous or wicked. Righteousness is not a status conveyed by a judge's decision.[10] The righteous person is the person who has done what is right, whether or not the judge acknowledges their righteousness. The sinner, the guilty party, is the person who actually did what is wrong, whether or not a judge pronounces them guilty. Human courts get it right sometimes, but they can also get it wrong. Sometimes innocent blood is shed. Naboth does not become unrighteous when he is falsely accused and condemned at the instigation of Jezebel (1 Kgs 21:1-19). Conversely, murderers do not become righteous if a corrupt judge acquits them. Warnings against declaring righteous the guilty, or declaring guilty the righteous (cf. Exod 23:7; Deut 25:1; Prov 15:17; Isa 5:23), make clear that whether one is righteous or guilty depends on what one has or has not done, regardless of any judicial decision in the matter. To quote the well-known pragmatic philosopher Bill Belichick, the defendant's integrity or guilt "is what it is." Neither righteousness nor its opposite, wickedness or guilt, is a status conveyed by a judge's decision.

The language of righteousness as basic ethical vocabulary is abundantly attested in Paul, now of course in the form of the Greek adjective δίκαιος, "righteous"; the noun δικαιοσύνη, "righteousness"; and the verb δικαιόω, "declare innocent or righteous." Righteousness, in Paul, too, is what one ought to do, the equivalent of the good, the opposite of sin. To say that no one is righteous, Romans 3:10, is to

---

[10] For the opposing view, see Wright, *Justification*, 68–69, 90, 92, etc.; but already Rudolf Bultmann, *Theology of the New Testament* (vol. 1; New York: Scribner, 1951), 272.

say that no one does what is good, Romans 3:12. One must choose between serving righteousness or serving sin (Rom 6:18, 19). There is no fellowship between righteousness and wickedness, any more than there is between light and darkness (2 Cor 6:14). And for the apostle, too, the obligation to do what is right is universal; it is, indeed, the implicit basis for the universal outpouring of God's wrath on all ungodliness and "un*righteousness*" (Rom 1:18; cf. 1 Thess 1:10; 5:3). For the benefit of Jews, God has spelled out in the law the moral obligations of all human beings; as a result, the Jew who is instructed in the law is in a position to be a guide to the blind, a light to those in darkness, an educator of the foolish—in each case by instructing Gentiles in the moral obligations incumbent upon all: you shall not steal, you shall not commit adultery, and so on (Rom 2:17-22). And God will judge Jew and Gentile alike as to whether or not they have actually fulfilled these demands: whether or not they have done what is good (Rom 2:7-10), or—in an equivalent expression—whether or not they are doers of the law (Rom 2:13). God's judgment is impartial and makes no mistakes: it is the doers of the laws who *are* righteous, and God will declare them so (Rom 2:11, 13). So understood, the "righteousness of the law" is neither arbitrary nor negotiable; it belongs to the moral fabric of the universe. To transgress it is to alienate oneself not only from God, but also from God's good creation and one's intended place within it.

Paul thus shared with his fellow Jews the conviction, first, that the cosmos is ordered by God; second, that the righteous live in conformity with the wisdom of the created order; and third, that God has given Jews a law spelling out the righteousness he requires, so that the doers of the law will be found righteous. Where he differs dramatically from his fellow Jews[11] is in his belief that the circle of those who will be found righteous in the ordinary sense of the word—because they have done what they ought—is a circle devoid of occupants. There *is* none

---

[11] See Stephen Westerholm, "Paul's Anthropological 'Pessimism' in Its Jewish Context," in *Divine and Human Agency in Paul and His Cultural Environment* (ed. John M. G. Barclay and Simon J. Gathercole; London: T&T Clark, 2006), 71–98. Also Mikael Winninge, *Sinners and the Righteous: A Comparative Study of the Psalms of Solomon and Paul's Letters* (Stockholm: Almqvist & Wiksell, 1995), who argues that Paul introduces something "entirely new" to Judaism in speaking of "all Jews and Gentiles" as "sinners from the outset" (264). Of Rom 5:6-10, Winninge writes, "Whereas Paul's Jewish contemporaries could admit that all human beings occasionally committed sins, they would never have thought of classifying the basically faithful as sinners (status). In fact, Rom 5:6-10 revolve around this central point" (306–7).

righteous (Rom 3:10). *No* flesh will be found righteous by doing what the law requires (Rom 3:20). Two standard objections to this claim will serve to clarify its essence.

First, does Paul think there is *none* righteous because he has set the standard impossibly high, so that anything short of perfection fails the test? After all, as noted above, perfection was not expected in most Old Testament and later Jewish texts that speak of righteous individuals.[12] The question misses Paul's point. Within the apostle's horizons, there is no one who is 99 percent righteous—or 90 percent, or 75 percent, or 50 percent. All humanity, he believes, is *at heart* hostile to God (Rom 5:10), unsubmissive to God's laws, and incapable of being otherwise (Rom 8:7-8). Paul does not deny that people, even Gentiles, may do things that are right. But there is in human beings no good that is not tainted by the flesh (Rom 7:18). People sin because they *are* sinners, under the power of sin, enslaved by sin—though one must add that it is a slavery that they themselves embrace again and again each time they commit concrete wrongful acts; the desires of *the* flesh evidently correspond all too well with the desires of *their* flesh (cf. Gal 6:8; Rom 7:18). Thus, when God gives his righteous law to rebellious human beings, its practical effect, through no fault of the law, is to exacerbate their rebelliousness, to show the exceeding sinfulness of their sin (Rom 7:7-13). As a result, though the law was given with a display of God's glory, its administration, among sinners, is reduced to one of condemnation and death (2 Cor 3:7, 9).

Second objection. Has Paul forgotten the rites of atonement that are also provided for in the law?[13] That seems unlikely; he may well have believed—what other early Christian writers explicitly say—that the old covenant's rites of atonement were ineffective in themselves, serving only to foreshadow the once-for-all, effective self-sacrifice of Christ (cf. Rom 3:25; Col 2:17; Heb 10:1, 4). But we should also remember that, even among non-Christ-believing Jews, the rites of atonement were thought to apply, not to high-handed sinners, but only to those living basically within the terms of the covenant (cf. Num 15:30-31). For Paul, however, the sinfulness of *all humankind* is radical. His anthropology, we may say, when compared to that of most second-temple

---

[12] Cf. Claude G. Montefiore, *Judaism and St. Paul* (London: Max Goschen, 1914), 40–42, 70, 78; Krister Stendahl, *Paul among Jews and Gentiles and Other Essays* (Philadelphia: Fortress, 1983), 80–81; E. P. Sanders, *Paul and Palestinian Judaism* (Philadelphia: Fortress, 1977), 137–38, 175–76, 203.

[13] Cf. Sanders, *Paul and Palestinian Judaism*, 157.

Jews, is, quantitatively and qualitatively, more pessimistic; the universal human condition is, in his understanding, more dire.

And, of course, it had to be. Paul was no pessimist by nature. But he had come to see that the divine remedy for human sinfulness was the crucifixion of the Messiah. So catastrophic a remedy demands a catastrophic predicament. After all, if people *were* righteous in the ordinary sense of the word, because they did what they ought, then there was no reason for Christ to die (Gal 2:21). But Christ had died. So righteousness is not possible in the ordinary way. In short, the radical nature of human *un*righteousness and *un*godliness becomes apparent only in the light of the cross. And as the cross of Christ reveals the depths of human sinfulness, it serves at the same time as the divine answer to the dilemma. Logically, plight precedes solution; but *this* perception of the plight emerged clearly only in the light of the solution.[14]

So in the end, Paul's dire depiction of the human dilemma is only the backdrop for his proclamation of the divine solution. If human beings prove, individually and *en masse*, to be unrighteous, God remains righteous, committed to upholding—or, in this case, restoring—the goodness of his creation. The restorative act of God's righteousness is the atoning death of his Son. As a result, those who are *not* righteous in the ordinary sense of the word (i.e., by doing what they ought) can nonetheless be declared righteous by God—extraordinarily but nonetheless rightly, because the wrongs they have done and the bane that followed those wrongs were borne by, and exhausted on, the dying Redeemer (Rom 3:24-26). "God shows his love for us in that while we were yet sinners, Christ died for us": so Paul writes in Romans 5:8, and he goes on immediately to say, in effect, "We are declared righteous at Christ's expense, at the cost of his blood" (Rom 5:9).

In 1 Corinthians 1, Paul delights in the paradox of a gospel by which God chose what is foolish in the world to shame the wise, what is weak to confound the strong (1 Cor 1:27). Similarly, in Romans 3 to 5, Paul relishes the paradox of a gospel by which, for Christ's sake, God rightly declares righteous the *un*righteous. The startling claim that

---

[14] Frank Thielman is right to remind us that the movement from plight to solution is repeatedly traced in both biblical and postbiblical Jewish tradition. *From Plight to Solution: A Jewish Framework for Understanding Paul's View of the Law in Galatians and Romans* (Leiden: Brill, 1989). And Paul certainly drew on biblical texts in depicting humanity's plight apart from Christ (esp. Rom 1–3). But his reading of these texts, and his reconfiguration of standard views of humanity's plight, are doubtless the product of his post-conversion thinking. See Westerholm, *Perspectives*, 359.

God justifies the ungodly (Rom 4:5) must be given its full force, not allowed to be blunted either by familiarity or by a failure to distinguish between the essence of the claim and one of its implications, the inclusion of sinful Gentiles with sinful Jews in the people of God. A crucial Pauline paradox is lost when the moral dimension of his language of justification is downplayed or transformed into a message of liberation, family membership, or the breaking down of barriers between Jews and Gentiles. To repeat, justification is only one way in which Paul depicts salvation in Christ; but it is an essential way, highlighting as it does the moral nature of human beings, the awful reality and consequences of their sin, and that God, even in redeeming sinful human beings, underscores rather than overlooks the difference between good and evil.

And, again to repeat, justification is *by faith*. Christ invited all, even tax collectors and prostitutes, to the kingdom of God; but—by definition, we may say—those who will have nothing to do with God's rule exclude themselves from his kingdom. For Paul, too, those who remain unsubmissive to God's righteousness in the rebelliousness of their flesh remain—by definition, we may say—at enmity with God;[15] hence the urgent appeal, "Be reconciled to God" (2 Cor 5:20). Those, on the other hand, who have been declared righteous on the basis of faith enjoy peace with God, stand in the sphere of his grace, and rejoice in the hope of sharing God's glory (Rom 5:1-2). So far, then, the righteousness of Romans 5:1: righteousness, we may say, on the microcosmic level.

Cosmic Righteousness

Paul can at times write as though, given that this present evil age is beyond redemption, God in Christ is salvaging what can be salvaged

---

[15] Cf. Sam K. Williams, "The 'Righteousness of God' in Romans," *JBL* 99 (1980): 241–90, here 256: "If *God* is revealing his righteousness [Rom 1:17], how can Paul say that the revelation is 'on the basis of faith'? He does not mean that man's faith is the necessary precondition for the revealing of God's righteousness.... On the other hand, the apostle cannot conceive of the fulfilling of that purpose apart from the human reception and appropriation of the revelation. Indeed, one can ask whether in Paul's letters or elsewhere in the biblical tradition there can *be* any 'revelation' without the human act of receiving what God initiates. Does not the very notion of revelation imply two parties, revealer and recipient . . . ? In spite of God's initiative, man does not 'see' his righteousness, does not experience it as such, except on the basis of faith. Thus faith, which is both fruit of and response to the gospel, actually contributes to the carrying through of God's eschatological plan, even as faith—the sign and seal of the new humanity God is creating—is also the goal."

before its warranted destruction, just as a remnant in Isaiah's day was all that kept Israel from becoming like Sodom and Gomorrah (cf. Rom 9:27-29). First Thessalonians in its entirety reads that way. So does the stated goal of all Paul's mission, in 1 Corinthians 9:19-22 and again in Romans 11:14: all he does is done with the hope that "some" will be saved. Without pausing here to note other texts to this effect, we turn now to the rather different emphasis of Romans 5:12-19. Here the story is not that of rescuing a few from the *massa perditionis*, but of the reversal of Adam's sin and its consequences for humankind as a whole.

The story of humankind as here related begins with Adam, the one man by whose sin, sin entered the world, the representative man by whose sin all human beings became sinners. The instinct that prompted Paul to add the last words of Romans 5:12, "inasmuch as all sinned," may well have risen out of an anxiety to guard against the misunderstanding that Adam's fall removed culpability for sin from later generations. No, says Paul—without retreating from his claim that Adam's sin had universal consequences; all human beings descended from Adam re-enact his disobedience and make his sin their own. Some sin, as he did, by transgressing God's commands; others (those between Adam and Moses) sinned without transgression of an explicit law (5:13-14). But sin, having penetrated the race in its forebear, now rules all its members. To speak of humankind as humankind was created is no longer an adequate account of its condition. Humankind-in-Adam has both embraced sin and become sin's slaves. Humankind-in-Adam is a ruined creation, a condemned race.

But Adam is the type of Jesus Christ, whose righteousness proves as determinative of the character of the new humanity as Adam's disobedience was of the old. Elsewhere Paul will speak of Christ as *God's Son*, sent in the form of sinful flesh (8:3; cf. Gal 4:4). Here, where the reversal of (the one *man*) Adam's misdeed is in view, he speaks of the other *man* Jesus Christ, and of the humanity patterned after each. Our focus here is on the language of righteousness. Christ's righteous act, his δικαίωμα, verse 18, is paralleled with his obedience, verse 19, and contrasted with Adam's offense and disobedience. If one specific act is in view, it is presumably the climax of a lifetime's obedience in Christ's death on the cross, as in Philippians 2:8. That act of righteousness and obedience leads to righteousness for others, specifically, as a sentence of acquittal, declaring them righteous (so vv. 16 and 18), the reception of the gift of righteousness (v. 17), the constitution of the many as righteous (v. 19). The three expressions represent different ways of saying the same thing, which itself does not differ from what in verse 1 is referred to as being declared righteous. The forensic connotations usually found with the verb δικαιόω seem present throughout verses 15-19, as indicated by the noun δικαίωμα, contrasted as it is with the κατάκριμα, the condemnation that followed Adam's sin.

Paul cannot say everything every time he opens his mouth, and much left unstated in these verses can be filled in by what we have seen of Paul's righteousness language earlier in Romans. Nothing is said of *how* Christ's righteous act led to a gift of righteousness to sinners. But we have no reason not to supplement the cryptic reference here with the explicit language of 3:24-26: God put forward Christ Jesus to atone for sins, so that he might declare righteous the one who has faith in Jesus. Nothing is said directly in 5:15-19 of the *reception* of the gift of righteousness by faith, though it should be noted that the beneficiaries of the gift in verse 17 are identified as "those who *receive* the overflow of grace and the gift of righteousness." Recall that a positive response to the gospel proclaimed by Paul is often summed up as faith, but at other times as "receiving" (δέχομαι, λαμβάνω; the verbs are synonyms in 2 Cor 11:4) the message (1 Thess 1:6; 2:13) or the gospel (2 Cor 11:4); and with the reception of the message comes the reception of its benefits: grace (2 Cor 6:1), reconciliation (Rom 5:11), the spirit of adoption (Rom 8:15; cf. 1 Cor 2:12; Gal 3:2, 14), and so on. Presumably, the same steps are presupposed in Romans 5:15-19 as well: the reception of God's overflowing grace and gift of righteousness (5:17) follows from the reception of the gospel in faith.

But if Romans 5:15-19 does not repeat all that Paul had said about righteousness earlier in the letter, it is in order to emphasize an aspect of God's gift of righteousness to this point left unstated. More than a salvage operation is at work. In Galatians and 2 Corinthians, Paul had spoken of a "new creation," which is a reality for "anyone who is in Christ" (2 Cor 5:17; cf. Gal 6:16). Here we may say that Adam and Christ are prototypes of the old and the new in humanity. If Adam's sin and disobedience brought the rule of sin and death upon "the many" who constituted the old humanity, Christ's righteousness and obedience bring righteousness and life to "the many" who constitute the new.

To read the passage in this way implies that not all who belong to the old humanity necessarily belong to the new; the obvious advantage of such a reading is that it allows consistency to Paul, who, as we have seen, elsewhere and repeatedly distinguishes between those who are being saved, on the one hand, and those who are perishing, on the other (1 Cor 1:18); who, in 2 Corinthians 5:17, explicitly limits the new creation to those who are "in Christ"; and who, immediately after Romans 5, will imply in Romans 6 that those not baptized into Christ's death and resurrection—and who have thus not "died to sin"—continue to live in sin, a slavery that ends in death (6:16, 23). The alternative is to read Romans 5 (*and* 1 Cor 15:22: "In Adam all die; in Christ all will be made alive") as saying that the "all" who are made righteous by Christ's obedience are the same "all" who were made sinners by Adam's offense. Righteousness and salvation thus become truly universal. One could then cite in support Romans 11:32: "God has consigned all to disobedience, that he may have mercy upon all." If Colossians and Ephesians are allowed to be part of the picture, we could then add that Colossians speaks of God as reconciling to himself "all things, whether on earth or in heaven, making peace by the blood of his cross" (1:20) and that Ephesians sees the fulfillment of God's purposes in the uniting of "all things in Christ, things in heaven and things on earth" (1:10).

It is a vexed issue. As an interpreter of Paul, I think the former interpretation the more likely. Consistency is not to be bought at any price,[16] and perhaps we may say, as one recent commentator has said, that Romans 5 represents a "charismatic breakthrough"[17] not possessed by Paul when he wrote elsewhere of those destined for wrath. The problem with the charismatic-breakthrough proposal is that the same insight seems to have been reached already in 1 Corinthians 15:22 but then forgotten in 2 Corinthians when Paul speaks of his mission as bringing the aroma of Christ alike to those who are being saved and to those who are perishing (2:15), of his gospel as hid from those who are perishing (4:3), and of the importance, in this day of salvation, of not receiving the grace of God in vain (6:1-2). Again, if Romans 5 does indeed represent a charismatic breakthrough, it seems to have been forgotten in chapter 6 and chapter 8, where Paul warns that those who

---

[16] As elsewhere, so on this issue Heikki Räisänen is content to see Paul simply as inconsistent; see "A Controversial Jew and His Conflicting Convictions: *Paul, the Law, and the Jewish People* Twenty Years After," in *Redefining First-Century Jewish and Christian Identities: Essays in Honor of Ed Parish Sanders* (ed. Fabian E. Udoh, with Susannah Heschel, Mark Chancey, and Gregory Tatum; Notre Dame: University of Notre Dame Press, 2008), 319–35, here 325–26.

[17] Cf. Arland J. Hultgren, *Paul's Letter to the Romans: A Commentary* (Grand Rapids: Eerdmans, 2011), 234.

live according to the flesh will die (8:13). Ephesians and Colossians, too, are certain that wrath, rather than a place in God's kingdom, awaits the "children of disobedience" (Eph 5:5-6; Col 3:6).

The conversation on these issues continues,[18] but this chapter must not. I conclude by listing five points that seem accurately to reflect Paul's thinking on our topic, whatever uncertainties remain.

1. The old age marred by sin is destined to give way to God's new creation, a new age that has already dawned with the resurrection of Christ.
2. The new age can have no place for the sin that marred the old.
3. Hence the sinful inhabitants of the old age can participate in the new only if they are somehow made righteous.
4. The death of Christ is God's appointed means for that to happen.
5. It is incumbent on human beings who hear the call of God in the gospel to receive the righteousness of God freely, as a gift of God's grace, with an existential faith, like Abraham's.

---

[18] E.g., M. Eugene Boring, "The Language of Universal Salvation in Paul," *JBL* 105 (1986): 269–92; Sven Hillert, *Limited and Universal Salvation: A Text-Oriented and Hermeneutical Study of Two Perspectives in Paul* (Stockholm: Almqvist & Wiksell, 1999).

3
A Tale of Two Gardens
Augustine's Narrative Interpretation of Romans 5

Benjamin Myers

Paul and Augustine

It has been more than fifty years since Krister Stendahl published his landmark essay on "The Apostle Paul and the Introspective Conscience of the West."[*2] The essay announced that, ever since Saint Augustine, the church had got Paul wrong. Prior to Augustine, "the church was by and large under the impression that Paul dealt with those issues with which he actually deals"—namely, what happens to the Jewish Law now that the Messiah has come, and how does the Messiah affect the relation between Jews and Gentiles? Thanks to Augustine's pioneering misreading, these questions have all but disappeared.

Now, Christians read Paul not to find about the Law and the Gentiles, but to assuage a troubled conscience. Now our interpretive question has become—to quote Luther—"how can I find a gracious God?" This is a private question, an individual question, an introspective question, a question that has everything to do with the self and nothing to do with the great drama of salvation history. And it is Augustine's *Confessions*, Stendahl says, that forms "the first great document

---

[*] In preparing and revising this chapter, I benefited from conversations with Beverly Gaventa, Mary Schmitt, Jeff Aernie, and Steve Wright.

[2] Krister Stendahl, "The Apostle Paul and the Introspective Conscience of the West," in *Paul among Jews and Gentiles* (Minneapolis: Fortress, 1976), 78–96; repr. of "The Apostle Paul and the Introspective Conscience of the West," *HTR* 56 (1963): 199–215; rev. and trans. of "Paulus och Samvetet," *SEÅ* 25 (1960): 62–77.

in the history of the introspective conscience," Augustine's *Confessions* that has eclipsed Paul's concerns with its own.[3]

Contemporary scholarship on Paul is, I suspect, deeply shaped not only by the study of Paul's texts, but also by this polemical repudiation of what Robert Jewett conveniently calls "the Augustinian tradition," a tradition that "construes salvation as individual forgiveness."[4] It is, for instance, hard to imagine what Jewett's Hermeneia commentary on Romans would look like without this pervasive rejection of the shadowy figure of an Augustinian Paul. There are notable exceptions of course, such as Stephen Westerholm's careful reading of Augustine in his *Perspectives Old and New on Paul*[5] and the edited volume *Engaging Augustine on Romans*[6] (which, interestingly, was dedicated to Stendahl). However, in such cases of substantive engagement with Augustine, we tend only to hear of the later anti-Pelagian systematization of Augustine's interpretation of Paul—his theories of original sin, concupiscence, predestination, the enslavement of the will—and we don't get a clear enough picture of *how* Augustine reads Paul's text and how his imaginative landscapes were shaped by his reading of Paul.

It is sometimes forgotten that Augustine's deepest engagement with Paul came not at the end of his career, in the anti-Pelagian writings, but at the beginning, shortly after his conversion and ordination to the priesthood. In quick succession he produced three Pauline commentaries—two on Romans and one on Galatians—and this process of interpretation led directly to his great experimental essay in autobiography, the *Confessions*. In this chapter I will concentrate on this early period of Pauline interpretation. And I will try to show that Augustine was indeed a *reader* of Paul, not just a theologian riding roughshod over Paul's text with his own theories and agendas. Augustine's reading of the Epistle to the Romans—centered on the Christ–Adam typology of Romans 5—provides the blueprint for some of his most intricate and elaborate theological innovations. He does not merely interpret Paul; the categories of his imagination are reorganized by his encounter with Paul.[7]

---

[3] Stendahl, "Introspective Conscience," 83–85.

[4] Robert Jewett, *Romans* (Minneapolis: Fortress, 2006), 361.

[5] Stephen Westerholm, *Perspectives Old and New on Paul: The "Lutheran" Paul and His Critics* (Grand Rapids: Eerdmans, 2004).

[6] Daniel Patte and Eugene TeSelle, eds., *Engaging Augustine on Romans: Self, Context, and Theology in Interpretation* (London: T&T Clark, 2002).

[7] On the importance of Augustine's early encounter with Paul, see esp. Carol

Augustine's attention to Paul was not itself unique. The last decades of the fourth century witnessed an unprecedented interest in the letters of Paul. A century and a half earlier, Origen had written the first biblical commentaries in Greek, but not until around the time of Augustine's conversion did commentaries begin to appear in Latin, especially commentaries on Paul. And not only among Catholic authors: the heterodox sects such as the Manichees also based their teachings on huge mythological interpretations of Paul. In order to be part of the important discussions at the time, you had to talk about Paul: everyone claimed to be following Paul, and everyone seemed to be using him for their own purposes. For Augustine, as a recovering Manichee himself, a lot was at stake in the question of what Paul said and what he meant.

Augustine's conversion was brought about by a reading of the Epistle to the Romans. And after his conversion and baptism, the first thing he did was to establish a monastic community. It was the first monastery in North Africa, and there, in the company of his friends, Augustine began to expound Paul's letters. He completed a set of brief notes on every chapter of Romans, then began a full-scale commentary on Romans (which was never finished), and then completed a full commentary on Galatians. It was this process of Pauline interpretation that culminated in the *Confessions*, which Augustine wrote between 397 C.E. and 400 C.E.

In this chapter, I want to argue that Augustine's reading of Paul led to an immense re-imagining of what it means to be human. The philosophical traditions available in antiquity presupposed that the self is some manner of autonomous essence, with various powers and faculties at its disposal. Augustine departs radically from these traditions and develops what has been called a dependent doctrine of the self.[8] His reading of Paul marks a watershed in Western thought. It was Paul—especially the Paul of Romans 5—who taught Augustine to link together the personal and corporate dimensions of the self. By the time he wrote the *Confessions*, Augustine could view the self as simultaneously inhabiting two corporate personas, two agencies, two directions of life—Christ and Adam.

Harrison, *Rethinking Augustine's Early Theology* (Oxford: Oxford University Press, 2006); and Michael Cameron, *Christ Meets Me Everywhere: Augustine's Early Figurative Exegesis* (Oxford: Oxford University Press, 2012).

[8] Brian Stock, *Augustine's Inner Dialogue: The Philosophical Soliloquy in Late Antiquity* (Cambridge: Cambridge University Press, 2010).

Augustine the Commentator
Propositions from the Epistle to the Romans

In the series of notes on Romans completed in 394/95 C.E., Augustine sees Romans 9:24 as a summary of the letter's argument: "We whom he has called not only from the Jews but also from the Gentiles."[9] Paul's theme, he says, is the creation of one new people: "thus the Lord united both peoples," Jew and Gentile.[10] He insists that there is no simple contrast between Law and grace. By "believing in the Liberator," a person "ceases to be under the Law, but rather is with or within it, fulfilling it by the love of God."[11]

It is true that Augustine condemns the pride of the Jews.[12] But to leap to the conclusion that this is a supercessionist or anti-Semitic reading of Paul would be a mistake, for Augustine just as roundly denounces the pride of Gentile believers, explaining that Paul's letter was written "lest the Gentiles in their turn dare to grow haughty towards [the Jews]."[13] And again: "For just as [Paul] had to refute the pride of the Jews because they gloried in their works, so also with the Gentiles, lest they grow proud as if they had been preferred over the Jews."[14] In all this, Augustine takes for granted that faith in Christ is aboriginally a Jewish thing. It is not that the Jews have been set aside, but that the Gentiles have "put aside their gentileness [*gentilitatem*] through faith in Christ."[15] It is the Gentiles who are "sanctified through the gospel,"[16] the gospel that was really "sent to the Jews."[17]

In this commentary, the Epistle to the Romans is not viewed primarily in terms of individual forgiveness. Sin, Augustine writes, is a power that "captures" us.[18] Christ is most frequently described throughout the commentary as "the Liberator." He is *liberator noster dominus*

---

[9] Augustine, *Expositio quarundam propositionum ex epistula apostoli ad Romanos*, 64.1, in *Augustine on Romans: Proposition from the Epistle to the Romans, Unfinished Commentary on the Epistle to the Romans* (ed. Paula Fredriksen; Chico, Calif.: Scholar's Press, 1982). Hereafter cited as *Exp. prop. Rom.*

[10] Augustine, *Exp. prop. Rom.*, 64.3.
[11] Augustine, *Exp. prop. Rom.*, 44.3.
[12] Augustine, *Exp. prop. Rom.*, 64.2.
[13] Augustine, *Exp. prop. Rom.*, 66.1.
[14] Augustine, *Exp. prop. Rom.*, 66.2.
[15] Augustine, *Exp. prop. Rom.*, 68.3.
[16] Augustine, *Exp. prop. Rom.*, 82.4.
[17] Augustine, *Exp. prop. Rom.*, 82.1.
[18] Augustine, *Exp. prop. Rom.*, 47.2.

Iesus Christus, "our Liberator the Lord Jesus Christ."[19] Christ frees us from sin's dominion[20] by putting us to death and raising us to new life.[21] He has "cast aside the principalities and powers, vanquishing them in himself."[22]

On Romans 7:13—Paul's "I do not understand"—Augustine underscores the mystery of sin's power. Just as darkness is perceived only by not-seeing, so sin is discerned by not-understanding.[23] There is no positive content to our knowledge of sin; all we know is the liberating grace of Christ. To borrow E. P. Sanders' language, knowledge of the plight is derived from knowledge of the solution.[24]

Though Augustine shows no interest here in speculating on the mechanism of sin's transmission, he notes that sin and its power, death, have their "source" in the transgression of Adam.[25] We perform Adam's story as a "role"; Adam's fall is the plot of our own lives.[26] And though Adam and Christ are both corporate personas, there is an asymmetry between the two. Augustine writes: "in Adam one sin was condemned, but by the Lord many sins were forgiven."[27]

Unfinished Commentary on Romans

After these brief exegetical notes, Augustine set out to write a detailed commentary on Romans in 394/95 C.E. It was one of his many abortive projects. He got as far as Paul's greeting in Romans 1:7—"grace and peace to you"—and then gave up, "discouraged by the vastness and difficulty of the project" and eager to turn to easier things.[28]

In this unfinished work, there is the same emphasis on the one people of God created in Christ. The central question of Romans, Augustine argues, is "whether the gospel of our Lord Jesus Christ came to the Jews alone" or to "all nations."[29] Again he stresses both the

---

[19] Augustine, *Exp. prop. Rom.*, 48.4.
[20] Augustine, *Exp. prop. Rom.*, 35.2.
[21] Augustine, *Exp. prop. Rom.*, 36.5.
[22] Augustine, *Exp. prop. Rom.*, 58.4.
[23] Augustine, *Exp. prop. Rom.*, 43.2–3.
[24] E. P. Sanders, *Paul and Palestinian Judaism* (Minneapolis: Fortress, 1977), 497.
[25] Augustine, *Exp. prop. Rom.*, 46.7.
[26] Augustine, *Exp. prop. Rom.*, 32–34.3.
[27] Augustine, *Exp. prop. Rom.*, 29.6.
[28] Augustine, *Retractationes*, 1.25; in *Revisions* (trans. Boniface Ramsey; Hyde Park, N.Y.: New City Press, 2010).
[29] Augustine, *Epistulae ad Romanos inchoate expositio liber unus*, 1.1, in *Augustine on Romans* (ed. Fredriksen). Hereafter cited as *Ep. Rom. inch.*

Jewishness and the universality of Jesus. Christ assumes Jewish flesh,[30] he argues, in order to become "the salvation of all nations," "even" those who don't belong to the Jewish people.[31] Again he underscores the theme of boasting in relation to Jews and Gentiles. Paul, he writes, "permits neither the Jews to be proud because of the merits of the Law, nor the Gentiles to be haughty toward the Jews because of the merit of their faith in accepting Christ."[32] One can see here the simple exegetical basis of Augustine's later theory that faith is itself the gift of God. The idea arises not from an abstract contrast between grace and works but from Augustine's theological horror of pride—a horror that has much to do with the recurring Pauline injunction against "boasting." Augustine writes, "Paul unites in Christ through the bond of grace peoples from among the Jews and Gentiles both, taking away from both all pride because of merit, and bringing both together to be justified by the discipline of humility."[33]

In both these early commentaries on Romans, so-called "Augustinian" concerns about a tormented conscience and individual salvation are scarcely discernible. Rather, the really distinctive features of Augustine's interpretation are (1) the uniquely positive role he gives to the Jewish people, in contrast to all earlier patristic commentaries on Paul;[34] (2) his unique emphasis on the continuity between Old and New Testaments, again in contrast to early commentators, who often disparaged the Jewish Law as a mere shadow of Christ; and (3) the dual theme of pride and humility, which Augustine takes as a hermeneutical lens through which all Paul's concerns are viewed.

Commentary on Galatians

The commentary on Galatians, written in 395 C.E.,[35] is the only full-scale commentary that Augustine ever completed, aside from his huge collection of sermons on the Psalms. Coming hard on the heels of his

---

[30] Augustine, *Ep. Rom. inch.*, 4.3.
[31] Augustine, *Ep. Rom. inch.*, 6.4.
[32] Augustine, *Ep. Rom. inch.*, 1.4.
[33] Augustine, *Ep. Rom. inch.*, 1.4.
[34] Paula Fredriksen, *Augustine and the Jews: A Christian Defense of Jews and Judaism* (New Haven, Conn.: Yale University Press, 2010).
[35] Augustine, *Expositio epistulae ad Galatas liber unus*, in *Augustine's Commentary on Galatians: Introduction, Text, Translation, and Notes* (trans. Eric Plumer; Oxford: Oxford University Press, 2003). Hereafter cited as *Exp. Gal.*

two exegetical experiments on Romans, Augustine turns to Galatians, and he begins by comparing the two epistles:

> The point at issue in the Letter to the Romans is similar [to Galatians], but with this apparent difference: there he resolves an actual conflict, settling a dispute that had arisen between believers of Jewish and of Gentile origin. The Jews thought that the reward of the gospel had been paid to them for merits accruing from works of the Law and did not want this reward given to the uncircumcised, whom they regarded as undeserving. The Gentiles, on the other hand, desired to exalt themselves above the Jews, regarding them as murderers of the Lord.[36]

Commenting on Galatians 4:6—"God has sent the Spirit of his Son into our hearts, crying Abba! Father!"—Augustine suggests that Paul's use of two equivalent words for "father" is not redundant but is particularly "elegant" given the theme of the epistle: "it was on account of the whole people, called from both Jews and Gentiles into the unity of faith. The Hebrew word was used for the Jews, the Greek for the Gentiles." Thus the use of two words from two different languages points "to the unity of the same faith and Spirit."[37] It is an ingenious interpretive suggestion, echoed by many subsequent commentators. Even if one takes issue with the exegesis here, it could hardly be said that Augustine is foisting his own prefabricated theological agenda onto the Pauline text. If anything, he is perhaps *too* acutely sensitive to Paul's concerns in the epistle; he finds the motif of Jewish–Gentile unity even in the minutest details of the text.

Commenting on Galatians 3:13, Augustine presents salvation as Christ's victory over the curse of sin. Christ overcame "death by death" and "sin by sin" and the "serpent by the serpent" and "the curse by the curse." As a result, "all these things are triumphed over in the cross."[38] This soteriological picture of liberation from the objective power of sin is framed, even more explicitly than in the two Romans commentaries, by a schema of pride (*superbia*) and humility (*humilitas*). Augustine even draws a rhetorical contrast between two different mediators:

---

[36] Augustine, *Exp. Gal.*, 1.5. The last phrase ought to be taken not so much as gloss on Paul as a subtle critique of the anti-Jewish assumptions of other commentators on Paul in Augustine's day.

[37] Augustine, *Exp. Gal.*, 31.2.

[38] Augustine, *Exp. Gal.*, 22.16.

"anyone who was cast down with the proud mediator—the devil—urging him to pride, is raised up with the humble mediator—Christ—urging him to humility."[39] For it is humility "that calls us back from the place to which pride cast us down."[40]

Interpretive Themes

It is now possible to make some general conclusions about the distinctive features of Augustine's three early Pauline commentaries.

First, more than other patristic commentators Augustine emphasizes the positive place of Israel in God's redemptive plan. He repeatedly criticizes the Christian tendency to regard the Jews from a vantage point of disparaging superiority. For Augustine, this exegetical emphasis is a crucial tactic in dismantling the Pauline interpretation of the Manichees, an interpretation driven by an intense theological hostility toward Israel and the Old Testament.

Second, more than other patristic commentators Augustine articulates a complex relation of continuity and discontinuity between the Old and New Testaments. There is discontinuity, since in Christ everything is made new: a new humanity, a new human story, a new form of human community. But there is also continuity: as Augustine would later write in the *City of God*, "What is the Old Testament but a concealed form of the New? And what is the New Testament but the revelation of the Old?"[41]

Third, Augustine places great emphasis on the Christ–Adam typology of Romans 5. He sees the parallel between Christ and Adam as central to a Christian understanding of humanity. But he also argues that Christ and Adam are asymmetrically related. Really, it is not Adam who comes first, but Christ: that is the conclusion Augustine would later draw in his doctrine of predestination.[42] Christ precedes Adam; it is Christ, not Adam, who discloses the fundamental truth of humanity.

Though anti-Manichaean polemic is clearly an important part of the background to these early commentaries, it is the experience of

---

[39] Augustine, *Exp. Gal.*, 24.6.

[40] Augustine, *Exp. Gal.*, 25.10.

[41] Augustine, *The City of God* (trans. R. W. Dyson; Cambridge: Cambridge University Press, 1998), 16.26.

[42] James Wetzel, "Predestination, Pelagianism, and Foreknowledge," in *The Cambridge Companion to Augustine* (ed. Eleonore Stump and Norman Kretzmann; Cambridge: Cambridge University Press, 2001), 56.

monastic community that forms the immediate context of Augustine's interpretation of Paul in the 390s C.E.[43] He reads Paul not primarily as a guide to personal salvation, but "as a guide to building community."[44] This accounts for what Eric Plumer calls Augustine's "vital interest in the corporate dimensions of Paul's teaching on grace."[45] He wants to know what holds a Christian community together—and, indeed what holds human history together as a whole. Once this communal concern is in view, one can appreciate Augustine's early preoccupation with the Manichean and Donatist teachings: he treats them "not as abstract problems in theology but as concrete threats" to Christian community.[46] For Augustine, polemical concerns are always bound up with pastoral considerations about Christian unity.

Paul's account of the one new people of God is taken up by Augustine as a fundamental model for creating and sustaining Christian unity. Even Augustine's later obsession with Pelagian polemics should be understood as an extrapolation from this basic Pauline vision. The problem with the Pelagians is not simply that they have a faulty view of original sin or the human will. For Augustine, the real problem with the Pelagians—as with the Manichees and the Donatists—is that they want to turn the church into a spiritual aristocracy, with one group standing superior over the rest. Pelagianism was an austere monastic ideal; it insisted on severe standards of personal holiness and disparaged the moral struggles of ordinary Christians. Peter Brown speaks of the "icy puritanism" of the Pelagians; their aim was for all Christians to be monks.[47] They rejected Augustine's view of the corporate, cumulative nature of sin because they thought all individual Christians should be responsible for their own moral failings; if you sin, it's your own fault, and there are no mitigating circumstances, no occasion for sympathy or pastoral patience. Augustine's condemnation of this theology was a pastoral intervention that reflected his deep sympathy for the ordinary moral foibles of his parishioners. His doctrine of original sin—based on the corporate logic of Romans 5—was an attempt to lighten the burdens of ordinary flawed believers, to remind them that

---

[43] Plumer, *Augustine's Commentary on Galatians*, 71–88; Harrison, *Rethinking Augustine's Early Theology*, 122ff.

[44] Plumer, *Augustine's Commentary on Galatians*, 117.

[45] Plumer, *Augustine's Commentary on Galatians*, 81.

[46] Plumer, *Augustine's Commentary on Galatians*, 87.

[47] Peter Brown, *Augustine of Hippo: A Biography* (2nd ed.; Berkeley: University of California Press, 2000), 351.

we are not only agents of sin but also its victims. Behind every moral decision is a history—in the first instance, my own personal history with its elaborate apparatus of habit and repetition; and behind that, the history of the whole human family, all tangled up together in one lump, a sort of massive cumulative power of wrongdoing.[48] So where the Pelagians wanted to hold all Christians to the most exacting moral standards, Augustine's attitude was the opposite: to extend the greatest possible sympathy to fellow believers. He was able to adopt this pastoral position even while maintaining a very high ideal of the sanctity of the Christian community precisely because he was less concerned with individual freedom than with the shape of a whole moral community—a community that is slowly, painfully learning how to enter into the corporate persona of Christ instead of that of Adam.

All this supplies the necessary background for examining Augustine's real triumph of Pauline interpretation, the interpretive *tour de force* of the *Confessions*.

Confessions as a Narrative Commentary on Romans

James Joyce's modernist novel *Ulysses* follows one day in the life of one man, Leopold Bloom. The narrative of Bloom's day is superimposed over one of the best-known stories in ancient literature—Homer's *Odyssey*, the epic tale of Odysseus' journey home after the Trojan War. On the one hand, a reader finds in *Ulysses* one of the most particular novelistic narratives ever written—an almost unbearably detailed account of one ordinary day in the life of an ordinary man in Dublin. But on the other hand, the constant echoes of Homer's epic create a sense that something enormous is taking place, as though the events of Bloom's story are unfolding on a cosmic, world-historical stage.

Something very similar is going on in Augustine's *Confessions*. Augustine tells the story of his own life—from birth and infancy to his adolescence, his early adult years, and finally his conversion. He overlays this story with two biblical tropes: the story of Adam's fall, which took place in a garden, and the story of Christ's redemptive work, which also features a moment of crisis in a garden. Just as the Homeric epic seems to electrify the ordinary materials of Joyce's novel, so the Christ–Adam typology invests Augustine's story, even down to its smallest details, with theological significance. We begin to feel that

---

[48] See Stock, *Augustine's Inner Dialogue*.

more is at stake than just the autobiography of one life; we begin to feel that there are vast cosmic dimensions to Augustine's life story—that his own particular experiences of sin and grace, captivity and liberation are windows into universal truths about humanity.

The First Garden

In the second book of *Confessions*, Augustine describes the theft of some pears from a neighbor's garden. The scene is so memorable, so distinctive, that for many readers its theological significance is eclipsed by a sense of the sheer largeness of Augustine's personality. But this is far more than just an eccentric episode from Augustine's youth. From the first lines of book 2, Augustine introduces a tightly knit sequence of verbal echoes of the story of Adam's fall. In his adolescence, he tells us, he "ran wild in the jungle" of carnal pleasures;[49] he "tasted" forbidden pleasures,[50] and so became "fruitless."[51] He refers to youthful lusts as "the thorns of lust"[52] and as "the brambles which were excluded from your paradise."[53] Right from the outset, Genesis 3 is superimposed over Augustine's own story. Indeed Augustine informs us that he is about to relate this episode for the sake of all humanity: "I declare this to my race, to the human race."[54] Its significance is corporate, not merely personal.

The garden scene itself is introduced with the economical precision of Hebrew narrative: "Now there was a pear tree near our vineyard laden with fruit."[55] The main action is narrated in the same spare style: "To shake the fruit of the tree and carry off the pears, I and a gang of naughty adolescents set off late at night. . . . We carried off a huge load of pears. But they were not for our feasts but merely to throw to the pigs. Even if we ate a few, nevertheless our pleasure lay in doing what was forbidden."[56]

Next, Augustine proceeds to place himself on trial for the theft. In a courtroom, every crime is investigated to discover its motive.

---

[49] Augustine, *Confessions*, 2.1.1. For quotations, I have generally followed Henry Chadwick's translation, *Confessions* (Oxford: Oxford University Press, 1991).
[50] Augustine, *Confessions*, 2.2.4.
[51] Augustine, *Confessions*, 2.1.1.
[52] Augustine, *Confessions*, 2.3.6.
[53] Augustine, *Confessions*, 2.2.3.
[54] Augustine, *Confessions*, 2.3.5.
[55] Augustine, *Confessions*, 2.4.9.
[56] Augustine, *Confessions*, 2.4.9.

Typically even the most heinous crimes are motivated by something that is, in itself, good: for instance, if I kill someone to protect my property (which is good), or to acquire financial security (which is in itself a good thing), or because of love (which is good) for someone else's spouse. But nobody commits murder, Augustine says, just for the sake of it. Yet the theft of pears had no motive except evil itself; the fun of the thing lay solely in the fact that it was wrong.[57] With another pun, Augustine observes sadly that he had "no fruit" in these things;[58] and in a peculiar metaphor, he recalls that the pears would not have tasted good without the added "sauce" of criminality.[59] "Wretch that I was!" he exclaims, in the language of Romans 7.[60] "Who can untie this extremely twisted and tangled knot?"[61]

Throughout all this, the echoes of the Genesis story are unmistakable. And just to make sure we haven't missed the point, Augustine explicitly describes this adolescent episode as a "fall": "I had no motive for my wickedness except wickedness itself. It was foul, and I loved it. I loved the self-destruction, I loved my fall, not the object for which I had fallen but my fall itself. My depraved soul leaped down from your firmament to ruin."[62] All the echoes of Genesis 3 have led up to this moment; the allusions to the Genesis story gather like thickets around the pear tree. Augustine's fall appears as part of a larger corporate fall. And like the fall of Adam, this fall has devastating consequences: "What rottenness! What a monstrous life and what an abyss of death!"[63]

This is the first half of Augustine's narrative interpretation of Paul's Christ–Adam typology. We are all of us bound together in the solidarity of sin. Adam's fall is our fall; his death is our death. We are characters in Adam's story, wearing his mask, his persona. We enter Adam's garden, repeating his fall in our own personal histories.

The Second Garden

The second garden scene in the *Confessions*, in book 8, is a story not of the fall but of salvation. Augustine is internally torn and tormented.

[57] Augustine, *Confessions*, 2.5.11.
[58] Augustine, *Confessions*, 2.8.16.
[59] Augustine, *Confessions*, 2.6.12.
[60] Augustine, *Confessions*, 2.6.12.
[61] Augustine, *Confessions*, 2.10.18.
[62] Augustine, *Confessions*, 2.4.9.
[63] Augustine, *Confessions*, 2.6.14.

He wants to make a full conversion to the Catholic faith but lacks the will to do so. And then in a garden in Milan, he hears a child's voice singing *tolle, lege, tolle, lege*: "take up and read, take up and read." Nearby is a book; it is Paul's Epistle to the Romans. Obeying the voice, Augustine picks it up and lets it fall open at random, and when he reads Paul's words from Romans 13:13-14, he is immediately converted and feels at once that he has been set free and given a new life.

That is, at any rate, how we often remember the scene: as though Augustine just happened to have the Epistle to the Romans lying nearby; as though the whole conversion experience were quite random and unanticipated. But nothing could be further from the truth. Rather, as James O'Donnell notes, "the whole of Book 8 is a record of reading Paul, particularly Romans." At this turning point in Augustine's story, the narrative "progresses through the central Pauline text, to whose exhortations Augustine eventually succumbs."[64] The Epistle to the Romans is, in fact, the blueprint of book 8. It is tempting to call this book a narrative commentary on Romans, just as Bach's *St. Matthew Passion*, say, is a musical commentary on the Gospel of Matthew.

Every significant moment in this eighth book of *Confessions* is marked out by a quotation from Romans. Here is a list of all the quotations in order:[65]

8.1.2	Romans 1:21
8.1.2	Romans 1:22
8.4.9	Romans 4:17
8.5.11	Romans 7:16-17
8.5.12	Romans 7:22
8.5.12	Romans 7:24-25
8.10.22	Romans 7:17, 20
8.12.29	Romans 13:13-14
8.12.30	Romans 14:1

Augustine feels too weak to walk in Christ's way. He attributes this, once more, to his personal "fall," and he compares himself to the people described in Romans 1:21, who, "not knowing God, have not glorified him as God nor given thanks." "In this respect," Augustine says, "I had fallen." In all his learning, he has become one of those whom

---

[64] James J. O'Donnell, *Augustine: Confessions* (3 vols.; Oxford: Clarendon, 1992), 3:3.

[65] Adapted, with corrections, from O'Donnell, *Confessions*, 3:3.

Paul mentions in Romans 1:22—he has become foolish by asserting himself as wise.

Yet though Augustine wants to be converted and to follow the example of other converts, he feels a division within himself, an inability to choose the good. He is held in "chains," in a "harsh bondage," by habits that have hardened into necessity.[66] He feels—now Romans 7 is quoted for the first time—that it is "no longer I" who wills. He feels himself pulled ineluctably away from God, toward death, toward the way of Adam. Even though he wants to follow Christ's way, he says, quoting Romans 7:22, that he is "captive to the law of sin which was in my members." This whole tormented passage culminates in the exclamation of Rom 7:24-25: "Wretched man that I was, who would deliver me from this body of death except your grace through Jesus Christ our Lord?"[67]

At this point the second garden scene is introduced with a sentence that echoes the homely biblical language of the pear scene: "Our house had a garden."[68] Tormented with indecision, Augustine "went out into the garden." His friend Alypius stays nearby. Augustine sits down alone and begins to gesticulate wildly, tormented by his inability to follow Christ's way. The garden of Genesis is evoked explicitly: "What is the cause of this monstrous situation," Augustine asks himself. The answer: his moral enslavement has come about because he is in Adam; it is one of the "hidden punishments and secret tribulations that befall the sons of Adam."[69] In the theft of pears, Augustine had entered Adam's garden and shared in Adam's fall; now he is present in the garden once again, sharing in Adam's punishment. Yet across this scene another narrative has been overlaid, the narrative of Christ's agonies in Gethsemane. Augustine echoes the Gospel of Mark when he speaks of his "agony," of the way his friend stays nearby to keep watch, and of the fact that he "was deeply disturbed in spirit."[70] He tears his hair, strikes his forehead, wrings his hands, clasps his knee. He is "dissociated" from himself, and this reminds him again of Paul's words in Romans 7: it is, he says, "not I" but the sin of Adam exercising its influence, "because I was a son of Adam."[71]

---

[66] Augustine, *Confessions*, 8.5.10.
[67] Augustine, *Confessions*, 8.5.12.
[68] Augustine, *Confessions*, 8.8.19.
[69] Augustine, *Confessions*, 8.8.19.
[70] Augustine, *Confessions*, 8.8.19–20.
[71] Augustine, *Confessions*, 8.10.22.

What this scene so powerfully portrays is not merely Augustine's own inner torments, but also a colossal struggle between the two corporate personas of Christ and Adam. Christ is trying to raise Augustine up, but Adam is weighing him down with heavy chains—Augustine quotes Ephesians 5:14, "Arise, you who are asleep, rise from the dead, and Christ shall give you light"; yet, he laments, he is "dragged down and held" by sin.[72] His own life story is overlaid simultaneously by two corporate stories—a story in which Adam is the principal agent, and a rival story in which the principal agent is Christ. Caught in this struggle, Augustine feels himself to be powerless. In an allusion to Romans 8:11 and Galatians 5:20, he describes himself as caught between two antithetical directions of life; he has been living in death, but now he feels pulled toward "dying to death and living to life."[73] Thus "in the agony of death I was coming to life."[74]

Then at the climactic moment, Augustine throws himself down "under a certain fig tree."[75] By now the allusions both to the garden of Eden and to Gethsemane have become so prevalent that we cannot help seeing this as the fig tree of Genesis 3:7; and at the same time we cannot help imagining Augustine lying prostrated in the same position as Christ in Gethsemane. It is here, weeping beneath the fig tree, that Augustine hears the child's voice: "take up and read, take up and read." It is here that the two superimposed narratives become perfectly aligned—Adam's fall in the garden and Christ's agony in the garden. It is here, prostrate beneath the weight of both these narratives, that Augustine's mind becomes strangely clear. The flood of tears stops. He stands up. He takes "the book of the apostle" that he had been reading earlier. Then the conversion occurs—the great turning point of his life—and he relates it in just a few simple sentences:

> I seized [the book], opened it and in silence read the first passage on which my eyes lit: "Not in riots and drunken parties, not in eroticism and indecencies, not in strife and rivalry, but put on the Lord Jesus Christ and make no provision for the flesh in its lusts" (Rom 13:13-14). I neither wished nor needed to read further. At once, with the

---

[72] Augustine, *Confessions*, 8.5.12.
[73] Augustine, *Confessions*, 8.11.25.
[74] Augustine, *Confessions*, 8.8.19.
[75] Augustine, *Confessions*, 8.12.28.

last words of this sentence, it was as if a light of relief from all anxiety flooded into my heart. All the shadows of doubt were dispelled.[76]

In the first garden scene, by stealing the pears Augustine had "put on" Adam, adopted the persona of Adam, acted out Adam's role and shared in Adam's fall. In the second garden scene, he "puts on the Lord Jesus Christ," adopts Christ's persona, allows Christ's narrative to be re-enacted in his own life. It is here that the story of Adam gives way at last to the story of Christ.

Though Augustine is often described as the father of Western individualism, it is important to recall that both these garden stories are, in fact, depictions of corporate agency. The theft of the pears is not an individual act but a corporate one. Augustine insists that he never would have done it on his own. Alone, there would be no desire to vandalize a pear tree. "The pleasure was not in the pears; it was in the crime itself, done in association with a sinful group"; the pleasure came from "sharing the guilt with others."[77] The first garden scene, then, is set up as a collective fall, an act of corporate solidarity in sin.

In the same way, the conversion scene is intensely personal, but it forms part of a wider corporate experience of participation in Christ. Augustine's conversion in book 8 comes at the end of a long sequence of conversion narratives, most of them following the same pattern: a sudden transformation as a result of reading a particular text. In the period leading up to his conversion, one of Augustine's friends tells him the story of Victorinus, who was suddenly converted "after his reading" of something in the New Testament (presumably Luke 12:9).[78] Another friend tells Augustine the story of Antony,[79] who had been suddenly converted one day when he heard Matthew 19:21 read in church.[80] His friend tells him about entire monasteries formed by people moved by Antony's example. One man came across a copy of Athanasius' life of Antony and was suddenly "amazed and set on fire" and "filled with holy love" as he read it; then he "read on and experienced a conversion."[81] To this impressive catalogue of conversions, Augustine adds the story of Paul's own conversion and the way Paul's

---

[76] Augustine, *Confessions*, 8.12.29.
[77] Augustine, *Confessions*, 2.8.16.
[78] Augustine, *Confessions*, 8.2.4.
[79] Augustine, *Confessions*, 8.6.14.
[80] Augustine, *Confessions*, 8.12.29.
[81] Augustine, *Confessions*, 8.6.15.

pride was humbled "under the gentle yoke of your Christ."[82] At the end of this chain of conversion stories, Augustine recalls the "large numbers" of holy people who have gone into monasteries, "a multitude of all ages" who have devoted themselves to Christ's way.[83] In his own conversion, then, he is entering into solidarity with these multitudes of converts, just as he had earlier entered into solidarity with the gang of delinquent fruit thieves. He now comes to participate in the corporate personality of Christ, just as he had earlier participated in the corporate personality of Adam.

Romans 5 and the Invention of Autobiography

Augustine's autobiography has been described as a "reediting of the self in which one narrative, a life to come, was traced over another, a life already lived."[84] That is the literary and theological achievement of the *Confessions*. It is why, when Augustine really wanted to assimilate Paul's theology, he laid aside commentary and turned to (or rather invented) the genre of autobiography. The *Confessions* is an exercise of memory: Augustine remembers his old life but remembers it *as* the story of Adam gradually giving way to the story of Christ. He remembers his life but "traces" these narrative patterns over it, so that the story of Adam, the story of Christ, and Augustine's own story are all legible at the same time.[85]

Though he never says so explicitly, I think Augustine sees Romans 5:12-21 as the real center of Paul's Epistle. He reads Romans as a record of the way two great narratives have played out in world history and in the history of each human self. It is Romans 7 that Augustine returns to most frequently throughout his life; but he reads chapter 7 through the lens of chapter 5. Romans 7 is not just a record of the tormented individual conscience; it records the almost unbearable tension that occurs when a life is torn between two corporate personas.

But Christ and Adam are not equal powers; they are asymmetrical. For a precise statement on how this asymmetrical relation works, we have to turn to Augustine's commentary on the Psalms. Discussing Psalms 22:1—"My God, my God, why have you forsaken me?"—he

---

[82] Augustine, *Confessions*, 8.4.9.
[83] Augustine, *Confessions*, 8.11.27.
[84] Brian Stock, *Augustine the Reader: Meditation, Self-Knowledge, and the Ethics of Interpretation* (Cambridge: Belknap, 1996), 17.
[85] Stock, *Augustine the Reader*, 214.

asks: "Whose voice is this, then, if not that of the first human being? Christ proves that his flesh is true flesh inherited from Adam when he cries, *My God, my God, why have you forsaken me?*" Christ utters this cry—as though God had abandoned him—because he has appropriated Adam's story and absorbed it into his own:

> Christ had transferred the persona of the first human being to himself [*personam in se transfiguraverat primi hominis*]. We know this from the apostle's words, *our old humanity has been nailed to the cross with him* (Rom 6:6). We should never have been rid of our old nature, had he not been crucified in weakness. He came for no other purpose than that we should be renewed in him, for it is by longing for him and imitating his passion that we are made new. It was the voice of weakness, our voice, that cried out, *Why have you forsaken me?* And the next words were, *the tale of my sins*, as though Christ were saying, "Those words were the words of a sinner, but I have transformed them into my own."[86]

Christ takes over Adam's persona, wears the mask of Adam (the Latin term *persona* was used in the theater, like the Greek πρόσωπον). Christ absorbs Adam's identity; he adopts Adam's voice. That is why there is no real dualism, no ultimate opposition, between Christ and Adam—because Christ *becomes* Adam, incorporates Adam into himself, and then dies as Adam, crying out in Adam's voice for redemption. In the end, it is not Adam *and* Christ, but Adam *in* Christ.

Still, for the time being, each human self is identified by its relation to these two archetypal personas. The old man is being taken up into the new; the voice of Adam is giving way to the voice of Christ. Perhaps that is why, infamously, Augustine interprets Romans 7 in so many different ways throughout his life: sometimes as an account of Israel; sometimes as a picture of the self before conversion; and sometimes as a portrayal of the continuing struggles of the Christian life. Augustine's point is not to turn Romans 7 into a record of private introspection, but to show that both Adam and Christ are present in the world, that both their stories are superimposed over every other human story, and that everyone is always moving either in the direction of Adam (toward death) or in the direction of Christ (toward

---

[86] Augustine, *Enarrationes in Psalmos*, 37.27, in *Expositions of the Psalms* (trans. Maria Boulding; 6 vols.; Hyde Park, N.Y.: New City, 2000–2004), 2:166.

life). The "I" of Romans 7 is simultaneously the fallen cry of Adam, the voice of Christ, and the voice of every human person.

In short, for Augustine it is the Christ–Adam typology of Romans 5 that supplies the central logic of the Epistle to the Romans, as well as the blueprint for Augustine's own autobiographical narrative. Paul's typology gives Augustine a way of constructing a story not only of his own life but of human life as such. To be human is to participate in these two great archetypal narratives.

Why is autobiography even possible? How can we presume that the story of one life has any wider significance for other human lives? And why did it happen to be a Christian—and a reader of Paul—who created the genre of autobiography in its recognizable modern form? In Augustine, autobiography emerges under the influence of the Pauline claim that human lives are not fundamentally isolated but are bound together in the corporate personas of Christ and Adam. There are, fundamentally, only two human voices, the voice of Christ and the voice of Adam.

Conclusion
Learning Paul's Language

I have tried to show that the assumption of a crassly individualistic and introspective "Augustinian" reading of Paul is hopelessly inadequate. The extraordinary thing about Augustine is just how much he gets from Paul, and how much he is able to do with it. To think of him as imposing his own narrow theological agenda onto Paul's text seems very far from the truth. It would be more accurate to say that he imposes Paul's text onto everything else: the self, society, history, everything that belongs to the domain of humanity. Paul's Adam–Christ typology becomes, for Augustine, a sort of mythos, a metanarrative within which all human activity is situated.

Augustine's deep assimilation of Paul's theology, centering on the Christ–Adam typology, culminates in the *Confessions*, a personal narrative shaped by two corporate personas, and then later in the *City of God*, which traces these two corporate personas and their moral trajectories through world history. In the *Confessions*, the Christian life is simultaneously overlaid by the stories of Christ and Adam. Since infancy we have learned to play the role of Adam, but now we are more and more learning how to put on the persona of Christ and so to be liberated from the immense accumulated power of sin. In the *City of God*, these two personas become the organizing principles of a narration of world history: the entire human family since the beginning of time has been incorporated in the character of Adam and has been following the narrative trajectory of that character, which ends in the eternal misery of pride; but in Christ, a new corporate humanity is taking shape and moving toward a different goal, the eternal happiness of life in humility before God. For Augustine, then, the self is not an autonomous, individual essence, but a pattern embedded in two overlapping and intersecting narratives.

Ironically, the position typically assigned to Augustine is exactly the view that he worked so hard to overturn: the doctrine of an autonomous individual self, which he found in the Pelagian teaching and vehemently resisted, arguing instead that we must bear with one another's weaknesses since we are all tangled up together in the same corporate moral history. Augustine can seem like an austere figure; but by the standards of his time, there was something almost Dickensian in his defense of the ordinary person and of ordinary Christian piety.[87] Augustine resisted every claim that perfection is attainable in this life. With constant slips and mistakes, the believer is always still learning how to play the part of Christ instead of the part of Adam.

And it is precisely this commitment to the business of ordinary, flawed Christian living that supports Augustine's immense concern with Christian unity. Whatever segregates the church into separate spiritual communities, whatever sets the few above the many, whatever tends towards the formation of a spiritual aristocracy in distinction from ordinary believers—all this Augustine condemns as a return to "boasting." For him, the cure is always a simple return to Paul's teaching: there is no room for boasting, since proud Gentiles and proud Jews, proud lawbreakers and proud law-keepers are all brought and refashioned anew in community, divided by nothing and united solely by the humility of Christ.

God's power, Augustine reminds us—in another of his striking improvisations of Paul—is like "maternal love, expressing itself as weakness."[88] The powerful weakness of a humble God—this is the persona that we are slowly learning to adopt, as more and more we cast off the old self and put on the new, clothing ourselves in the Lord Jesus Christ.

---

[87] For a summary, see Henry Chadwick, *Augustine of Hippo: A Life* (Oxford: Oxford University Press, 2009), 57–61.

[88] Augustine, *Enarrationes in Psalmos*, 58.10.

4
Under Grace
The Christ-Gift and the Construction of a Christian *Habitus*

John M. G. Barclay

Imperatival Grace

When Paul pauses, midway through Romans 5, to redraw the map of the cosmos, he sees two, and only two, power structures at work within it (5:12-21). Viewed from the perspective of the Christ-event, all history, even Israel's history "under the law," has been subject to the power of sin and propelled toward death (5:12-14, 20). But in Christ, and because of Christ, a new reality has emerged, powerful enough to reverse the tendency to death, and to propel its recipients, contrariwise, towards "eternal life" (5:17, 19, 21). In line with earlier statements in this letter (Rom 3:24; 4:4, 16), Paul refers to this counter-momentum with the term χάρις (5:15, 17, 21), but also, for rhetorical purposes, with a variety of synonyms, χάρισμα (5:15, 16), δωρεά (5:15), and δώρημα (5:16). The extraordinary proliferation of this group of terms (ten times in 5:14-21) matches the motif of "super-abundance" (περισσεία), which also reverberates through this section (5:15, 17, 20).

However, the emphasis lies not just on the quantity of this divine gift, but also on its incongruity (cf. 5:5-8). God's gift in Christ is given not, as one might expect, as a reward to the righteous, but precisely in the depth of sin, out of "many transgressions" (5:16) and following the increase of sin stimulated by the law (5:20). The Christ-gift does not match the worth of its recipients but is given precisely in their abject worthlessness. By this miracle of counterintuitive gift, where sin had thus far "reigned" in death there is now a counter-reign, the reign of "grace," which operates through "righteousness" in the direction of eternal life (ἵνα . . . ἡ χάρις βασιλεύσῃ διὰ δικαιοσύνης εἰς ζωὴν αἰώνιον διὰ Ἰησοῦ Χριστοῦ τοῦ κυρίου ἡμῶν, 5:21).

Romans 6 spells out the phenomenology of this counter-reign. In baptism, believers are wholly reconstituted. The "old human nature" (the residue of Adam) is put out of action by participation in the crucifixion of Christ, so that believers are released from slavery to sin (τοῦ μηκέτι δουλεύειν τῇ ἁμαρτίᾳ, 6:6). At the same time, drawing on the miraculous resurrection life of Christ, they enter a "newness of life" with a new structure of allegiance (6:4). They are no longer to let sin reign in their mortal bodies (μὴ . . . βασιλευέτω ἡ ἁμαρτία ἐν τῷ θνητῷ ὑμῶν σώματι, 6:12). The echo here of 5:21 (note the common terms, βασιλεύειν, ἁμαρτία, θάνατος/θνητός) implies that instead of sin something else will reign, and from 5:21 we know what that is: χάρις. That implication is confirmed by 6:14, where, using variant language for the same phenomenon, Paul says that "sin will not lord it over you (ὑμῶν κυριεύσει), because you are not under the law but under grace" (ὑπὸ χάριν; cf. 5:20-21). Once again, grace is described as a power, this time more explicitly as a "power over." Accordingly, the subsequent verses (6:15-23) are replete with the language of "slavery" and "obedience": everyone is subject to one power or another, sin or righteousness, and Paul pointedly thanks God that they have been freed from one in order to be enslaved to the other (6:18, 22). There is no neutral zone in Paul's cosmos, no pocket of absolute freedom, no no-man's land between the two fronts. The gift of God in Jesus Christ has established not liberation from authority or demand, but a new allegiance, a new responsibility, a new "slavery" under the rule of grace. Although not itself an imperative, grace is imperatival: it bears within itself the imperative to obey.

To make such a claim will elicit in some circles howls of protest, on both theological and exegetical grounds. The theological objections will come from those influenced by the rich theology of Martin Luther. Concerned to liberate his contemporaries from their image of Christ as a hyper-demanding legislator, who was preparing to judge them on the final Day, Luther insisted that God comes to us in Christ *only* as Savior: "Christ is not Moses, not a taskmaster or a lawgiver; he is the dispenser of grace, the Savior, and the Pitier."[1] Drawing a general contrast

---

[1] From the 1535 lectures on Galatians: *Luther's Works* [LW] (55 vols.; St. Louis: Concordia Publishing House; Philadelphia: Fortress, 1955–1986), vol. 26, p. 178; *Dr Martin Luthers Werke* [WA] (69 vols.; Weimar: Böhlau, 1883–1993), vol. 40¹, p. 298, lines 19–20.

between gospel as gift and law as demand, Luther insists: "The Law is a taskmaster; it demands that we work and that we give. . . . The Gospel, on the contrary, does not demand; it grants freely; it commands us to hold out our hands and to receive what is being offered. Now demanding and giving, receiving and offering, are exact opposites and cannot exist together."[2] On closer inspection one would see that what really concerned Luther was not the bare notion of obedience or demand, but the idea that God demands anything which is *necessary for salvation*. Outside of this sphere there is plenty of scope for the language of obedience and duty (see Luther's Catechisms!), but this obedience is never instrumental: it does not acquire any further gain or favor from God.[3] Nonetheless, such statements of Luther as those just quoted have been taken to mean that grace carries no obligations and issues no commands: it is gift, purely gift, and in principle outside the domain of reciprocity or return. The modern, Western notion of the "pure" gift, wholly disinterested and without strings attached, indeed owes a lot to Luther (among other influences) and has become deeply entrenched in some theologies of grace. Romans 6, however, is a thorn in its side, and I shall argue that although Paul in this chapter encapsulates a theology of the *incongruity* of grace, grace given without *prior conditions of fit or worth*, he does not, and does not need to, perfect the notion of grace as "gift without return."[4] When he says that believers are "under grace" he means that grace carries demands.

Exegetically, any underlining of the language of obedience and slavery in Romans 6 is frequently challenged by one reading of 6:19, where Paul follows his strong statement that "you have been enslaved to righteousness" with the phrase "I speak in a human fashion because of the weakness of your flesh" (ἀνθρώπινον λέγω διὰ τὴν ἀσθένειαν τῆς σαρκὸς ὑμῶν, 6:19). This is often read as a kind of apology: Paul does not really mean anything so straightforward as believers being subject to imperatives like slaves—after all, he later says they have received

---

[2] *LW* 26.208; *WA* 40¹ 337.15–19.

[3] Although Luther is sometimes understood (and criticized) as holding a notion of gift without reciprocity, careful readers have recently insisted this is not so. There is at least the return to God of gratitude and honor; see Oswald Bayer, "The Ethics of Gift," *LQ* 24 (2010): 447–68. But the crucial point is that this return is never instrumental, in the sense that it is never a means to a subsequent favor or gift from God.

[4] For the notion that "grace" can be "perfected" (drawn to a fullness or extreme) in various directions, see John M. G. Barclay, *Paul and the Gift* (Grand Rapids: Eerdmans, forthcoming).

a spirit of adoption, not of slavery (8:15). He really expects them to serve God willingly, "from the heart" (6:17), without having to submit to external pressure or demand, but he speaks in this "human fashion" to make a point in an unfortunately exaggerated fashion.[5] I am not convinced. The metaphor of slavery is repeated with such force in this passage, both before and after 6:19, and is used so un-self-consciously elsewhere in Romans both for Paul's (1:1) and for the Roman believers' relationship to God (12:11; 14:4), that it would be hard to conclude that Paul thought the metaphor fundamentally inappropriate. He may be excusing the rather odd expression "slavery to righteousness" (6:18; cf. 6:22: enslaved to God), or he may be not excusing himself at all, but explaining why he insists on this figure, lest they be tempted by pride (in "fleshly weakness") to think themselves above any kind of enslavement (cf. 12:3).[6] In any case, the sense of submission and obligation runs very strongly through 6:11-23, and Paul has no difficulty in describing the "newness of life" as a life lived under the rule of grace.

Ernst Käsemann has been the Pauline scholar most insistent on this *Gnadenherrschaft*, in his linkage between "grace" and the lordship of Christ.[7] Combating a danger in the Lutheran understanding of gift (exemplified, for him, in Bultmann's existentialist interpretation), Käsemann insists that it is inadequate to think of grace as "gift" unless we also recognize its character as divine power:

> The gift which is being bestowed here [in salvation] is never at any time separable from its Giver. It partakes of the character of power, in so far as God himself enters the arena and remains in the arena with it. Thus personal address, obligation and service are indissolubly

---

[5] See, e.g., C. E. B. Cranfield, *The Epistle to the Romans* (2 vols.; ICC; Edinburgh: T&T Clark, 1975, 1979), 1:325–26, though the apology is only for the figure of slavery not for the sense of "total obligation, total commitment" that characterize the life under grace; Troels Engberg-Pedersen, *Paul and the Stoics* (Edinburgh: T&T Clark, 2000), 235–37: they should want to do God's will of themselves (like Stoics), not because they have to.

[6] Ernst Käsemann, *Commentary on Romans* (trans. G. W. Bromiley; Grand Rapids: Eerdmans, 1980), 182–83, insisting that "δουλεία is the key word in the passage" (182). Although the identical phrase occurs in Gal 4:12, it is not clear how it could here, as there, refer to some physical weakness; but a good short paper by Emerson Powery at the Princeton conference usefully explored this possibility.

[7] For the term, see Ernst Käsemann, *An die Römer* (HNT; Tübingen: Mohr Siebeck, 1980), 175; for the theme, see especially idem, "The Righteousness of God in Paul," in *New Testament Questions of Today* (London: SCM Press, 1969), 168–82.

bound up with the gift. When God enters the arena, our experience is, that he maintains his lordship even in his giving; indeed it is his gifts which are the very means by which he subordinates us to his lordship and makes us responsible beings.[8]

This captures very well the sense of powers, submissions, and slaveries that permeate Romans 5–6, reflecting also Käsemann's reading of the cosmic warfare which forms the framework for Paul's theology. It is notable that he does not find it easy to identify the sense of obligation in *gift itself*, deriving it primarily from the Lord who comes with and in the gift, rather than from the structure of gift-giving itself. I suspect this represents a Western disinclination to recognize gifts as carrying obligations, whereas everyone in antiquity knew (like most people know in most cultures today) that gifts create ties of obligation between the giver and the recipient—indeed the creation of ties is precisely why gifts were given. It was extremely common in antiquity for recipients of gifts to feel themselves obliged to their donors; in fact this is so much taken for granted that it forms the subject of delicate negotiation from both sides (see Seneca, *De beneficiis* passim).[9]

Paul naturally figures his Gentile converts as under obligation (ὀφειλέται εἰσίν) to the Jerusalem church for the spiritual goods they have shared (Rom 15:27; cf. 1:14 of his own obligation to preach). It is probably because he did not want to be seen as the donor of the gospel (putting its recipients under obligation *to him*, rather than *to God*) that he refused to take fees while founding a church.[10] But the idea that God gives gifts that put us under obligation to him does not seem to be a problem for Paul: his phrase ὑπὸ χάριν is paralleled by similar phrases in antiquity, such as the notice in Manetho that the king of Ethiopia was under obligation to Amenophis, king of Egypt, out of gratitude (χάριτι ἦν αὐτῷ ὑποχείριος).[11] One may add to this an anthropological notion that comes close to the statements of Käsemann, that some gifts are so invested with the personality and interests of the giver (in our culture,

---

[8] Käsemann, "The Righteousness of God," 174.

[9] On the structures of benefaction and obligation in antiquity, see, e.g., F. W. Danker, *Benefactor: Epigraphic Study of a Graeco-Roman Semantic Field* (St. Louis: Clayton, 1982); James R. Harrison, *Paul's Language of Grace in its Graeco-Roman Context* (WUNT 2.172; Tübingen: Mohr Siebeck, 2003). The seminal anthropological study of gift remains Marcel Mauss, *The Gift* (trans. W. D. Halls; London: Routledge, 1990).

[10] See David E. Briones, "Paul's Financial Policy: A Socio-Theological Approach" (Ph.D. diss., Durham, 2011).

[11] In Josephus, *Apion* 1.246.

one thinks of heirlooms) that they constitute "inalienable" gifts, given but in important senses still belonging to the giver.[12] None of Paul's hearers would thus be the least surprised that God's supreme gift in Christ (the χάρις here spoken of), even if it was given without regard to worth (given, indeed, to the utterly sinful and ungodly), carried with it expectations and obligations which resulted from the gift. It was, if you like, *unconditioned* (based on no prior conditions) but not *unconditional* (carrying no subsequent demands). As we begin now to investigate the nature of this gift we shall see eventually why this is not theologically problematic for Paul, whatever it may seem to us.

Grace
Christ's Life from the Dead— in Mortal Human Bodies

The theology of Romans is built around the shocking, and in ancient terms bizarre, fact that God's gift (in Christ) has been given without regard to the worth of the recipient. Divine grace did not have to be figured this way: in most ancient ideologies of grace, both Jewish and non-Jewish, God's gifts are given well precisely in being given to the fitting and the worthy.[13] But Paul has come to understand (and experience, in his life and in the Gentile mission) that God has acted in Christ by giving without regard to ethnic, cultural, or moral worth, and thus on the same basis to Gentile and Jew alike. (χάρις does not mean undeserved gift, in normal Greek usage; it only takes that meaning in certain contexts, most notably in Paul.) This incongruity between the gift and its recipients is what is demonstrated in Romans 1–3, and it forms the core of Romans 4 where the God who (bizarrely) justifies the *ungodly* is the God who promises to give offspring not to a young and virile couple but to Abraham (as good as dead) and Sarah (whose womb was defunct). Incongruity—the disregard of worth, capacity, or work—is also the hallmark of Israel's story, as traced in Romans 9–11, which is why Paul is not reduced to despair at the unbelief of his fellow Jews, because God's mercy operates without regard to prior

---

[12] See, e.g., Maurice Godelier, *The Enigma of the Gift* (trans. N. Scott; Chicago: University of Chicago Press, 1999); Annette B. Weiner, *Inalienable Possessions: The Paradox of Keeping while Giving* (Berkeley: University of California Press, 1992).

[13] This is as true of Philo as it is of Seneca; on the former, see John M. G. Barclay, "Grace within and beyond reason: Philo and Paul in Dialogue," in *Paul, Grace and Freedom: Essays in Honour of John K. Riches* (ed. P. Middleton, A. Paddison, and K. Wenell; London: T&T Clark, 2009), 9–21.

obedience, indeed precisely on behalf of the disobedient. This same dynamic—God's something out of a human nothing—permeates the second main section of the letter (5:12–8:39). The Christ-gift has arisen not in response to human obedience, but out of an avalanche of sin (5:12-21), and it takes its grip on human lives not by enhancing or supplementing their natural capacities but in an act of burial and new life: the old life is brought to an end and an impossible new life—life out of death—begins (6:1-11).

Crucial to Paul's theology is that this new life is not in the first place an anthropological phenomenon: it is experienced by human beings only inasmuch as they share in, and draw from, a life whose source lies outside of themselves, the life of the risen Christ. Their identity is recentered, since their life is now wholly dependent on the life of Another, the One who is risen from the dead. Paul repeatedly draws attention to the resurrection of Jesus throughout these chapters (6:4, 5, 8, 9; 7:4; 8:11) because he wants to make clear that this "newness of life" (6:4; cf. 7:6) is not some reformation of the self, or some newly discovered technique in self-mastery; it is an ectopic phenomenon, drawing on the "life from the dead" that began with Jesus' resurrection. Believers "live to God" (6:11) as walking, sleeping, eating, breathing miracles. This new creation life begins, in their case, not the other side, but this side of their mortality; hence it is not quite describable as ἀνάστασις, which remains a future hope (6:5). It is not for nothing that Paul emphasizes several times in these chapters the mortality of the body: "let sin not reign in your *mortal* bodies" (ἐν τῷ θνητῷ ὑμῶν σώματι, 6:12); the Spirit will finally vivify "your *mortal* bodies" (τὰ θνητὰ σώματα ὑμῶν, 8:11); the present body is "*a corpse* on account of sin" (νεκρὸν διὰ ἁμαρτίαν, 8:10) and a "body *of death*" (τὸ σῶμα τοῦ θανάτου, 7:24). Whereas Christ has finished with death (6:9), believers have not: they are dead to sin (6:11) but not to death. This puts their lives into a state of permanent incongruity: in one respect they are bound to death ("on account of sin," that is, as a residue of their Adamic heritage, 8:10); in another they are alive, in a "life from the dead," the eternal life that is at source uniquely Jesus-life.

Luther attempted in several ways to express the permanent, structurally basic, incongruity of grace in the believer's life, most famously in the phrase *simul justus et peccator*.[14] The strongest exegetical base for that notion comes from Romans 6–8, but it draws on what seems

---

[14] E.g., in the 1535 Galatians lectures, WA 40¹ 366.26; LW 26.232.

now to many exegetes a faulty reading of Romans 7–8, as a dialectical depiction of two dimensions of the Christian life.[15] If, to the contrary, 7:7-25 describes life "in the flesh" outside of Christ (cf. 7:5), not life in Christ, Luther's *simul peccator* looks less convincing. Nonetheless, Romans 6–8 *does* express the permanent paradox of grace in the life of the believer, only in a different form. The believer is here described as both mortal and eternally alive, *simul mortuus et vivens*. On the one hand doomed to death, in a body that is bound by mortality, the believer is also the site of an impossible new life, whose origin lies in the resurrection of Jesus and whose goal is their own future resurrection (8:11). "If Christ is in you," says Paul (note the recentering of the self from "outside"), τὸ μὲν σῶμα νεκρὸν διὰ ἁμαρτίαν τὸ δὲ πνεῦμα ζωὴ διὰ δικαιοσύνην (8:10).[16] At the same time dead and alive—the life operative through the Spirit (capital "S"), which is another way of saying that this "newness of life" is established, sustained, and governed not by believers themselves, but by God. That paradox is the sign that God's grace is permanently at odds with the natural (post-Adamic) condition of the human being, however much believers may (and should) grow in holiness.

We should be careful to note here the importance of *the body* as the site of this paradoxical co-existence of mortality and life. After insisting that the σῶμα τῆς ἁμαρτίας is rendered inoperative (καταργεῖσθαι)

---

[15] Several papers at the Princeton conference were inclined to the later Augustinian view, shared by the Reformers, that Rom 7:7-25 expresses, in some respects, the continuing experience of the believer. This has the strong weight of Christian experience behind it, but the antithesis of 7:5-6 (corresponding in terminology to 7:7-25 and 8:1ff) and the language of enslaved captivity under sin (7:14) seem to me to identify 7:7-25 as a description (from a believer-viewpoint) of life "when we were in the flesh" (7:5). The "groaning" of 8:23 is not at all the same as the cry of despair in 7:24.

[16] I take the ἁμαρτία here to be not their own present sin as believers but the sin of Adam and of their past, in the cosmos infected by sin and thereby doomed to death (5:11-21; 7:5, 7-11). That this cannot mean their sinfulness as believers is indicated by the fact that they are now "dead to sin" (6:11) and "freed from sin" (6:19) in being enslaved to God. Cranfield's traditional Reformed reading of 7:7-25 leads him to take διὰ ἁμαρτίαν as referring to the sin of the believer (*Romans*, 1:389). Others rightly resist this but find instead reference to the believer's death *to sin* in baptism (6:11: the expression is tellingly different) or to the condemnation of sin at the cross (8:3); see the discussion in James D. G. Dunn, *Romans 1–8* (WBC 38a; Waco, Tex.: Word, 1988), 430–31. Although Paul can juxtapose multiple ways of relating "death" to "sin," the μὲν . . . δέ construction suggests a strong contrast between two antithetical but coexisting realities.

in baptism (6:6), Paul urges the Roman believers to consider themselves "dead to sin and alive to God in Christ Jesus" (6:11) and *explicates* what this "considering" (λογίζεσθαι) looks like in the following imperatives (6:12-13). These verses form four clauses, two negative (A) and two positive (B):

A¹ Μὴ οὖν βασιλευέτω ἡ ἁμαρτία ἐν τῷ θνητῷ ὑμῶν σώματι εἰς τὸ ὑπακούειν ταῖς ἐπιθυμίαις αὐτοῦ, (v. 12)
A² μηδὲ παριστάνετε τὰ μέλη ὑμῶν ὅπλα ἀδικίας τῇ ἁμαρτίᾳ,
B¹ ἀλλὰ παραστήσατε ἑαυτοὺς τῷ θεῷ ὡσεὶ ἐκ νεκρῶν ζῶντας
B² καὶ τὰ μέλη ὑμῶν ὅπλα δικαιοσύνης τῷ θεῷ. (v. 13)

It is striking that in three of these four clauses what is ruled or presented is *the body* (as τὸ σῶμα or τὰ μέλη, the second a particularization of the first). That the first positive command (B¹) concerns "yourselves" (ἑαυτούς) should not be read in an idealist or dualist frame, as if "the self" is something anterior to, or separable from, the body; to the contrary, the fact that "yourselves" is embedded here in statements about the body suggests that the self can be "ruled" or "presented" *only as* the body is "ruled" or "presented." It accords with this that Paul's puts stress on the μέλη as slaves of either uncleanness or righteousness again in 6:19 and identifies the power of sin (which goes so far as to co-opt the law) as operative in the μέλη no less than three times in chapter 7 (7:5, 23, 25). The body, unambiguously identified in its physicality by the term μέλη, is thus the site where "the self" is identified and defined.[17]

Bultmann's famous discussion of σῶμα as an anthropological term rightly noted how "the body" in Paul can be synonymous with the person ("man does not *have* a soma; he *is soma*"). He then quite wrongly took this to mean that we can empty the term (in most places, including Rom 6:12-13) of any overtones of materiality or physicality, since σῶμα means "the self," as the subject of human action, or the object to whom something happens.[18] Käsemann rightly objected that this made

---

[17] I will continue to use the traditional translation "limbs" for μέλη, though "organs" might be better (Paul imagines under this category ears, eyes, and sexual organs, as well as feet and hands, 1 Cor 12:12-26); there is a danger that the term becomes dephysicalized if it is taken to mean something as vague as "natural capacities" (e.g., Cranfield, *Romans*, 1:317–18). For proper emphasis on the physicality of the term, see Robert Jewett, *Romans* (Hermeneia; Minneapolis: Fortress, 2007), 410–11.

[18] Rudolf Bultmann, *Theology of the New Testament* (2 vols.; London: SCM Press, 1952), 1:192–203, here 194.

a nonsense of most of Paul's uses of the term σῶμα, and that *Leiblichkeit* (corporeality or physicality) was an essential component of Paul's anthropology, which could not be conjured away by Bultmann's existential wand. Käsemann himself put stress on the body as the sign of human "creatureliness," and as the signal of our participation in, and solidarity with, entities much larger than the individual; in particular he stressed the condition of belonging to "powers," the body being a part of the world which is always beholden to a sphere of sovereignty (*Herrschaftsbereich*), either divine or antidivine.[19] He thus insists that in our Romans texts the body language is crucial to Paul's theology: "that part of the world which we are in our bodies" (*das Stück Welt, das wir in unserm Leibe sind*)[20] is what God lays claim to, wresting it from its enslavement to sin for obedience to righteousness. Moreover, as he adds, "bodily obedience is necessary as an anticipation of the reality of bodily resurrection. Otherwise it would not be clear that we are engaged in the eschatological struggle for power."[21]

We can perhaps sharpen this further. The body is, for Paul, the site where the "I" is expressed and enacted; his commitment to the notion of the "resurrected body" (8:11; cf. 1 Cor 15:42-44) suggests that the self cannot be operative or communicative in any other way. If so, the body is the place where the resurrection life of Jesus (the new self) becomes visible and active in human lives: the renewal of the mind that Paul speaks of in Romans 12:2 cannot take effect, in fact cannot be real in any meaningful sense, unless it is expressed in "the presentation of your bodies" as a living sacrifice (of which he had spoken *first* in 12:1). This means that the body is the site of that fundamental incongruity of which we spoke just now: it is here in the body that the believer is both visibly on the path to death *and* visibly and demonstrably to display the presence of the miraculous resurrection of Christ, in service of righteousness and holiness. It is precisely in his/her corporeality that the believer is *simul mortuus et vivens* (cf. 2 Cor 4:10-11). It is not for nothing that Paul here uses military language ("weapons," 6:13, 19; cf. 13:14) since the body is the critical site of

---

[19] See esp. Ernst Käsemann, "On Paul's Anthropology," in *Perspectives on Paul* (trans. M. Kohl; London: SCM Press, 1971), 1–31. For further critique of Bultmann, see Robert H. Gundry, *Sôma in Biblical Theology, with emphasis on Pauline Anthropology* (Cambridge: Cambridge University Press, 1976).

[20] Käsemann, *Commentary on Romans*, 178.

[21] Käsemann, *Commentary on Romans*, 177; idem, *An die Römer*, 169–70.

resistance. Once appropriated by sin, the body is reappropriated by Christ. The very location where sin once held most visible sway, and where its former grip still draws our bodily selves towards death, is now the location where the "newness of life" breaks through into action, displaying in counterintuitive patterns of behavior the miraculous Christ-life which draws our embodied selves towards the "vivification" (8:11) or "redemption" (8:23) of the body. In this tug-of-war between death and life, Christian obedience *in the body*, the former stronghold of sin, displays the fact that a miraculous counterforce is already at work. By "putting to death the deeds of the body" (8:13)—that is, killing the killer at the site of the crime (see 8:13 with 7:24)—the obedience to righteousness demonstrates that the believer is on a trajectory toward a victory whose finale will be the resurrection of the body and the redemption of the cosmos.

The Construction of a Christian *Habitus*

Thus far I have spoken of the body as the necessary expressive medium of the Christ-sourced life in theological terms, remaining relatively close to Paul's own diction. I now want to add some observations from a different angle of vision, from the anthropology of culture. These observations are not intended to replace or to surpass the theological analysis, but they give some conceptual clarity to one dimension of the text which is apt to puzzle interpreters.

It has often been remarked that Paul seems to encroach on what we call "ethics" in Romans 6–8 in a way that seems to anticipate Romans 12–15 (note the vocabulary links between Rom 6:12-21 and 12:1-2) yet without the specificity of ethical instruction and example given in those later chapters. There are imperatives here (6:11-13; 8:12-13), but the chapters are concerned not so much with norms or practices as with ethic-structuring orientations, allegiances, and dispositions. Even when speaking of the body, Paul is talking about a system of loyalties and alignments which appears to go "deeper" than this or that particular practice: at issue is what he calls τὸ φρόνημα—either of the Flesh or of the Spirit (8:6-8)—which governs the body while being expressed not outside or behind it, but precisely in the physical deployment of its "limbs." What is he talking about here? Can we interpret it in terms that make some sort of sense to us?

One of the best analysts of this level of "structuring structures" is the anthropological theorist Pierre Bourdieu, who developed the much-discussed and still useful concept of the *habitus*.[22] In an effort to go beyond the sterile dualisms of "structure" and "free agency," of "objective" and "subjective" forces in human action, Bourdieu suggested that, at a level deeper than articulated norms and specified rules, cultures operate by a *habitus*, "a system of lasting, transposable dispositions which, integrating past experiences, functions at every moment as a *matrix of perceptions, appreciations, and actions* and makes possible the achievement of infinitely diversified tasks."[23] These dispositions concern the unspoken, and often unconscious, systems of classification by which we order reality, as well as the taken-for-granted limits of the possible, the sensible, the proper, and the imaginable, which limit our action without articulation in rules of behavior. In a kind of unending circularity, these dispositions and conceptual schemas are produced by practices but also, in turn, govern practices, at a level so deep that they are very hard to change unless (Bourdieu thought) there are major shifts in physical or economic conditions.[24] They represent what we take to be necessary and self-evident, "what goes without saying because it comes without saying." The *habitus* defines the sense of reality, of responsibility, of beauty, of value, and of the sacred and profane.

For Bourdieu, the *habitus* is crucially *embodied*, inscribed in all manner of bodily habits and expectations: "nothing seems more ineffable, more incommunicable, more inimitable, and, therefore, more precious, than the values given body, *made* body by the transubstantiation achieved by the hidden persuasion of an implicit pedagogy, capable of instilling a whole cosmology, an ethic, a metaphysic, a political philosophy, through injunctions as insignificant as 'stand up straight' or 'don't hold your knife in your left hand.'"[25] In this respect, "what is

---

[22] See, e.g., Pierre Bourdieu, *Outline of a Theory of Practice* (trans. R. Nice; Cambridge: Cambridge University Press, 1977), 72–95; idem, *The Logic of Practice* (trans. R. Nice; Stanford: Stanford University Press, 1980). For discussion and criticisms, see, e.g., Richard Jenkins, *Pierre Bourdieu* (London: Routledge, 1993), 74–84; Anthony King, "Thinking with Bourdieu against Bourdieu: A 'Practical' Critique of the Habitus," *Sociological Theory* 18 (2000): 417–33.

[23] Bourdieu, *Outline*, 82–83 (emphasis in original).

[24] The ultimate causality attributed to material, physical, and economic conditions indicates the pull of Marxist determinism in Bourdieu's work; critics often note that he finds it hard to explain how the *habitus* can be altered. For this reason, it may be that we need to go beyond Bourdieu to explain the change in *habitus* envisaged in Rom 6, while utilizing his thought to illuminate how the *habitus* functions through the medium of the body.

[25] Bourdieu, *Outline*, 94.

'learned by body' is not something that one has . . . but something that one is"[26]—a nice complement to Bultmann's famous statement about σῶμα in Paul ("man does not *have* a *soma*; he *is soma*"), but this time much nearer to Paul's conception of the physical body. It is at this level of the "structuring structures" of thought and action that Bourdieu places the body not as a medium of some prior, purely mental, activity but as a constitutive ingredient of how we perceive, order, and practice reality itself.[27]

When Paul talks about "the body of sin" (Rom 6:6), we would be unwise either to "spiritualize" this phrase as signifying something vague like "the sinful person" or to limit its range of meaning to certain physical acts (for instance, the μέθαι and κοίται of 13:13). He seems to have a sense that the body has been commandeered by sin, such that its dispositions, emotions, speech patterns, and habitual gestures are bound to systems of honor, self-aggrandizement, and license which are fundamentally at odds with the will of God. Thus even the Law, good and holy as it is (7:12), ends up "bearing fruit for death" (7:5). When received by a body "inhabited" by sin (7:17, 20)—endued with a deeply inculcated *habitus* of sin—it cannot achieve what it promises. The "law" that is at work in the members (7:23) is a set of predispositions and orientations too deep to be altered by the instructions of the Torah, however much the mind may approve of them. What is needed is "rescue from this body of death" (7:24)—a new φρόνημα of cognitive and practical schemas operative in physical deportment, corporeal practice, and bodily appetites.

One could hardly imagine a more effective demonstration of this "rescue" than the physical rite of baptism, which Paul interprets as a transition from death to life *performed on and with the body*. Henceforth believers give themselves over to this new life ("as alive from the dead," 6:13), that is, they "present their limbs as weapons of righteousness to God" (6:13; cf. 12:1)—in other words, they are committed to instantiate a new embodied *habitus*. This commitment could never be

---

[26] Bourdieu, *Logic*, 73.

[27] The point is well expounded by Troels Engberg-Pedersen, *Cosmology and the Self in the Apostle Paul* (Oxford: Oxford University Press, 2010), esp. 141–42 and 185: "ideas should in principle *always* be seen as part of practices. Together with all other less articulated types of cognition, they enter into the bodily habitus that is expressed in practices" (emphasis in original). This represents a shift from his earlier discussion of Rom 6, which suggested that the cognitive "I" was logically separate from and prior to the body (*Paul and the Stoics*, 228, 238).

a solo affair: while the body is individual, it is also shaped in and by its social interaction. The attempt to break with the old schematizations (μὴ συσχηματίζεσθαι τῷ αἰῶνι τουτῷ, 12:2) and to express a new, transformed νοῦς (12:2) will require collective practices that challenge the old taxonomic systems (the structuring "antinomies" of the present age) and embody new apperceptions and goals. That is why the bodily reorientation described in Romans 6 is given some exemplification in Romans 12–15, which concerns the formation of a *community* oriented to the gospel. It is in this community that new social habits are formed; new patterns of speech are practiced (prophecy, teaching, encouragement, prayer, 12:6-7, 12); new emotional commitments are formed ("weep with those who weep, rejoice with those who rejoice," 12:15); a new countercultural quest is inculcated for the giving, not the receiving, of honor (12:10); a strong resistance is built up against the instinctual quest for revenge (12:14-21); and the body is deployed in new abstentions from the normal licenses of food, drink, and sex (13:13-14). In relation to food, Paul announces a significant shift from the Jewish taxonomic system of clean and unclean foods (14:14, 20), but only to insist on a new way of perceiving and practicing "strength," which is to support the burdens of the weak (15:1-5). With enormous sensitivity to the difficulty of changing from one *habitus* to another, Paul requires of all the Roman believers, both Jewish and non-Jewish, an overriding commitment to their common Master, and thus to each other, which will alter the default setting of their *habitus* in food consumption and hospitality at just enough strategic points to remind them that they belong ultimately not to the Law but to the Lord (cf. 7:1-4).[28] In one sense, the kingdom of God is not about food and drink (14:17), but in another sense it is precisely in practicing a culturally relativized ethic of food and drink, performed exclusively to the Lord and in gratitude to God (14:6-8), that believers are now to show their ultimate allegiance in corporeal practice.

In all such ways, Paul demonstrates what it means to "present your limbs as weapons of righteousness to God" (6:13). The new Christian *habitus* can be expressed and reinforced only in practice; it requires to be embodied, not simply conceptualized. The impossible "life from the dead," externally sourced in Christ, necessarily entails a new set of

---

[28] See John M. G. Barclay, "'Do we Undermine the Law?': A Study of Romans 14:1–15:6," in *Paul and the Mosaic Law* (ed. James D. G. Dunn; Tübingen: Mohr Siebeck, 1996), 287–303; repr. in John M. G. Barclay, *Pauline Churches and Diaspora Jews* (WUNT 275; Tübingen: Mohr Siebeck, 2011), 37–59.

orientations and dispositions which structure new patterns of behavior, and Paul seems instinctively aware of what anthropologists have labored to clarify: the refashioning of the self cannot take effect without refashioning the practices of the body.

Grace, Obedience, and Christian Agency

If we draw these observations together, the following eight conclusions emerge:

A. Christian "obedience" responds to the prior, incongruous gift of God in Christ; it is symptomatic of a new life which runs clean contrary to the death-doomed life of the "natural" human being. That incongruity is evident in the fact that this life is present precisely in the *mortal* human body and is dramatized in the baptismal break with the past. Christian life is an impossible newness given as an unfitting gift, such that everything in this life refers back to its source and foundation in the Christ-gift, and forward to its eschatological fulfillment as eternal life. Everything that can be said about Christian action, obedience, and obligation arises from this generative basis because the very life that believers now live is created and sustained by the resurrection life of Christ, who is present in power.[29]

B. Hence the obligation now incumbent on believers is not to "gain" grace (or salvation), nor to win another installment of grace: there is a single χάρισμα of eternal life (6:23) which runs from the Christ-event to eternity (cf. 8:32), not a series of "graces" won by increases in sanctification. Paul certainly expects that the *moral* incongruity at the start of the Christian life will be reduced over time, as the believers' slavery to righteousness draws them toward holiness (6:19). In that sense, what began as a morally incongruous gift will be completed as a morally congruous gift for those rendered somewhat worthy of the kingdom of God (cf. 1 Thess 2:12; 3:13).[30] But this does not reduce the essential incongruity of

---

[29] Understandably nervous about the language of "obligation," lest it become another condition laid on an autonomous but incompetent agent, J. Louis Martyn has stressed to me the importance of the notion that Christ *continues to be present* with the gift and in its demand—present to empower, and not just to demand. I am happy to underline this same point, but within that frame I consider "obligation" still an appropriate term to express the Pauline imperative and his associated metaphors of slavery.

[30] See my attempt to explore this phenomenon in John M. G. Barclay, "Believers

grace, since the very life in which this holiness emerges is not the believers' own life (which is doomed to death) but the resurrection life of Christ: right up to the moment of their resurrection a believer remains *simul mortuus et vivens*.

C. Since the "newness of life" by which the believer now lives is a miraculous gift, there is no possibility of imagining their resulting obedience as their own achievement, self-initiated or independently governed. Their new competence is wholly dependent on the life of Christ, present within. What is given to them is not a new set of competencies added to their previous capacities, nor an enhancement of their previous selves: what is given is rather a death, and the emergence from that death of a new self, essentially ectopic in dependence on the resurrection life of Christ.

D. Because he operates within this frame of thought, Paul does not have to say that the agent operating in and through the believer's agency is *really* the Spirit or Christ. He can certainly speak of the presence of Christ (or the Spirit) within (8:9-11) and can talk of Christian action as taking place generically in the Spirit (πνεύματι, 8:13-14). But he does not have to articulate this on each occasion when he speaks of believers as agents. He gives genuine exhortations to genuinely freed agents who are urged to more than passive acquiescence in the work of another. In other words, Paul does not "perfect" the efficacy of grace into a formula of monergism because it is clear for him from the baptismal event that the very life in which the believer acts and decides is a life sourced, established, and upheld by Christ (a "life from the dead"). Within this frame and on this basis, plenty of statements can be made regarding believers as responsible agents, required to present their bodies in one direction rather than another.

E. The theological logic of the Pauline imperative is to live the life that has been given. Paul is not requiring them to turn theory into practice, or possibility into reality: joined to Christ in baptism they really and actually share his risen life.[31] Nor is he requiring them to turn an "objective" truth into a "subjective"

---

and the 'Last Judgement' in Paul: Rethinking Grace and Recompense," in *Eschatologie-Eschatology* (ed. H.-J. Eckstein, C. Landmesser, and H. Lichtenberger; Tübingen: Mohr Siebeck, 2011), 195–208.

[31] In this sense, if we may speak of an "ontological change," that is primarily true of Christ, and only secondarily, and derivatively, applicable to believers.

reality since they are "alive to God" in every dimension of their subjectivity by participation in Christ. Nor is the imperative the supplement to the indicative in the sense that something incomplete has to be completed in further degrees. The theological logic of indicative and imperative is in one sense much simpler than all of these inadequate conceptualizations. They have been given a new life which can be lived only in activity and practice: this "newness of life" is essentially and not just contingently a matter of περιπατεῖν (6:4). Practice, action, and obedience are the mode of this new life. In every move they make, believers are either living this new life or living according to the flesh (8:13), the latter still possible because, for as long as they live in the realm of mortality they can fall back into the force-field of sin and death and repudiate the power that tugs them towards life. The imperative is thus to practice (and thereby demonstrate) the new life given, which cannot be said to be active *within* them unless it is acted out *by* them.

F. Sociologically, one may put this in other (partly complementary) terms. The new *habitus* of the believer—the new perceptions, goals, dispositions, and values—can become effective only in practice: outside of practice it is not clear that they would mean anything at all. The believer has a new identity as a slave to God and a slave to righteousness: it is hard to know what that identity could mean if he/she does not actually obey God in everyday practice. Everything one does every moment of time contributes to the formation of one *habitus* or another: if you do not sow to the Spirit, you are certainly sowing to the Flesh (Gal 6:8). The imperative to *live in practice* the new life one has been given has, thus, a kind of sociological as well as a theological logic.

G. From both theological and sociological perspectives, the body has emerged as a crucial component of Christian obedience, understandably prominent in Romans 6, as elsewhere in Paul. From a theological point of view, it is the site where the new life headed to eternity and the old life headed for death meet and clash: that it is precisely here the new obedience is displayed provides a vivid demonstration and foretaste of the triumph in Christ of life over death. Sociologically, the new *habitus* requires embodiment if it is to be effective at all: the body is already pretrained to all sorts of harmful effects and needs to be disciplined and reoriented for the new identity in Christ to take effect. If Christians are to present themselves to God, this has to involve their "organs" or "limbs."

H. Finally, we can comprehend better now the role of obedience "under grace." Christian obedience is only ever in a responsive mode: it arises in conjunction with faith and gratitude as the answer to a prior gift. The gift is entirely undeserved but strongly obliging: it creates agents who are newly alive, required to live the life they have been given. This obedience is not instrumental (it does not acquire the gift of Christ, or any additional gift from God), but it is integral to the gift itself, as God graciously wills newly competent, freed agents who express in practice their freedom from sin in slavery to righteousness. God's grace does not exclude, deny, or displace believing agents; they are not reduced to passivity or pure receptivity. Rather, it generates and grounds an active, willed conformity to the Christ-life, in which believers become, like Christ, truly human—that is, obedient agents (5:19).[32] Without this obedience grace is ineffective and unfulfilled.

---

[32] For a careful analysis of this theme in Barth, see John Webster, *Barth's Ethics of Reconciliation* (Cambridge: Cambridge University Press, 1995).

5
The Shape of the "I"
The Psalter, the Gospel, and the Speaker in Romans 7

Beverly Roberts Gaventa

Few scholarly works have influenced my understanding of a text more than has Paul W. Meyer's essay "The Worm at the Core of the Apple: Exegetical Reflections on Romans 7." Meyer argues that the interpretation of Romans 7 has been seriously misled by the assumption that Paul must be referring here *either* to the "religious person" or to the "irreligious" (the regenerate *or* the unregenerate, the saved *or* the lost). In contrast to most customary readings, Meyer demonstrates that in Romans 7, Sin continues to be the major "character" in the argument. As in chapters 5–6, where Sin enters the world, Sin increases in power, Sin reigns like a king, and Sin enslaves, so also in chapter 7 Sin makes use of the Law, Sin deceives and kills, Sin takes captive the human being. Sin actually produces a kind of rupture, not in the self but in the Law (as indicated by 7:25b; see also 8:2). On Meyer's reading, then, the primary concern in Romans 7 is neither the Law nor the "I" but the way in which Sin's power can reach into and use even the holy and right and good Law of God.[1] This is one of those rare essays that rearranges the furniture in our exegetical houses.

---

[1] Paul W. Meyer, "The Worm at the Core of the Apple: Exegetical Reflections on Romans 7," in *The Conversation Continues: Studies in Paul and John in Honor of J. Louis Martyn* (ed. Robert T. Fortna and Beverly R. Gaventa; Nashville: Abingdon, 1990), 62–97; repr. in *The Word in This World* (ed. John Carroll; Louisville: Westminster John Knox, 2004), 57–77. As the present chapter emerged from the celebration of Princeton Theological Seminary's bicentennial, it is appropriate to observe that Meyer is the Helen H. P. Manson Professor of New Testament Emeritus.

Whenever I teach Romans, Meyer's essay is among the required readings. In class, I work through his argument carefully, making sure that students follow along. (I specify "carefully" not because the argument is hard to follow, but because it leads us down a path that diverges so sharply from the usual interpretive ruts as to be stunning to first-time readers.) And, almost every time, someone responds by asking, "Well, then, what does this mean about the 'I'? Why is it that I find myself so drawn to the 'I'?" Normally I have responded to that question with a few comments about the power of interpretation, especially the interpretations we inherit from our ecclesial communities.

Yet the persistent questions from my students return me to Meyer's essay and, more importantly, they return me to Romans 7. For all that I have learned from "The Worm at the Core of the Apple," there is still the matter of the "I" in this passage. The puzzle arises not simply because Paul shifts to first person, but because when he does so he introduces the emphatic pronoun ἐγώ, which has previously appeared in the letter only at 3:7.[2] And he does so not once but repeatedly (at least seven times),[3] in a more concentrated fashion than anywhere else in his extant letters. To put the question directly: Why the concentrated use of ἐγώ? Why, on Meyer's interpretation, would Paul not simply say, "Do you not know that Sin can use even the Law, and then people find that they cannot do what they want to do?"

Consideration of this question has prompted me to push a step further. In what follows, I argue that the "I" of Romans 7 is shaped by the "I" of the Psalter, although here the "I" of the Psalter has itself been reshaped, perhaps even distorted, through the lens of the gospel. And I further argue that the "I" has the potential to shape its hearers, so that they join with that "I" in crying out for deliverance from the enslaving power of Sin.

A few preliminary words about the "I" of Romans 7 are in order. The scholarly literature abounds with arguments about the "I," most of

---

[2] The first-person singular pronoun does appear several times in 1:8-15, but in the genitive and accusative cases, not as the emphatic ἐγώ.

[3] There are eight instances of ἐγώ if the one in v. 20a is included, but there the manuscript evidence is divided. For my purposes, the presence or absence of that single instance of ἐγώ scarcely matters, but it could have been omitted accidentally to harmonize with the ὃ θέλω that appears in v. 19. Or, as Robert Jewett suggests, the ἐγώ may have been omitted because of its similarity to the immediately preceding θέλω (i.e., reading θελωεγω a scribe could have missed the final three letters). See the helpful discussion in Robert Jewett, *Romans* (Hermeneia; Minneapolis: Fortress, 2007), 454–55.

which revolve around two issues.⁴ The first is the question of autobiography: is the speaker Paul? If so, then from what chapter of his memoir is this statement drawn; is it pre- or post-conversion? The second issue has to do with the rhetoric of the passage: is this or is it not an instance of speech-in-character? That is, is Paul self-consciously giving voice to the stance or experience of another person or group of people?⁵ Throughout this study, I am raising a different sort of question, less about rhetorical analysis as such or the identity of the "I" than about its workings, what I have called in my title the "shape" of the "I."

The word "shape" is admittedly and deliberately vague. I have chosen it under the influence of the work of linguistic theorists Emile Benveniste and Kaja Silverman on the peculiarities of first- and second-person pronouns.⁶ Unlike nouns, which refer to a class of "objects" (say, a tree or a room or even a feeling), the pronouns "I," "we," and "you" (whether singular or plural) have no definable referent. They have their point of reference only within a particular discourse, a particular context.⁷ This much is obvious in daily experience, even if it is seldom isolated for discussion: the word "I" in the context of a scholarly paper given at a conference might be that of the paper presenter, that of the session's moderator, or that of the respondent to the paper, but those "I"s are not identical and are unlikely to be confused with one another.

---

⁴ Informative surveys of the extensive debate about Romans 7 are readily available in C. E. B. Cranfield, *Romans 1–8* (ICC; Edinburgh: T&T Clark, 1975), 342–47; and Arland Hultgren, *Paul's Letter to the Romans: A Commentary* (Grand Rapids: Eerdmans, 2011), 681–91.

⁵ See esp. Stanley K. Stowers, "Romans 7.7-25 as a Speech in Character (προσωποιία)," in *Paul in His Hellenistic Context* (ed. Troels Engberg-Pedersen; Minneapolis: Fortress, 1995), 180–202; Thomas H. Tobin, S. J., *Paul's Rhetoric in Its Contexts: The Argument of Romans* (Peabody, Mass.: Hendrickson, 2004), 227–45.

⁶ Emile Benveniste, *Problems in General Linguistics* (trans. Mary Elizabeth Meek; Coral Gables, Fla: University of Miami Press, 1971), 217–30; Kaja Silverman, *The Subject of Semiotics* (New York: Oxford University Press, 1984), 43–53, 194–201.

⁷ Benveniste, *General Linguistics*, 218. Benveniste distinguishes between first- and second-person pronouns and those of third person, which serve as "abbreviated substitutes" in that "they replace one or another of the material elements of the utterance" (221). As the protagonist of David Lodge's novel *Deaf Sentence* observes: "Pronouns are tricky for kids, of course, because they're shifters, as we say in the trade, their meaning depends entirely on who is using them: 'you' means you when I say it, but me when you say it. So mastery of pronouns always comes fairly late in the child's acquisition of language." (London: Harvill Secker, 2008), 10.

We can take yet another step: in every discourse, there are (at least theoretically) two "I"s, the one who is speaking (in Benveniste this "I" is identified as "the speaking subject") and the subject of that speech.[8] In ordinary conversation, this distinction usually makes no difference, but there are occasional exceptions. For example, someone who arrives in the middle of an ongoing conversation may not know that the speaker (in Benveniste's terms "the speaking subject") is reporting speech from an absent third party (the subject of the speech). In such an instance, there is a potentially significant difference between the "I" who is speaking and the "I" who is being reported, the one who is the subject of the speech.[9] To take a textual example, when the book opens with, "Whether I shall turn out to be the hero of my own life," the identity of the "I" is by no means clear. Only as the story develops can the reader understand that Charles Dickens is speaking (or is writing) the subject "I" of David Copperfield.

Things become still more complicated when we consider the relationship between the "I" written within a text and the audience of that text. When an audience or the reader identifies "with the subject of the speech," that is, the "I" in a discourse, as Silverman observes, she "permits the signifier 'I' to represent" her as well.[10] And in so doing, she may be changed in some way by that "I."

These highly theoretical distinctions come into focus when we think of the work of hymns or prayers or creeds.[11] "Amazing Grace," for example, was written by an individual "I" by the name of John Newton, who articulated those moving lines about the "I" who was once lost and is now found. When I (Beverly Gaventa) sing those lines, I may or may not align myself with the "I" of that text. That hymn works especially well for illustrative purposes, since there are people who decline to sing "Amazing Grace," protesting that they have never been "wretches" in need of salvation. They resist the implicit invitation of the "I" of that hymn. One reason the content of hymns and prayers and other liturgical acts is sharply contested is precisely because we know their power to shape what people believe (as in the ancient maxim, "*lex orandi lex credendi*").

---

[8] Benveniste, *General Linguistics*, 218.

[9] As Carol Newsom notes, the distinctions being made here are similar to those between the author/implied author and the narrator; *The Self as Symbolic Space: Constructing Identity and Community at Qumran* (STDJ 52; Leiden: Brill, 2004), 200.

[10] Silverman, *The Subject of Semiotics*, 198–99.

My contention is that these observations about pronouns in general can shed light on the shape of the "I" in Romans 7 in particular, namely, that this "I" is shaped by the "I" of the Psalter as it is reinterpreted by the gospel. This new "I" in turn may shape the audience to identify with Paul's analysis of the enslaving power of Sin and its capacity to take even God's holy Law as its captive. I begin with the role of the ἐγώ in the Psalter and its possible connections with Romans 7.[12] Then I turn to the ἐγώ of Romans 7 in relation to the argument of the letter, and finally I consider the relationship of the ἐγώ to the cosmic horizon of the letter.

The ἐγώ of the Psalter

The overwhelming majority of occurrences of ἐγώ (here specifically the nominative singular form) in the Septuagint's translation of the Psalms involve a human speaker rather than the voice of God.[13] Of the seventy-nine instances of ἐγώ in the Psalms, God is the speaker in only eight instances.[14] In all the other instances, the voice of the ἐγώ is that of a human being, the psalmist.[15] And overwhelmingly, the psalm is a

---

[11] Here I am drawing on Carol Newsom's discussion of the formation of subjectivity in the Hodayot; *Self as Symbolic Space*, 190–286, esp. 196–204.

[12] Others have made brief suggestions about possible connections between the lament psalms and Rom 7: Meyer, "The Worm at the Core," 65; Peter Stuhlmacher, *Paul's Letter to the Romans: A Commentary* (trans. Scott J. Hafemann; Louisville: Westminster John Knox, 1994), 109, 113; Mark A. Seifrid, "The Subject of Rom 7:14-25," *NovT* 34 (1992): 322–33. More extensive is J. Gerald Janzen's discussion of Rom 7 in light of Ps 119 in "Sin and the Deception of Devout Desire: Paul and the Commandment in Romans 7," *Encounter* 70 (2009): 29–61. Janzen connects Romans 7 with Paul's "pre-conversion self" (53) who reflected the moral world of Psalm 119 (along with Psalm 19 and 4 Maccabees). I am grateful to Professor Janzen for his generous comments on an earlier draft of this chapter.

[13] To be sure, ἐγώ appears extensively elsewhere in the LXX outside the Psalms, but given the importance of the Psalms in Romans, it seems reasonable to focus there. See Moisés Silva, "The Greek Psalter in Paul's Letters: A Textual Study," in *The Old Greek Psalter: Studies in Honour of Albert Pietersma* (ed. Robert J. V. Hiebert, Claude E. Cox, and Peter J. Gentry; JSOTSup 332; Sheffield: Sheffield Academic, 2001), 277–88; Sylvia C. Keesmaat, "The Psalms in Romans and Galatians," in *The Psalms in the New Testament* (ed. Steve Moyise and Maarten J. J. Menken; London: T&T Clark, 2004), 139–61; J. Ross Wagner, "Paul and Scripture," in *The Blackwell Companion to Paul* (ed. Stephen Westerholm; Chichester: Blackwell, 2011), 154–71, esp. the table on 155–57.

[14] Psalms 2:6, 7; 35:3; 46:10; 50:7; 75:2, 3; 81:10.

[15] Given the work of Benveniste introduced above, there is a distinction to be

lament, or at least the psalm contains elements of lament. That fact in itself should not be even mildly surprising: if a psalm is an individual lament, then we would expect it to be written in first person (although notice that I specify the use of the emphatic pronoun).[16] In addition, ten of the lament psalms use the emphatic ἐγώ more than once (as is the case in Romans 7).[17] And twenty-three times the emphatic ἐγώ is coupled with *de*: "but I," i.e., setting the speaker apart from what (or more often *who*) has preceded (as also in Romans 7:9, 10, 14).[18] And in many of these instances, other language that figures importantly in Romans 7 or its context also occurs. Constraints of space preclude a discussion of every instance of ἐγώ in the Psalter; instead, I shall focus on a few psalms for brief comment (namely Psalms 17, 69, 119) and then reflect on those psalms in relationship to the "I" of Romans 7.

Psalm 17 [LXX 16] is a relatively straightforward call for God's help in the face of those who have sought to do harm to the speaker. It appears to be a textbook example of the individual lament. The petitioner asserts that her cause is just, that she is innocent; she seeks God's vindication, characterizes the "wicked" enemies who are bent on her destruction, and closes with a call for God to destroy the enemy and a confident claim that the speaker herself will be found in God's presence. The word ἐγώ appears twice, first in verse 6:

I (ἐγώ) cried aloud, because you will listen to me, God,
Turn your ear toward me and hear my words.[19]

The second ἐγώ comes in the final verse of the psalm, following a forceful depiction of what should happen to the enemies. Not only should God fill up their stomachs with God's wrath, but there should

---

made also between the "I" of the psalmist and the "I" who speaks in the psalm, but that theoretical distinction does not seem particularly relevant in the Psalter.

[16] And even the use of the emphatic ἐγώ is not surprising, since in the Psalter ἐγώ consistently translates the Hebrew 'ani and 'anoki.

[17] Ἐγώ appears more than once referring to a human speaker in 16:4, 6, 15; 25:1, 11; 30:7, 15, 23; 37:14, 18, 19; 38:5, 11, 13; 54:17, 24 (twice); 68:14, 30; 70:14, 22; 108:4, 22, 25; 118:19, 63, 67, 69, 70, 78, 87, 94, 125, 141, 162 (LXX numbering). (Psalm 118 is not usually categorized as a lament psalm, but it does include features of lament.)

[18] Ἐγώ δε appears in 5:8; 12:6; 16:15; 21:7; 25:11; 30:7, 15, 23; 34:13; 37:14; 39:18; 54:17, 24; 55:4; 58:17; 68:14; 69:6; 70:14; 108:4; 118:69, 70, 78, 87 (LXX numbering).

[19] Translations are my own unless otherwise indicated.

be enough vengeance left over for their children to have a share. Then:

> But I (ἐγώ δε) in [my] righteousness will see your face,
> I will be satisfied when I see your glory.

In addition to the "I," Psalm 17 speaks of those ungodly people who "cause me to be wretched" (ταλαιπωρέω, v. 9) and seeks God's rescue (ῥύομαι, v. 13). This usage of "wretchedness" and "deliverance" sits interestingly alongside Romans 7:24, with its anguished call for deliverance by the self-identified "wretched" speaker. And there are other connections between Psalm 17 and important terms in Romans: righteousness/rectification, ungodly, enemy, glory (although, of course, some of these terms are ubiquitous in the psalms, so their appearance in this particular psalm is not unusual).

A second psalm that is pertinent for this discussion is Psalm 69 [LXX 68]. Here the speaker details his distress, perhaps resulting from illness. Although the speaker admits briefly to some wrongdoing (v. 5), he also claims that he is accused falsely by enemies. He is insulted because of his zeal for God's house (presumably to be understood as the temple[20]). He calls on God to pour out vengeance on his enemies and to protect him (e.g., "May the rage of your wrath overtake them," v. 25 [LXX]). The speaker promises to praise God and closes by invoking praise of God who will rescue God's people. As in Psalm 17, the emphatic ἐγώ appears twice in this psalm, the first time in verse 13 [LXX14]. Having said that

> Against me, those who sit in the city gate chatter,
> And against me the wine-drinkers sing.

The speaker then insists,

> But I [ἐγώ δε] say in my prayer to you, Lord
> Hear me . . . save me . . . deliver me from those who hate me.[21]

Later, having asked God to wipe the enemies from the book of the living, in verse 29 [LXX 30], the speaker again contrasts himself:

---

[20] Adele Berlin connects this psalm with mourning for Zion in the context of the exile, mourning that evokes the ridicule of others; "Psalms and the Literature of Exile: Psalms 137–44, 69, and 78," in *The Book of Psalms: Composition and Reception* (VTSup 99; Leiden: Brill, 2005), 74–75.

[21] Note the contrast of speech here: the enemies speak harshly against the speaker of the psalm, but the speaker's words cry out to God.

I am [ἐγώ] lowly and in pain,
Let the salvation of your presence assist me, O God.

Again, as in Psalm 17, we find in Psalm 69 both "wretched" as a description of the speaker's life (v. 21 LXX), and the plea for "deliverance from those who hate me" (v. 15 LXX). There can be no doubt that Paul knows this psalm: he quotes verse 9 in Romans 15:3 ("The insults of those you insult you have fallen on me," NRSV), and he quotes verse 22 at 11:9-10 ("Let their table become a snare and a trap," NRSV). What I will suggest below is that the wretched "I" of Romans 7 has been shaped—consciously or otherwise—by the outlook represented in this psalm.

A third example, and perhaps the most suggestive, is the longest of all the psalms, Psalm 119 [LXX 118]. Unlike Psalm 17 or 69, here there is little sense of movement from one place or position to another. James Luther Mays aptly observes that this psalm says the same thing 167 different ways.[22] This complex composition is sometimes characterized as a meditation on the Law; indeed, William P. Brown describes the speaker as "lovesick" over God's Law.[23] Although it is not typically classified as a lament, it does contain elements of lament (see, e.g., vv. 42, 61, 78, 82-84, 86, 95).[24]

The emphatic ἐγώ appears eleven times in Psalm 119 (LXX 118). Given the sheer length of the psalm, that number may seem less impressive, but nonetheless the psalm is a single unit. In a couple of instances, the ἐγώ speaks to identify herself as one in need of instruction in the Law:

v. 19:   I am (ἐγώ) an alien in the land,
        Do not hide from me your commandments.
v. 125:   I am (ἐγώ) your slave.
        Instruct me,
        And I will know your decrees.

---

[22] James Luther Mays, *Psalms* (Interpretation; Louisville: John Knox, 1994), 382.
[23] William P. Brown, *Psalms* (IBT; Nashville: Abingdon, 2010), 78.
[24] Patrick D. Miller, *They Cried to the Lord: The Form and Theology of Biblical Prayer* (Minneapolis: Fortress, 1994), 113. See also the careful discussion of Psalm 119 and genre in Kent Aaron Reynolds, *Torah as Teacher: The Exemplary Torah Student in Psalm 119* (VTSup 137; Leiden: Brill, 2010), 21–29. Janzen's provocative essay "Sin and the Deception of Devout Desire" also connects Psalm 119 with Romans 7. Our approaches differ in that Janzen connects Romans 7 more closely to Paul's conversion than I do, and I attend more to the larger context of Romans.

At one point the ἐγώ confesses to have failed in following the Law (v. 67, and see the closing verse of the psalm). For the most part, however, the ἐγώ claims both to delight in the Law and to observe it:

> v. 63: I am (ἐγώ) a companion of all those who fear you and keep your commandments.
> v. 94: I (ἐγώ) am yours, save me, since I have sought out your statutes.
> v. 162: I (ἐγώ) rejoice at your words, like one who finds much spoil.

And the ἐγώ distinguishes herself from others who do not behave rightly:

> vv. 69, 70: Wrongdoing by the arrogant increases against me, but I (ἐγώ δε) with my whole heart search out your commandments.
> Their hearts are like curdled milk, But I (ἐγώ δε) study your Law.
> v. 78: Let the arrogant be put to shame, since they have acted wrongly against me, but I (ἐγώ δε) will meditate on your commandments.
> v. 87: They have nearly put an end of me in the earth, but I (ἐγώ δε) have not neglected your commandments.
> v. 141: I am (ἐγώ) young and disdained, but I do not forget your statutes.

These three psalms provide some texture and specificity to the argument, but they are by no means the only ones that might be adduced, especially if we extend the discussion to consider all usage of first-person speech in the Psalter. Rather than extending the investigation at this point, however, I want to turn to the question, what can be said about this "I" who speaks in the psalms?

The speaker in these psalms knows and delights in God's Law. Although the speaker does at some points confess to wrongdoing, on the whole the speaker not only delights in God's Law but observes that Law and reflects a sense of confidence in his ability to do so. That is emphatically not to identify the speaker as what is usually termed "self-righteous," an expression that is saddled with numerous complications and, indeed, susceptible of malicious abuse. What the speaker displays is a fairly robust understanding of his own capacity to hear the Law, to understand it, and to carry out God's demands as reflected in the Law.

The speaker also knows that his obedience to the Law sets him apart, making him different from others, those repeatedly referred to as "they" who do not keep God's Law. They too apparently have the ability to keep the Law, but they choose not to do so. Indeed, these others emerge as the speaker's enemies, whom God will punish.

In addition, the speaker regularly occupies a situation of danger. She is confronted with a range of hardships, including deprivation, assault, illness, and abandonment. Yet, however severe the isolation and threat, however disempowered the speaker claims to be, she nevertheless calls out to God with confidence. She knows that God will intervene and even employs her own faithfulness as leverage to provoke God's action. As William P. Brown observes, even in situations of extreme deprivation, the psalmist still "speaks from a position of power, a position of covenantal kinship that calls God to account for divine negligence or abuse."[25]

The Shape of the "I" of Romans 7

When we return to Romans 7 after pondering these psalm texts, certain things stand out. Like the speaker of the psalms, this "I" also knows that the Law is holy, right, and good (v. 12). This "I" recalls coming to know the Law (v. 9). This "I" also gives voice to delight in the Law (v. 22).

This "I" also has enemies, or perhaps it is more accurate to claim that this "I" has *an* enemy. This enemy is not human; it is, rather, the power of Sin. The fourth-century commentator traditionally identified as Ambrosiaster understands the enemy status of Sin in this passage so well that he repeatedly identifies Sin with the Devil.[26] Sin takes advantage of the Law to produce enslavement. The takeover by this enemy is nearly complete: twice the "I" declares, "Sin lives within me." The "I" endeavors to keep God's Law. And the "I" of Romans 7 cries out for deliverance from wretchedness, just as does the "I" of the Psalter using, as I have indicated, similar terminology.[27]

---

[25] Brown characterizes the relationship between God and the speaker as "intensely personal, trusting, and empowering" in *Psalms*, 138. See also Amy Cottrill's important discussion of the self in the laments, which argues for a more ambivalent relationship between the speaker and God. *Language, Power, and Identity* (Edinburgh: T&T Clark, 2008), 100–137.

[26] J. Patout Burns, trans. and ed., *Romans Interpreted by Early Christian Commentators* (The Church's Bible; Grand Rapids: Eerdmans, 2012), 163–65, 173–75.

[27] Stuhlmacher notes that the passage ends abruptly, as do the laments (*Paul's Letter to the Romans*, 113), citing especially Psalms 22, 51, 69.

There are also differences between the two uses of ἐγώ, however, differences produced by the gospel as it refracts the "I" of the psalmist. Although this "I" in Romans 7 knows that the Law is holy, right, and good, that the Law is spiritual, this "I" also knows that Sin can make use of the Law, that Sin can even take control of the Law in order to produce more wrongdoing.[28] And Sin has already enslaved the "I," who declares himself to be "sold under Sin's power" (v. 14). As a result of Sin's action, this "I" can make no claim to be observant of the Law. From the lips of this "I," we will hear no confident assertion to be a "companion of all those who fear you and keep your commandments" (as in Ps 119 [LXX 118]:63). Neither will this "I" report that "I have not neglected your commandments" (as in 119 [LXX 118]:87).[29]

A striking feature of the speech of this ἐγώ is the absence of reference either to God or to Jesus. There is no confident call for God to rescue the speaker, no expectation of God's help. The "I" appears to be so utterly *dis*empowered that he can make no claim on God; the wretchedness of v. 24 seems total. It is only with v. 25a that God and Jesus Christ enter the picture. And it is only after 8:1-4, with its declaration that God has now condemned (defeated) Sin in the fleshly body of Jesus Christ, that Paul turns finally to a depiction of life in the Spirit.

This is not to claim that the "I" of Romans 7 is either citing or intentionally echoing the "I" in any or all of these psalms. What I am claiming instead is that the "I" of Romans 7 is—in part at least—shaped by the "I" of the Psalter. The "I" of Romans 7 knows this tradition; indeed, the speaker is shaped in some important ways by identification with this tradition.[30] The Psalms form part of the imaginative world of this speaker. Just as I may have hymn tunes or lines from Jane Austen or lines from the Apostle Paul playing in my head, the imaginative world of the "I" in Romans 7 is furnished with the stance of the Psalmist. And just as I may employ those lines in ways that would be unrecognizable, perhaps even deeply offensive, to their authors, the ἐγώ of Romans 7 recasts the ἐγώ of the Psalter. Perhaps it should even be said that the ἐγώ of Romans 7 is a new character introduced by Paul, a character shaped by the psalms but powerfully reshaped by the Christ event.

[28] On this point, again see Meyer, "The Worm at the Core of the Apple."
[29] This "I" is also far removed from the Paul who confidently depicts himself in Phil 3:6 as "blameless" with respect to the Law.
[30] Reynolds suggests that Psalm 119 is "suasive" in that it does not so much "define the righteous" as to encourage readers to obey Torah (*Torah as Teacher*, 57 and *passim*).

Precisely at this point, some may find it tempting to conclude that the "I" in Romans 7 represents the Jewish Christian.[31] If the ἐγώ is a new character produced by a collision between the gospel and the desire to fulfill the Law of Moses, then presumably that "I" is a Jew who has come to see Jesus of Nazareth as the Messiah of Israel. A narrow identification of the ἐγώ is problematic, however. To begin with, it is not only Jews who are concerned with the Law; there may well be Gentiles among the Roman congregations who have been associated with the synagogue for some time and who themselves know the Law. More to the point, any move to connect the "I" with a *particular* individual or group neglects the relationship between the ἐγώ and the πᾶς, between the "I" and the "all." Clarifying that relationship requires attention to the role of Romans 7 in the letter as a whole.

The "I" of Romans 7 in Context

Among the persistent challenges that confront proposals about Romans 7 is the problem of understanding what role this passage plays in the larger argument of the letter. Attending to the work of the pronouns in these chapters may shed light on exactly that question.

In the initial, scathing indictment in 1:18-32, Paul speaks of "*those* people" who suppress the truth about God with their own lies. "*They*" withhold worship from God. As a result, Paul insists—not once but three times—that God "handed *them* over." He concludes, "Those who do such things are worthy of death." Paul and the audience of the letter stand together outside this accusation, or so it seems. Of course, at 2:1, the letter takes a sharp turn toward the accusation of the "you" who judges (second-person singular) and again in 2:17-24 toward the singular "you" who claims to be a Jew (whether Jewish or Gentile, this "you" names himself/herself as Jew). And in chapter 3, Paul again speaks in third person, but this time of "all" who are under the power of Sin.

Apart from a few formulaic expressions (e.g., "We know," 2:2; 3:19; "What do we say?" 3:5), the account in 1:18–3:20 is dominated by this accusation of "they" and "you" singular. There is, however, an important shift to first-person plural in chapter 4, when Paul introduces Abraham as "our forefather." The first-person plural carries over into chapter 5, with "we have peace," and "we have access to grace,"

---

[31] E.g., see Ann Jervis, "Reading Romans 7 in Conversation with Post-colonial Theory: Paul's Struggle Toward a Christian Identity of Hybridity," *Theoforum* 35 (2004): 173–93.

and "we boast in the hope of God's glory." Romans 5 is widely characterized as the beginning of Paul's discussion of the Christian life, yet an odd detour appears on the way to depicting the Christian life. As it turns out, "we" are not only the people who have peace with God, "we" are also those who were "weak" and "ungodly," we were "sinners," we were "enemies of God" who required God's reconciliation (5:8-11).

This is strong language, stronger than is generally acknowledged. The claim that "we" are—or even were—weak, ungodly sinners at enmity with God may well prompt a negative reaction, especially if the Roman congregations are populated with God-fearing Jews and Gentiles who were already associated with the synagogue. Not unlike those who decline to sing "God saved a wretch like me," they may object to this characterization. If Paul understands this possibility—perhaps is even provoking it—then what follows in the second half of chapter 5 is not so much intended to explain the Adam–Christ relationship as it is to show the inescapability of the claim that "we" were weak, ungodly sinners at enmity with God. If Adam's disobedience opened the door for the entry of the powerful rulers Sin and Death, then no one can claim to be exempt. In any case, the second half of Romans 5 abounds with language about the "all" who were subject to the twin rule of Sin and Death.

At 6:1, however, Paul moves again to first-person plural. "We" no longer belong in the territory governed by Sin because "we" were baptized into Christ's death so that "we" might have new lives (6:4). Second-person plurals dominate the second half of the chapter, with its contrasts between slavery to Sin and slavery to righteousness. Second-person plurals continue into the opening of chapter 7, but at 7:4 Paul shifts to first-person plural again: "We bear fruit to God. . . .We were in the flesh and ruled by the Law, we now have our service in a new spirit."

This movement brings us back to 7:7.[32] Here, finally, Paul takes up the provocative comments about the Law that he has so skillfully

---

[32] Verse 7 cites the commandment against desire, which prompts some to connect this verse with the understanding of desire as a vice in Greco-Roman moral philosophy (see esp. Tobin, *Paul's Rhetoric in Its Contexts*, 228–38, and the literature cited there). That there is a strong concern in the philosophical tradition about desire running out of control makes it more valuable to Paul's argument, but the tenth commandment is especially helpful to Paul quite apart from contemporary moral philosophy. As Patrick D. Miller has shown, the commandment is connected to a large strand

sprinkled throughout his argument, but his concern with the cosmic power of Sin again comes to the foreground. As Meyer argues, the problem is not with the Law itself but with Sin's overpowering even of God's holy and good and right Law. And this final time, when Paul limns the activity of Sin, he does so with the "I," first as a depiction of past events (vv. 7-13) and then in the present tense (vv. 14-25), which further vivifies the depiction.[33] Paul shows that Sin has reached all the way down, even into the person of the archetypal "I" who delights in God's Law, producing not simply disobedience but despair. The voice of the psalmist is here contorted by the inability to do what is desired, an inability produced by Sin. And the deliverance comes, not because the "I" has successfully observed the Law and set himself apart from others, but because God has acted unilaterally in the case of all humanity.

Conclusion

This argument is intended as an appreciative modification of Meyer's groundbreaking interpretation, not a return to the pitfall of perseverating about the identification of the "I." Meyer is surely right in his claim that Romans 7 concerns Sin's powerful use of even the good and holy and right Law of God to produce enslavement and destruction. By doing so with an ἐγώ that is shaped by the Psalter, Paul gives a power to his argument that has the capacity to draw in its audience.[34] As Paul brings to a culmination his long argument about Sin, he does so neither by telling nor by showing but by drawing his audience into the experience of the collision between the psalmist's voice and the workings of Sin as those workings have been revealed in the gospel.

This means that, when my students ask about the "I," it is because the text is actually doing its work of evoking our identification with the wretched one who cries out for deliverance. The problem is that we identify with the "I," but that we do so without attending to the

---

of biblical tradition for which "*the human predicament begins with desire let loose and uncontrolled*"; *The Ten Commandments* (Louisville: Westminster John Knox, 2009), 400 (emphasis in original). Miller reflects also on the relationship between the tenth and the first commandments, in that "coveting and taking arise out of the lack of trust in the God who has made and provided for the human creature" (406).

[33] The use of ἐγώ also intensifies in vv. 14-15; it appears twice in vv. 7-13 (vv. 9 and 10) but at least five times vv. 14-15 (vv. 14, 17, 20, 24, and 25).

[34] Interestingly, Stuhlmacher (*Paul's Letter to the Romans*, 109) contends that use of the present tense in vv. 14-25 "invites one to repeat the verses for oneself."

context in which it emerges, so that it becomes merely a claim about "me," not "me" in the context of a cosmic conflict.

Over the last several years, as I have endeavored to contribute to an apocalyptic interpretation of Paul's letter to the Romans, I have emphasized the cosmic horizon of the letter.[35] By that phrase I mean that Paul's understanding of the gospel is not addressed *solely* to the individual or *solely* to Israel or *solely* to Gentiles. Instead, the gospel has to do with a conflict between God and antigod powers; these powers go by various names, in Romans they are most prominently named Sin and Death. That concern about the cosmic horizon of the letter can be heard as a claim that Romans has little or nothing to do with the life in the present (the so-called real world), much less with the lives of individuals. This contribution should allay at least some of those concerns. As I see it, Romans 7 demonstrates that the conflict between God and the powers of Sin and Death is not just about some other "they" or about a privileged "us" that somehow has been removed from Sin's grasp. It is also about the "I" who delights in God's will and faithfully undertakes what is holy and right and good, since the cosmic power of Sin reaches even into our best selves and produces despair.

---

[35] See in particular, Beverly Roberts Gaventa, "Neither Height nor Depth: Discerning the Cosmology of Romans," *SJT* 64 (2011): 265–78; and idem, "Romans," in *Paul, John, and Apocalyptic Eschatology: Studies in Honour of Martinus C. de Boer* (ed. Jan Krans et al.; SuppNovT 149; Leiden: Brill, 2013), 61–75.

6
Double Participation and the Responsible Self in Romans 5–8

Susan Eastman

"I am because we are, and because we are, I am."

This African proverb has become widely known in the west, and embraced as an antidote to American individualism. It expresses the simple truth that we need a community to be human. But it also raises important questions about the relationship between the "I" and the "we," between a self shaped in different communal identities, and a community constructed of such selves. In the following essay, I hope to explore this relationship in the context of Romans 5–8 and see what light Paul sheds on the formation of persons. I use the term "double participation" to describe human existence in the realm of sin and death on the one hand, and life in Christ under the dominion of grace on the other. In turn, "the responsible self" indicates my thesis: I shall argue that in Romans Paul depicts not only communal identity but also distinct selves in a constitutive interaction with both sin and God in Christ. Such selves undergo a diminishment of personal agency under the tyranny of sin and death, and a reconstitution of agency in the dominion of grace, thereby becoming responsible actors in the service of God. The movement from Romans 7:7-25 to 8:1-2 is the turning point in this story of the self, under the banner of "no condemnation" (8:1).

In Romans 7:15-17, Paul writes, "I do not know what I am doing. For what I want—this I do not do, but what I hate—this is what I do. Now if I do what I do not want, I agree that the law is good. So then it is no longer I doing it, but sin which dwells within me (ἀλλὰ ἡ οἰκοῦσα ἐν ἐμοὶ ἁμαρτία)." In verses 19-20, he repeats the same claim of self-negating double agency: "For I do not do the good I want, but the evil I do not want, this is what I do. Now if I do what I do not want, it is no longer I doing it, but sin that dwells within me (οὐκέτι ἐγὼ κατεργάζομαι αὐτὸ ἀλλὰ ἡ οἰκοῦσα ἐν ἐμοὶ ἁμαρτία)." These claims are a haunting reversal of the double agency in Gal 2:20, where Paul proclaims, "I have been crucified with Christ; it is no longer I who live, but it is Christ who lives in me (ζῶ δὲ οὐκέτι ἐγώ ζῇ δὲ ἐν ἐμοὶ Χριστός)."

In the Galatians passage, Paul speaks directly about himself and his own experience. In the Romans passage, he places a speech in the mouth of an anonymous *I* (ἐγώ) whose relationship to Paul himself is debated. Taken together, however, these statements evoke a picture of persons formed in relationship to entities that are external to and distinct from human beings, yet operate intrinsically within and through them. There is an "I, yet not I, but Christ," and an "I, yet not I, but sin," acting in these confusing statements. Furthermore, in both statements this "double agency" is a new development; it has not always been so: "It is *no longer I* (οὐκέτι ἐγώ) who does evil," and conversely, "It is *no longer I* (οὐκέτι ἐγώ) who lives, but Christ lives in me." These observations in turn raise the question of whether the *I* in either case is a responsible actor, and if so, in what way. There are further questions, such as whether these two modalities or realms of existence are sequential or simultaneous; that is, whether selves (if indeed Paul has a notion of individual selves rather than only corporate identity) can simultaneously be in relationship to both sin and Christ, or not.

The Self in Paul's Theological Anthropology

Is there a self in Paul's functional anthropology? Is there an account of either personal responsibility for sin, or of the flourishing of individuals within the body of Christ? In the first half of the last century, the usual answer to that question would have been an unqualified "Yes," perhaps accompanied by puzzlement that it should even be asked. Paul was seen as the champion of the individual, even sometimes the discoverer of the individual. Almost fifty years ago, Ernst Käsemann wrote,

> Bultmann rightly draws attention to the importance which Paul assigns to the individual. The other New Testament writers view a person more or less as the representative of a group. . . . For Paul, too, this aspect has its relevance, and he always has it in mind. But at the same time, with unusual emphasis and by no means merely

paraenetically, he brings the individual, as believer or unbeliever, into prominence.[1]

Nonetheless, Käsemann went on to describe the cosmic and corporate contours of Paul's anthropology: "existence is always fundamentally conceived from the angle of the world to which one belongs. . . . even the believer has neither being, existence, nor power in himself. His continuity and identity also rest outside himself."[2] Summarizing the tension between these individualistic and cosmic views of humanity, Käsemann wrote, "We started from the position that Paul, more than any other New Testament writer, viewed man as an individual. We went on from this to call anthropology crystallized cosmology and to term every person the projection of his respective world and that world's Lord. How is this antithesis to be bridged?"[3]

Since Käsemann's time the antithesis has not been so much bridged as abrogated, to the neglect or even denial of any individual existence. To give one example, in his 1995 book, *The Corinthian Body*, Dale Martin claims:

> [F]or most people of Greco-Roman culture the human body was of a piece with its environment. The self was a precarious, temporary state of affairs, constituted by forces surrounding and pervading the body, like the radio waves that bounce around and through the bodies of modern urbanites. In such a maelstrom of cosmological forces, the individualism of modern conceptions disappears, and the body is perceived as a location in a continuum of cosmic movement. The body—or the "self"—is an unstable point of transition, not a discrete, permanent, solid entity.[4]

---

[1] Ernst Käsemann, *Perspectives on Paul* (Tübingen: J. C. B. Mohr, 1969; repr., trans. M. Kohl; Mifflintown, Pa.: Sigler, 1996), 1–31, here 2.

[2] Käsemann, *Perspectives on Paul*, 26–27.

[3] Käsemann, *Perspectives on Paul*, 29.

[4] Dale B. Martin, *The Corinthian Body* (New Haven, Conn.: Yale University Press, 1995), 25. Earlier, Martin discusses Cartesian notions of body/soul dualism and individual notions of existence in order to clarify how different Paul's worldview is from ours. He suggests that we "try to imagine how ancient Greeks and Romans could see as 'natural' what seems to us bizarre: the nonexistence of the 'individual,' the fluidity of the elements that make up the 'self,' and the essential continuity of the human body with its surroundings" (21). I note in passing that in the discourse of contemporary science, psychology, and philosophy of mind, to speak of the fluidity of the elements that make up the self, and some sort of continuity between the self and its environment,

To give another example, less extreme but nonetheless telling, Robert Jewett comments on Romans 12:1-2: "The Pauline concept of transformation . . . in contrast to the philosophers and mystery religions, . . . is corporate rather than individual."[5]

Note that Jewett does not agree with Martin's general statement regarding the lack of an individual self in the ancient world; rather, he attributes such individual concerns precisely to the philosophers and mystery religions, in contrast with Paul. My quibble here is not with the corporate focus, but rather with the presumed dichotomy between corporate and individual identity—a dichotomy that reflects, I would argue, the legacy of Cartesian thinking about individual existence only in discrete and autonomous terms. But why should we assume that Paul thought in such an either/or fashion in regard to the construction of the person? While I agree that there is in Paul no self-creating, non-embedded, nonembodied self, to say therefore that there is no responsible self is to confuse responsible agency with autonomy. One may deny mind/body dualism and qualify bounded identity without necessarily claiming that the self is only "an unstable point of transition."[6]

My question is simply this: what happens to the self in Paul's account of the gospel in Romans 5–8? Is there any room for either personal responsibility under the tyranny of sin, or the flourishing of individual selves in the dominion of grace?

---

is anything but bizarre. Such notions of the self intersect in intriguing ways with current neurological research that suggests we are physically "wired for relationship," and with the idea of intersubjective identity formed through empathic mirroring between infant and parent. The literature on this subject is vast; for helpful introductions, see *On Being Moved: From Mirror Neurons to Empathy* (ed. Stein Bråten; Amsterdam: John Benjamins, 2007), and *Perspectives on Imitation: From Neuroscience to Social Science*, vol. 2 (eds. Susan Hurley and Nick Chater; Cambridge, Mass.: MIT Press, 2005). Some philosophers now talk about the notion of the "extended mind" which is not only "intimately embodied" but "intimately embedded in its world." See Andy Clark, *Supersizing the Mind: Embodiment, Action, and Cognitive Extension* (Oxford: Oxford University Press, 2011), xxvii, quoting John Haugeland, who writes, "If we are to understand mind as the locus of intelligence, we cannot follow Descartes in regarding it as separable in principle from the body and the world. . . . Mind, therefore, is not incidentally but intimately embodied and intimately embedded in its world." "Mind Embodied and Embedded," in *Having Thought: Essays in the Metaphysics of Mind* (ed. J. Haugeland; Cambridge, Mass.: Harvard University Press), 207–40, here 236–37.

[5] Robert Jewett, *Romans* (Hermeneia; Minneapolis: Fortress, 2007), 733. See also James D. G. Dunn, *Romans 9–16* (WBC 38b; Dallas: Word, 1988), 715.

[6] Martin, *The Corinthian Body*, 25.

To sharpen the point, I share a conversation with an African woman whom I met on a cross-country flight. She told me she had immigrated to the United States. I asked how she found American culture and society, in comparison with her own, and she said that she much preferred it. That surprised me a bit, so I inquired further: don't you find our culture isolated and individualistic, in comparison with a more communal society? I added that I always had been impressed by the well-known African saying, "I am because we are, and because we are, I am." "I hate that saying!" she exclaimed. "Don't talk to me about community! I came here to get away from that! Here, I create myself; no one tells me who I am or what I can do. I want autonomy. I celebrate American individualism! I love it! I could never go back."

Life in community is not always good news![7]

So we come back to the question of the self in a new light: what does Romans 5–8 have to say to the woman on the plane? Might Paul's account of the self constructed in relationship to sin speak to her experience of the communal culture from which she came, and the supposedly autonomous culture she has embraced? And might his account of the self in relationship to Christ name a place in which the self flourishes? If so, in what way?

Tracing the "I" and the "You"

In the following remarks I will trace a "history of the singular" in Romans, focusing on chapters 5–8, but with side looks at the rest of the letter.[8] I note briefly that Paul often refers to himself in the first-person

---

[7] As my colleague Esther E. Acolatse has written about pastoral care with African women, "what is termed 'relational ethos' benefits only some of the people." "Unraveling the Relational Myth in the Turn toward Autonomy: Pastoral Care and Counseling with African Women," in *Women Out of Order: Risking Change and Creating Care in a Multicultural World* (ed. J. Stevenson-Moessner and T. Snorton; Minneapolis: Fortress, 2010), 219. She continues, "[T]he need of the female for connectedness is seen as essential for the survival of the self, and yet this need in certain cases also becomes the source of the death to the self" (222). Connection may mean death, not life. Acolatse is speaking about a particular gendered cultural experience, but surely her observations can be applied more widely; in any community, social harmony in effect may be maintained by an unequal distribution of burdens and goods. Furthermore, corporate solidarity can issue in violence every bit as much as individualism can. The idea of the self-in-relation *per se*, let alone communal solidarity or corporate identity, is no panacea for humanity's ills.

[8] The first-person singular occurs in 1:8-16; 7:7-25; 9:1-3; 10:1-2; 11:1, 11, 25; 12:1, 3; 15:14-32; 16:1, 17, 19. The second-person singular form appears in 2:1-11,

singular, as in his lengthy introduction of himself to the Roman Christians: he thanks God, serves God in the Spirit, prays for the Romans, longs to be with them, wants them to know his intention to visit them, and is under obligation and eager to preach the gospel to them (1:8-15). Indeed, despite saying in Galatians that he has been crucified with Christ and no longer lives, Paul certainly has a strong sense of himself as a thinking, intending, emoting, and acting self with a distinctive history and vocation. That he sees others also as distinct persons and not simply in collective groups is amply clear from his extensive greetings to individuals by name, with personal descriptions, in 16:1-16.

Elsewhere in the letter, the singular functions in a variety of ways. Within chapters 5–8, there are two striking instances of the grammatical singular—the famous *I* of Romans 7, and the remarkable singular *you* (σε) in Romans 8:2: "The law of the Spirit of Life in Christ Jesus has set you free from the law of sin and death." Few people pay attention to the sudden intrusion of the second-person singular here, perhaps because it so often is translated either as *me*, which accords with the singular *I* in Romans 7:24, or as *us*, which matches the first-person plurals that follow. These translations follow textual variants, yet the strongest textual evidence, as well as the difficulty of the second-person singular, argues for its priority.[9] So then, whom is Paul addressing here?

Stanley Stowers has argued, persuasively in my view, that the *you* receiving good news of liberation from the law of sin and death is the same person as the *I* who in 7:24 cries out for deliverance.[10] Indeed, who else could be signified, in the immediate context of the verse? Following the dramatic performance of the anonymous individual's plight under sin's use of the law, in 8:1 the authorial voice returns to the

---

17-23; 8:2; 10:4-5, 8-13; 11:17-22; 12:3-8, 21; 13:1, 3, 4; 14:1-12, 15-16, 20-22. With the exception of 7:7-25 and 11:1, the first-person singular usages are simply Paul expressing his actions and intentions. In 11:1 he uses himself as a sign of God's ongoing election of Israel; in 7:7-25 he uses speech-in-character, although not, in my view, to the exclusion of his own experience.

[9] σε is supported by both Alexandrian and Western witnesses—ℵ B F G 1506 1739 ar b sy^p Tert Ambst. Bruce M. Metzger comments, "it is much more difficult to choose between με and σε. The latter, as the more difficult reading, is more likely to have been replaced by the former (which harmonizes better with the argument in chap. 7) than vice versa"; *A Textual Commentary on the Greek New Testament* (2nd ed.; Stuttgart: German Bible Society, 1994), 456.

[10] Stanley K. Stowers, *A Rereading of Romans: Justice, Jews, and Gentiles* (New Haven, Conn.: Yale University Press, 1994), 282.

stage, and in 8:2, it speaks news of liberation and assurance precisely to the self enslaved by the law of sin and death (7:24). Stowers puts it this way: "The character's speech ends when Paul addresses him in words of encouragement."[11] This means that the person addressed in 8:2 has a history, and that history has come to a desperate climax in the cry for deliverance from "this body of death" in 7:24.

In fact, by the time we get to this part of the letter, we have heard a complex and layered story of the self in relationship to both sin and grace. In 1:18–5:21, human beings are the subjects of the verbs, doing evil, sinning, and therefore justly deserving of God's wrath (1:18; 2:5, 16; 3:5-7; 5:9). As such, human beings are responsible agents. Employing the second-person singular, the apostrophes of 2:1-11 and 17-27 cumulatively pronounce judgment on all humanity, both Gentile and Jew, precisely highlighting culpability for judging others when one does the same things: "Therefore you are without excuse, O human being, whoever you are who passes judgment, for in judging another you condemn yourself" (2:1). As Jewett notes, the language anticipates Paul's exhortation against mutual judgment in the Roman churches, in 14:3, 4, 5, 10, 13, 22.[12] The effect of the singular address, regardless of whether Paul has Gentiles or all humanity in mind here, is to challenge his Roman auditors to examine themselves.

At the same time, however, human actors have been handed over by God into the grip of destructive passions and distorted cognition (1:24, 26, 28), and as such they are "under the power of sin" (3:9). This aspect of the human relationship to sin comes to the fore in the narrative of 5:12–7:6, which overlaps in 5:12-21 with the previous account. Now sin and death come onto the scene as subjects of the verbs, and henceforth act as enslaving powers that use even God's good law as a lethal weapon against humanity itself. Within this account, humanity as a whole is bound up in the destiny of the one person (ἄνθρωπος), Adam, and the one person (ἄνθρωπος), Christ (5:12-19). The language is thoroughly corporate; as Robert Tannehill puts it: "Paul is not speaking of the death of individual believers one by one. He is speaking of the destruction of the dominion of sin, of which all believers were a part."[13] Adam and Christ inaugurate and instantiate two reigns—on

---

[11] Stowers, A Rereading, 282.

[12] Jewett, Romans, 197.

[13] Robert C. Tannehill, Dying and Rising with Christ: A Study in Pauline Theology (Berlin: Töpelmann, 1967; repr., Eugene, Ore.: Wipf & Stock, 2006), 30.

the one hand, the dominion of sin and death (5:14, 17, 21); on the other hand, the dominion of grace (5:21).[14]

This corporate language runs throughout 5:12–7:6, depicting a communal bondage under the enslaving reign of sin, and a communal liberation through the reign of grace, which also entails a powerful capacity to act corporately against the power of sin: "For if, through the trespass of the one, sin reigned through the one, how much more those who receive the overflowing abundance of grace and of the gift of righteousness will reign in life through the one, Jesus Christ" (5:17). The outworking of this new power is seen in the (again plural and corporate) presentation of the community's bodily members to God as weapons of righteousness (6:12-14, 17-19) under the liberating authority of grace (6:14). If it were not for the singular *you* in 8:2, one could move easily from 7:6 to that verse: "Now we are discharged from the law, dead to that which held us captive, so that we serve in newness of the Spirit and not in oldness of the letter.... For the law of the Spirit of life in Christ Jesus has set you free from the law of sin and death."

But the *you* in 8:2 is singular, and it is anticipated by the agony of the singular *I* in 7:7-25. Why then does Paul interrupt his victorious account of Christian liberty in chapter 6 with an anguished expression of bondage under sin's use of the law, in chapter 7? Why does he switch from the plural to the singular here, in the present tense? These are familiar questions, with some familiar answers: Paul revisits the discussion of sin, death, and the law in order to exonerate God's good law, and to intensify the sinfulness of sin.[15] But Paul could defend the law and bring sin itself to the bar of judgment without using the first-person singular. I suggest, therefore, a further purpose in Paul's striking language: he dramatizes the situation of the self (and not only of humanity in general) in the grip of sin's lethal and deceptive power, in order to bring home to his Roman auditors, empirically and personally, both that power and the even-greater power of God's deliverance through Christ.[16] Along the way, he dramatizes in individual terms what happens to personal agency in relationship to the agency of sin.

---

[14] Tannehill, *Dying and Rising*, 39.

[15] Leander E. Keck, "The Absent Good: The Significance of Rom 7:18a," in *Text und Geschichte: Facetten theologischen Arbeitens aus dem Freundes und Schülerkreis, Dieter Lührmann zum 60 Geburtstag* (Marburger Theologische Studien 50; ed. Stefan Maser and Egbert Schlarb; Marburg: Elwert, 1999), 67.

[16] See Leander E. Keck: "[W]hat makes Romans 1–8 tick is the inner logic of having to show how the gospel deals with the human condition on three ever-deeper

Now sin as an agent performs actions previously accomplished by human beings: whereas in chapters 1–3, evil is what humans do, in 7:19-21 evil is what sin does, counter to the wishes of the self. The falsehood and violence previously attributed to human beings now become the province of sin itself (7:11). In the first account, human beings are sinners, but now sin itself is the surpassing "sinner" (7:13). And whereas in 1:30 human beings are "inventors of evil," now indwelling sin itself accomplishes evil through its unwilling human minions (7:14-20). I want to do the good, serving it with "the law of my mind." But sin wrests the law of God to its own purpose of death, making it "the law of sin and death" (7:22-25; 8:2).[17] The human actor recedes curiously into the background here, particularly in regard to the performance of evil.

Yet there is not a complete erasure of the self, which continues to "know" (v. 18), to "want" (vv. 15, 16, 19, 20), to "find" (v. 21), to "delight" (v. 22), and to "see" (v. 23). This self watches its own actions with horror and ascribes them to sin, with an "I, yet not I" agency. The self operates in tandem with a lethal partner, sin, and the partner is stronger. This is a participatory, noncompetitive account of the human self as constituted in relationship to sin, yet not completely conflated with it: the self is still a responsible agent, still the subject of verbs. It also is separated from the results of its actions—the language drives a wedge between what this I wants and what it accomplishes—or rather, indwelling sin accomplishes through it.[18] To conceptualize this self, we need to set aside any Cartesian notions of a freestanding individual and think rather in terms of self-in-relationship, corporately constituted yet still a distinct self.

---

levels, each understood as a dimension of the Adamic condition: the self's skewed relationship to God in which the norm (law) is the accuser, the self in sin's domain where death rules before Moses arrived only to exacerbate the situation by specifying transgression, the self victimized by sin as a resident power stronger than the law"; "What Makes Romans Tick?" in *Pauline Theology*, vol. 3: *Romans* (ed. David M. Hay and E. Elizabeth Johnson; Minneapolis: Fortress, 1995), 3–29, here 26.

[17] For a discussion of the relationship between Rom 1 and Rom 7 in regard to agency, see Simon J. Gathercole, "Sin in God's Economy: Agencies in Romans 1 and 7," in *Divine and Human Agency in Paul and His Cultural Environment* (ed. John M. G. Barclay and Simon J. Gathercole; London: T&T Clark, 2001), 158–72.

[18] See Paul W. Meyer's chapter, "The Worm at the Core of the Apple: Exegetical Reflections on Romans 7," in *The Word in This World: Essays in New Testament Exegesis and Theology* (ed. John T. Carroll; Louisville: Westminster John Knox, 2004), 57–77.

This is a personal identity that exists in inescapable bodily participation in the realm of sin and death—"this body of death"—and yet still is able to witness the effects of this participatory action as evil. Here is a depiction of radically diminished personal agency, a crippled capacity for effective action for the good, but not a complete erasure of the self. Furthermore, this anonymous self speaks with tremendous pathos, drawing the letter's auditors into the same experience.[19] In Stowers' words, "The characterization of 7:7-25 reads like someone personally witnessing to the statement 'when we were in the flesh, our sinful passions worked in our bodily parts through the law' (7:5)."[20]

Thus the speaker, *whoever it is*, describes in profoundly personal and empirical terms what chapters 5–6 describe as the cosmic and corporate reality of human bondage to sin. Does the identity behind this I matter? Or does the experiential, emotional speech and the anonymity of the speaker allow the listener to locate his or her self in relationship to the plight of the I, so that, as the saying goes, "If the shoe fits, wear it"?[21] In other words, the speaker who talks as if he or she suffers under the tyranny of sin (and indeed, as if he were Paul himself) makes it possible to name a slippage between the cosmic, corporate realities of sin and grace and the discrete experiences of Paul's auditors. Naming that slippage prepares his auditors, in turn, to hear repeatedly and to appropriate personally the news of deliverance in chapter 8. They are invited to find themselves in the story of the I; not only were we in bondage to sin, but you and you—yes, even you—know this dilemma as well. As Engberg-Pedersen writes, "Indeed, the whole point of Paul's account seems to lie in making his readers themselves experience the experiences of the self that he is recounting."[22]

---

[19] Leander E. Keck, "*Pathos* in Romans? Mostly Preliminary Remarks," in *Paul and Pathos* (SBLSymS 16; ed. Thomas H. Olbricht and Jerry L. Sumney; Atlanta: Society of Biblical Literature, 2001), 71–96.

[20] Stowers, *A Rereading*, 270.

[21] In his work on *prosopopoiia*, Stowers notes its use by ancient rhetoricians to "depict and elicit emotion" (*A Rereading*, 20). In his recent work *Cosmology and the Self in the Apostle Paul*, Troels Engberg-Pedersen rightly attends to the paraenetic function of this passage, including its use of the singular first person, asking, "Is there a self to be found in Rom 7:7-25? Definitely yes! The word ἐγώ (an emphatic Greek form of 'I') is used extensively throughout the passage and towards the end Paul even uses the phrase αὐτός ἐγώ, meaning 'I myself'"; *Cosmology and Self in the Apostle Paul: The Material Spirit* (New York: Oxford University Press, 2010), 164.

[22] Engberg-Pedersen, *Cosmology*, 168.

Whether this account reminds the Roman believers of their past bondage under sin or reminds them of their present susceptibility to sin's power is less important than the experience itself—the narrative time here is not chronological, but empirical. That is, rather than depicting sequential events, here we find depicted the ways in which past and present mingle in human experience. As my colleague, Stanley Hauerwas, often says, "The past isn't past until it's redeemed." Yes, it was redeemed cosmically and corporately on the cross, but the recognition and reception of this redemption in personal understanding and practice requires its repeated narration. This is what Paul does in Romans, spiraling back over the same territory from different angles— here, a vivid portrayal from below of the anguish of sin and the power of no condemnation. The result is a deepened personal recognition of both the horror of sin, and ultimately, the deliverance of God through the work of Christ. So when in Romans 8:1-2 Paul announces that there is no condemnation for those who are in Christ Jesus, for "the law of the Spirit of life in Christ Jesus has set you free from the law of sin and death," we may hear each person addressed as an individual— you, and you, and you—who has been set free from the judgment of condemnation, the power of sin's use of the law to kill.

It is important to emphasize the paraenetic function of Paul's language here. Paul is not making a claim about the ontological status of the Roman believers, as if they still are slaves of sin and have not "died to sin" through being buried with Christ in baptism (6:2-3). Such an interpretation would render nonsensical Paul's earlier affirmation that "our old self was crucified with [Christ] so that the sinful body might be destroyed, and we might no longer be enslaved to sin. For he who has died is freed from sin" (6:6-7). Nonetheless, as the many imperatives in chapter 6 imply, this death to sin in union with Christ does not automatically or magically change Paul's auditors. Rather, it engages them in the struggle to bring this new reality to bodily expression in their lives: "So also you must consider yourselves dead to sin and alive to God in Christ Jesus" (6:11). Again, Paul says, "now yield yourselves to God as those who have been brought from death to life, and your bodily members to God as weapons of righteousness" (6:13). Hence his subsequent vigorous affirmation, "For sin will not rule over you, for you are not under law but under grace" (6:14), is not the final word ("mission accomplished"), but a call to arms in an ongoing conflict in which the Roman Christians are personally involved. The battle is ongoing because, although those in Christ are no longer enslaved by sin, they still live in a cosmos dominated by sin and death.

What then will bring home to Paul's auditors the reality of that struggle and their part in it? I suggest they become active participants through an existential realization of what it is to be ruled by sin, under law, and what it is to be liberated under the reign of grace, precisely so as to "reckon" themselves "dead to sin and alive to God" (6:11). Romans 7:7-25 functions precisely to elicit such existential recognition. As the anonymous I vividly expresses the anguish of the self co-opted by sin's use of the law, and then receives the freedom from condemnation announced in 8:1-4, the affective language draws Paul's auditors personally into the same experience, so that they each may know and reckon themselves as liberated agents and act accordingly.[23] Only after this dramatic portrayal of deliverance does Paul stop talking about sin in the course of the letter. It drops out of the picture after chapter 8.

Corporate and Singular Redemption

What then of the self that participates in the reign of grace? Is it freed now for autonomy? Is it able to be self-creating? Has it moved from Africa to the United States?

Not at all. Paul immediately enfolds the singular *you* of 8:2 into the *we* in whom the righteous deed of the law (δικαίωμα τοῦ νόμου) is being fulfilled (8:4), in and among whom the Spirit dwells corporately (8:11), and who walk according to the Spirit. This liberated self is also constituted relationally and only finds freedom in and through its

---

[23] Engberg-Pedersen rightly highlights Paul's paraenetic purpose: "Paul aims in the two passages [Rom 7:7–8:11] to make the Romans both see and feel the change that they have ex hypothesi already undergone—and should indeed now show in practice" (*Cosmology*, 246–47). Engberg-Pedersen's discussion of the self disclosed in Rom 7 is fascinating but omits any serious reckoning with the role of sin as an agent acting on and through persons. Hence he reads the text in terms of a divided self with an "uppermost 'I' which describes its own ineffectual attempts to control itself" (*Cosmology*, 166), and bypasses Paul's statement, "It is no longer I doing [evil] but sin dwelling in me" (7:20). Self-control is not the issue (and certainly not the solution!); the issue is sin's invasion of the self and lethal use of the law. *Pace* also Stowers, *A Rereading*, 272, who also reads Rom 7:7-25 as a speech about *akrasia*. Behind the similarities between Paul's language and that of Greco-Roman moral discourse lies a much larger difference in worldviews. See John M. G. Barclay, "Stoic Physics and the Christ-event: A Review of Troels Engberg-Pedersen, *Cosmology and Self in the Apostle Paul: The Material Spirit*," *JSNT* 33 (2012): 406–14, esp. 413. See Meyer, *The Word*, 74–75.

bodily membership in the new community in Christ. The priority of the community is abundantly clear through the plurals that dominate the rest of the chapter.

If I were to stop here, however, we would have a narrative of the self as moving from a participatory existence under the dominion of sin into a participatory life in Christ, with only a fleeting glance at individual agency. I would talk only in terms of an addressable community, a corporate agent, and the wonders of life in the church. And I would put aside the question of whether there is an erasure of the individual within this community.

The woman on the plane will not allow me to do this. And happily, neither will Paul, because in Romans 12–14 there is a striking reappearance of the addressable individual in the midst of the addressable community. I note this first in the singular imperatives of 12:21: "Do not be conquered by evil, but conquer evil with the good (μὴ νικῶ ὑπὸ τοῦ κακοῦ ἀλλὰ νίκα ἐν τῷ ἀγαθῷ τὸ κακόν)." This singular admonition is the climax of a series of plural exhortations to communal up-building (12:9-13) and forbearance in the face of persecution (12:14-21). It sums up the immediately preceding quotation (12:20) from Proverbs 25:21-22, which also employs singular imperatives. Hence the turn to the singular could simply follow from the citation.

Yet the singular imperative also functions in another way. Its military imagery hearkens back to the military language in Romans 7:11, in which sin uses the law as a base of operations for its lethal assault on the self (7:19-21). The contrast is sharp: now sin is absent from Paul's exhortation, and the liberated self of Romans 8:2 is called to victorious action in conquering the evil that sin once accomplished through it. If the singular speech of 7:7-25 articulated on an individual level the experience of being under sin's power, the singular imperatives of 12:21 articulate personally the reality of presenting one's members to God as weapons of righteousness.

Again, this personal defeat of evil is not the triumph of a lone ranger, an autonomous individual, but of a self whose agency is constructed within a community of both "solidarity and difference," as Paul already has made clear by depicting the Roman churches as made up of one body in Christ, and individually members of one another (12:3-8).[24] For Paul, persons are responsible actors in the fact of their

---

[24] David G. Horrell, *Solidarity and Difference: A Contemporary Reading of Paul's Ethics* (New York: Continuum, 2005).

mutual belonging in a corporate life indwelt by the Spirit and under the dominion of grace. But conversely, this community is made up of addressable selves.[25]

A brief look at chapter 14 will conclude this story of the self in Romans. The chapter is replete with singular description and address, including the apostrophes at 14:4—"who are you who judges (σὺ τίς εἶ ὁ κρίνων) the servant of another?"—and verse 10—"You! (emphatic position) Why do you judge your brother? Or you! Why do you despise your brother?" Both in style and in the criticism of human judgment these verses recall 2:1—"Therefore you are without excuse, O human being, whoever you are who passes judgment, for in judging another you condemn yourself (Διὸ ἀναπολόγητος εἶ ὦ ἄνθρωπε πᾶς ὁ κρίνων ἐν ᾧ γὰρ κρίνεις τὸν ἕτερον σεαυτὸν κατακρίνεις)." Now, however, the matter of mutual judgment becomes concrete and particular in the life of a community that stands under the sign of "no condemnation" (οὐδὲν ἄρα νῦν κατάκριμα—8:1), and the basis on which it is rejected is that each person stands or falls before her Lord, who is able to make her stand (12:4, 7, 12). Indeed, "Each of us (ἕκαστος ἡμῶν) will give a word concerning him or herself to God" (14:12).[26] Notably, here the certainty of divine judgment constrains mutual criticism in the community and enforces a place for individual differences. But also notably, here the singular comes into play in relationship to God's judgment.[27] Surely this language of facing God as individuals and not simply as a group implies the constitution of a responsible self within

---

[25] It is striking that commentary after commentary ignores the singular imperative of v. 21, merging it into the communal exhortation that leads up to it, under the heading of corporate identity and mutual service. See, e.g., Dunn, *Romans 9–16*, 833; Leander E. Keck, *Romans* (ANTC; Nashville: Abingdon, 2005), 346–47; Jewett, *Romans*, 868; Ernst Käsemann, *Commentary on Romans* (trans. Geoffrey W. Bromiley; Grand Rapids: Eerdmans, 1980), 378; Meyer, *The Word*, 208. An exception is Stowers, *A Rereading*, 319.

[26] Jewett reads all this as concerning groups, not individuals, but even so he must resort to talking once more about the place of the individual before God (*Romans*, 852). John M. G. Barclay notes explicitly the individual thrust of Paul's instruction at this point: "Thus each Christian can act, even if with opposite effect, 'in honour of the Lord'. . . . The individual definition of morality could hardly be more plainly stated, and is further reinforced towards the end of the discussion: 'the faith that you have, keep to yourself before God' (14:22)." In "'Do We Undermine the Law?': A Study of Romans 14:1–15:6," in *Paul and the Mosaic Law* (ed. J. D. G. Dunn; WUNT 89; Tübingen: J. C. B. Mohr, 1996; repr., Grand Rapids: Eerdmans, 2001), 287–308, here 301.

[27] Paul also uses the singular in Gal 6:4-5 to talk about facing divine judgment.

the community of grace. There is emphatically no diminishment of personal agency (as in chapter 7), but rather its establishment in responsible selves who are capable of being judged, because the Lord will make them stand—for, as the Roman Christians know, "there is now no condemnation for those who are in Christ Jesus" (8:1).

Reprise

These remarks have traced a sort of story of the self, from acting agent to a diminished and compromised (but not dissolved) agency under sin, to a reconstitution of the responsible self under the dominion of grace. This is a double narrative, from condemnation to no condemnation, and from bondage to freedom. As I have laid out the texts, they seem to portray a progressive development. But as we have noted, this is not simply the case. The ordering of Paul's thought is notoriously confusing when we try to map it onto a sequential chronology: 7:7-25 comes after 5:1–7:7, and even within chapter 7, 7:25b comes after the victory cry of 7:25a. This is a spiral structure in which Paul repeatedly revisits and amplifies both sin and the saving power of God. On the one hand, the objective redemption accomplished by Christ's action on the cross is sure, and the victory is accomplished (8:3). On the other hand, continued existence in the realm of the flesh seems to mean a continued vulnerability to the powers of sin and death, entailing—this side of the eschaton—a life of double participation. I suggest that precisely in this life of double participation the self is trained as a responsible agent, indeed as a soldier who is to present her bodily members as "weapons of righteousness" (6:13) and thereby to conquer evil with good, and death with life.

The Transformed and Responsible Self
A Parable

I will close with a parable of one way, among many, in which we might conceptualize such liberation. The parable comes from *Biting the Hand That Starves You*, which is a marvelous account of a kind of narrative therapy for victims of anorexia and bulimia (hereafter referred to simply as a/b).[28] The psychologists who have developed this therapy teach girls and women in the grip of a/b a "manner of speaking" that (unbeknownst to the therapists) is very similar to Paul's manner of speaking in Romans 7–8.

---

[28] Richard Maisel, David Epston, and Ali Borden, *Biting the Hand that Starves You: Inspiring Resistance to Anorexia/Bulimia* (New York: W. W. Norton, 2004).

Conventional treatments of a/b label its sufferers with the term *anorexic* or *bulimic*, and then tell them to change. This creates a catch-22, because the self that is merged with a/b itself has no place to stand. As the authors observe, "In this manner of speaking, the distinction between the person and problem is blurred. . . . 'I have bulimia' or 'she's an anorexic.' When the problem is seen to arise from within the person or the 'self,' it becomes easy to think about the person as the problem."[29] Furthermore, this labeling occurs in a judgmental context that exacerbates rather than alleviates the grip of a/b. As the authors explain:

> Labeling such as this takes place within a framework of norms and expectations regarding how people *should* think and act. The judgments that arise from these norms exist on a continuum of merit. . . . A/b thrives upon this way of thinking, which allows it to promote itself as the means to cultivate and perfect those qualities that are highly valued by the dominant culture. . . . This all too often prompts the "patient" to try to be a "perfect anorexic" for the doctor or other professional, because a/b fosters in many a desire to please others and live up to their expectations.[30]

Hence there are two problems with this conventional narrative: first, it merges the voice of the young woman with the disease itself, diminishing the self's role as an acting agent, or even as a witness. Second, the language of "shoulds" and of rules (How much did you eat today? You need to eat more!) is ineffective if not downright harmful when addressed to someone who has lost any sense of self as agent.

Alternatively, narrative therapy personifies and objectifies a/b as a hostile and alien enemy of the person, which lodges within and uses its victim's own desire to do the right thing to deceive and literally kill her. There are striking similarities between this description of a/b and Paul's language about sin in Romans 7. For example:

> A/b secures its authority as jailer by relying on certain implicit assumptions about morality. We use the term *morality* in a broad sense to refer to those qualities and ways of being in the world that are regarded as virtuous and meritorious. . . . [A]/b's promises revolve around its vision of the morally virtuous, whereas its

---

[29] Maisel, Epston, and Borden, *Biting the Hand*, 76.
[30] Maisel, Epston, and Borden, *Biting the Hand*, 76–77.

chastisements, threats, and dire predictions revolve around its vision of the morally flawed. . . . [W]e are not making the case that a/b is a moral discourse or a moral problem. Rather, we are discussing the ways in which a/b *uses* moral arguments to achieve its highly immoral ends—the murder of women and men."[31]

Such a lethal appeal to morality is similar to Paul's own complaint about sin's use of the law to deceive and to kill: "Sin, finding an opportunity in the commandment, deceived me and by it killed me" (7:11).

Anorexia also takes over the agency of the person so that she thinks she's acting and choosing freely but is actually following orders. Its sufferers describe it this way: "I was at one with anorexia. . . . The voice you heard was not mine."[32] Or this: "You become almost like a tool. Like someone is just using you. It's not really you. I felt the whole time like I'm not Jennifer, I'm just Jennifer's body. Something else is in charge of what I'm thinking and doing. It feels like you are possessed by the devil. Whenever I smiled I felt like the devil smiling."[33] In Paul's terms, "it is no longer I doing it, but sin which dwells in me" (7:17, 20).

To combat this lethal takeover, the therapists develop an "anti-a/b language."[34] I will note very briefly several aspects of this language and its similarity to Romans 7. First, it distinguishes between the voice of the person and the voice of a/b. This is rather similar to the way in which the self of Romans 7 retains a separate voice that witnesses to the evil actions of sin residing within. Secondly, anti-a/b language is replete with images of combat. A/b is an enemy to be fought with every resource available. In another woman's letter to her therapist, she wrote: "I now had to confront evil as evil along with you. I knew I had to prepare for mortal combat as anorexia intended to murder me."[35] And as in Romans 6–8, the site of this combat is at least partially the body itself.

Furthermore, just as the person whom Paul commands to conquer evil does not act alone, but is part of the new community in Christ, the captive of a/b is strengthened in her battle for liberation by a gracious communal matrix of allies. There is a new vision of the person, "widely distributed among and supported by ongoing relationships in

---

[31] Maisel, Epston, and Borden, *Biting the Hand*, 32.
[32] Maisel, Epston, and Borden, *Biting the Hand*, 119.
[33] Maisel, Epston, and Borden, *Biting the Hand*, 65.
[34] Maisel, Epston, and Borden, *Biting the Hand*, 75–76.
[35] Maisel, Epston, and Borden, *Biting the Hand*, 92.

the person's life."³⁶ The "I in relationship to others" is stronger than the "I in relationship to a/b." Or as a young woman wrote about the support of family and friends in her fight against anorexia, it was "Ten voices against one."³⁷ The noncondemning quality of these voices is crucial in their power to combat a/b's judgments and rules.

Finally, the goal of this manner of speaking is most emphatically not to inculcate a victim mentality in those who suffer from anorexia or bulimia, but rather to strengthen them as responsible agents who can choose and act, and face the consequences of their choices and actions, out from under the deception of a/b's false narrative of the world. It does this by giving them a vocation to use their experiences to help others in anorexia's grip, initially simply by witnessing to their own experience. While they never are entirely free of the lure and power of a/b, through the struggle itself, and through their own participation in the community of fellow fighters, they increasingly own and take responsibility for their actions. They join the community of the living.

I offer this brief description of a form of narrative therapy as a partial parable of Paul's account of the self in Romans. It is a description from below—from the depths of human experience—and certainly not a full account of Paul's emphasis on divine causality and the lordship of Christ over every competing lordship. Nonetheless, perhaps it can help us imagine how Paul's gospel, far from submerging persons in communal identity alone, creates a place where we can flourish as liberated selves under the banner of "no condemnation," for "the law of the Spirit of life in Christ Jesus has delivered you—yes, even you—from the law of sin and death."

---

[36] Maisel, Epston, and Borden, *Biting the Hand*, 100.
[37] Maisel, Epston, and Borden, *Biting the Hand*, 114.

7
The Love of God Is a Sovereign Thing
The Witness of Romans 8:31-39 and the Royal Office of Jesus Christ

Philip G. Ziegler

Lord our God, other lords indeed rule over us besides you, but we invoke only you and your name.
—Isaiah 26:13

Introduction
The Spiritual Character of the Munus Regnum Christi

The doctrine of Christ's offices has long served, particularly in Protestant theology, as an important device by which to organize exposition of his saving work.[1] In its best-known form, that of the *munus triplex* or "threefold office," Jesus Christ is acknowledged as the prophet, priest,

---

[1] Karin Bornkamm, "Amt Christi," in *Religions in Geschichte und Gegenwart 4* (Band 1; ed. Hans D. Betz et al.; Tübingen: Mohr Siebeck, 2007–), 439–40. Though it does not originate in the work of the Reformers, the threefold office came to particular prominence in Calvin's work (see his *Institutes of the Christian Religion* II.15) and went on to provide the scheme through which to analyze the work of Christ in both Lutheran and Reformed orthodoxy. See Heinrich Heppe, *Reformed Dogmatics* (trans. G. T. Thompson; London: George Allen & Unwin, 1950), 481–82; Heinrich Schmid, *The Doctrinal Theology of the Evangelical Lutheran Church* (3rd ed.; trans. C. A. Hay and H. E. Jacobs; Minneapolis: Augsburg, 1961), 370–71. Alongside its close study of Luther's theology of the "twofold office," Karin Bornkamm also provides extensive discussion of the history of the idea of Christ's offices in the ancient, medieval, and early modern periods. *Christus-König und Priester: Das Amt Christi bei Luther im Verhältnis zur Vor- und Nachgeschichte* (Tübingen: Mohr Siebeck, 1998). The formative role of this teaching is evident by its appearance in Protestant catechetical texts including Calvin's *Geneva Catechism*, articles 37–38; the *Heidelberg Catechism*, Questions 31–32; Luther's *Small Catechism*, Question 132; *Westminster Catechism*, Questions 23–26.

and king of divine salvation, the singular concentrated fulfillment and antitype of these roles as they are depicted in the scriptural history of ancient Israel. By means of this scheme, the manifold character of his saving activity as the "one Mediator between God and humankind" is ordered and displayed. The scheme of the threefold office has been subject to sustained criticism since the nineteenth century on various grounds, chief among which are its alleged failure to do justice to the historical reality and activity of Jesus of Nazareth and the inappropriateness of applying the titles of prophet, priest, and king to him when these are understood in rigorously *religionsgeschichtliche* terms.[2] Not all historical-critical scholarship supports such a judgment, and recent Christian dogmatics has shown itself willing to continue to work with the scheme on the far side of such criticism. The most significant example of this is Karl Barth's creative use of a variant of the *munus triplex* as an essential architectural feature of his massive account of the doctrine of reconciliation, where it affords a means by which to overcome what the Swiss theologian considered deeply unhelpful divisions between Christology, soteriology, and hamartiology which dog the theological tradition.[3] Others working since Barth have also continued to find the formula valuable in ordering comprehensive accounts of Christ's saving work.[4]

---

[2] Albrecht Ritschl wrote of the "purely arbitrary analysis of the word 'Christ'" and "superficial formalism" which underwrote the traditional account of the *munus triplex* with the result that modern theology must adjudge that "the doctrine of the three offices spells failure"; *The Christian Doctrine of Justification and Reconciliation* (trans. H. R. Mackintosh; Edinburgh: T&T Clark, 1902), 427, 431. On related grounds, the doctrine was rejected by Wolfhart Pannenberg in his *Jesus-God-Man* (trans. L. L. Wilkins and D. A. Priebe; Philadelphia: Westminster, 1976), 212–25. In his more recent *Systematic Theology* ([trans. G. W. Bromiley; London: T&T Clark/Continuum, 2004], 2:445–49), he reiterates the earlier criticism that "The historical Jesus, then, was neither priest, nor king nor, in the strict sense, prophet" (445). But he now also sees more dogmatic value in the teaching of the threefold office on the basis of the significant admission that "[t]he earthly activities [of Jesus] have contexts other than those that appear on a purely historical approach" (446).

[3] See Karl Barth, *Church Dogmatics* (trans. G. W. Bromiley; Edinburgh: T&T Clark, 1956–69), 4:1–3.

[4] For three examples of quite different kinds, see G. C. Berkouwer, *The Work of Christ* (trans. C. Lambregtse; *Studies in Dogmatics*; Grand Rapids: Eerdmans, 1965), 58–87; Geoffrey Wainwright, *For Our Salvation: Two Approaches to the Work of Christ* (Grand Rapids: Eerdmans, 1997), 99–186; and more extensively Robert J. Sherman, *King, Priest and Prophet: A Trinitarian Theology of Atonement* (London: T&T Clark, 2004).

It is thus still largely with reference to this scheme that doctrinal reflection upon Christ's lordship, his *munus regnum* or royal or kingly office, has taken and continues to take place. The theme of the lordship of Christ, together with its wide-ranging ecclesial and political consequences, proved a central preoccupation of ecumenical work within the World Council of Churches in its first two decades.[5] Extended treatments of the theme from the postwar period typically were set out as correctives to longstanding neglect of the royal motif in Protestant soteriology, a neglect rooted in nearly exclusive concentration upon Christ's priestly or prophetic work, and so also upon substitutionary atonement or salutary teaching respectively.[6] Yet already around the turn of the twentieth century, when Weiss and Schweitzer were putting the centrality of the Kingdom of God as an apocalyptic reality back on the christological agenda, others were also moving in a parallel way to reassert the primacy of the *munus regnum* within the threefold scheme. So, E. F. Karl Müller writing just before the outbreak of the First World War concluded his brief article on the doctrine by asserting that

> the permanent union and simultaneous exercise of the three functions do not exclude, however, a fixed aim, namely the kingdom. To this as the organizing purpose of the whole points before everything the Biblical basis of the formula, the starting-point and essential content of the Messianic office is royal dominion over and for God's people, the peculiar modification of which is described by the other titles.[7]

It could be argued that the substance of this claim was already borne out in Calvin's own seminal account of the threefold office in the 1559 *Institutes of the Christian Religion*, where it is the *munus regnum* which

---

[5] Indicatively, see the working paper prepared by the Division of Studies of the World Council of Churches, "The Lordship of Christ over the Church and the World," *Ecumenical Review* 11 (1959): 437–49; cf. Niels Hasselmann, "The Lordship of Christ in Ecumenical Discussion," *Lutheran Forum* 14 (1967): 93–101.

[6] As examples, see Jean Bosc, *The Kingly Office of the Lord Jesus Christ* (trans. A. K. S. Reid; Edinburgh: Oliver and Boyd, 1959); and W. A. Visser't Hooft, *The Kingship of Christ* (London: SCM Press, 1948).

[7] E. F. Karl Müller, "Jesus Christ, Threefold Office of," in *New Schaff-Herzog Encyclopedia of Religious Knowledge* (vol. 6; ed. S. Macauley Jackson; repr., Grand Rapids: Baker, 1953); cf. Bosc, *The Kingly Office*, 10: "Without doubt, the character which dominates the eschatological Messiah is that of the King."

in fact dominates the compressed presentation of the doctrine of the threefold office.[8] And Calvin's teaching here could well be characterized as "messianic" in as much as he acknowledges that Christ combines in his person the roles of king and pastor as the one through whom God wills to protect, direct, bless, and secure the "everlasting preservation" of his covenant people the church. Moreover, Calvin argues expressly that "Christ was called Messiah especially with respect to, and in virtue of, his kingship."[9] In support of this understanding of Christ's kingship and in order to display, as he says, its "efficacy and benefit for us, as well as its whole force and eternity," Calvin is at great pains to emphasize its *spiritual* character. Calvin's glosses on the meaning of "spiritual" concern the eternal, incorruptible character of Christ's reign and focus upon the distribution of the gifts and power the Holy Spirit by means of which he secures victory for his people over "the devil, the world, and every kind of harmful thing." The spiritual work of Christ's reign is to "share with us all that he has received from the Father" and to do so with salutary power to the end that "launched into history" the church be built up and believers advanced in assurance and sanctity until the time when the glory of the Kingdom will be manifest.[10] As Calvin summarizes, Christ "rules—inwardly and outwardly—more for our own sake, than for his."[11] Thus, Christ's kingship is spiritual, in other words, because the power by which he reigns is heavenly and not "of this world"; Christ's kingship is spiritual because his dominion is accomplished not by worldly means but rather in virtue of his own

---

[8] John Calvin, *Institutes of the Christian Religion*, II.xv.1–6, where §§3–5 treat of the royal office. Citations from Calvin in the following exposition are taken from these paragraphs in the *Library of Christian Classics* edition: *Institutes of the Christian Religion* (ed. J. T. McNeil; trans. Ford Lewis Battles; Philadelphia: Westminster, 1960). Emil Brunner remarks that "[t]he fact that in his presentation the largest part is given to the office of King, is in harmony with the whole of Calvin's outlook, and also with that of the earliest creed of the Church, *Kyrios Christos*"; *The Christian Doctrine of Creation and Redemption* (trans. O. Wyon; London: Lutterworth, 1952), 314.

[9] Cf. Calvin, *Institutes*, II.vi.3.

[10] "Launched into history, [the church] grows and increases until the advent of Christ"—so T. F. Torrance, who identifies these two motifs of *aedificatio ecclesiae* and *profectus fidelium* as hallmarks of Calvin's understanding of the reign of God in and through Christ. See idem, "The Eschatology of Hope: John Calvin," in *Kingdom and Church: A Study in the Theology of the Reformation* (Edinburgh: Oliver and Boyd, 1956), 96, 116; cf. 113ff.

[11] Calvin, *Institutes*, II.xv.4.

[12] Torrance, "The Eschatology of Hope," 123.

priestly and prophetic work;[12] Christ's kingship is spiritual because he is "armed with eternal power" such that "the devil, with all the resources of the world, can never destroy the church."[13] We do well to note in all of this the public, gracious, agonistic, and eschatological force of Christ's spiritual rule as Calvin sets it forth. Calvin's exposition of the spiritual nature of Christ's lordship bears the imprint of the witness and language of the concluding verses of Romans 8, and shares their eschatological, even apocalyptic, tone.

We find something similar when we consider Martin Luther's influential treatment of this same motif. Like Calvin, Luther too is at pains to emphasize the *spiritual* character of Christ's kingship. Citing John 18:36 ("My kingdom is not of this world"), Luther considers that Christ is true king "but not after the fashion of the flesh and the world, for . . . He reigns in heavenly and spiritual things and consecrates them—things such as righteousness, truth, wisdom, peace, salvation, etc."[14] However, in his work, *The Freedom of a Christian,* Luther also shows himself to be concerned that firm stress upon the spiritual character not be taken to imply the impotence of Christ in the world— quite the opposite. In a cardinal passage which amounts to a sustained gloss on Romans 8:28 and following and its Pauline parallels, he speaks of the decisive effectiveness of Christ's reign in the world. To speak of Christ's kingship as spiritual "does not mean that all things on earth and in hell are not also subject to him—otherwise how could he protect and save us from them? but his kingdom consists neither in them nor of them."[15] To speak of Christ's kingship is to speak of his *power*, a power by means of which the Christian is secured and made radically free within the world; indeed, it is an "inestimable" power that reigns "in the midst of enemies and is powerful in the midst of oppression."[16] To say that this power is spiritual, as Luther consistently stresses, is therefore not to mitigate or delimit it, but rather to specify its form and aim. The purpose of Christ's royal power is ever to secure human salvation, and its form is the communication of a radical liberty for human service which is grasped by confident faith in the evangelical promises of God even—and especially—amidst weakness, suffering, and

---

[13] Calvin, *Institutes*, II.xv.3.
[14] Martin Luther, "Freedom of a Christian," in *Martin Luther: Selections from His Work* (ed. J. Dillenberger; New York: Anchor, 1961), 62.
[15] Luther, "Freedom of a Christian," 62.
[16] Luther, "Freedom of a Christian," 63–64.

persecution in the world.[17] Importantly, Luther here elects to interpret Romans 8:28—a *locus classicus* for reflection on general divine providence—by referring it specifically to Christ's exercise of his royal office. It is also notable that Luther's discourse on this motif, like Calvin's, reflects the agonistic and apocalyptic tenor of Paul's discourse from the final verses of the eighth chapter of Romans.

It must be said, however, that the subsequent career of this Reformation emphasis on the spiritual character of Christ's royal office leads in a direction very different indeed from that seemingly pursued by Calvin and Luther themselves. In later debates concerning the nature of Christ's kingship, an ambiguity attends the meaning of "spiritual": with what is it rightly contrasted? As "soul" with "body"? As "inner" with "outer"? As "church" with "world"? As "future" with "present"?[18] The leading resolution of these ambiguities in modern Protestant theology when it comes is decisive and of lasting influence. Schleiermacher's important and influential account of the *munus regnum* conceives that "nothing remains as the immediate sphere of His kingship but the inner life of men individually, and in their relation to each other, this reign being exercised entirely in virtue of "the inner vital relationship in which each individual stands to Christ."[19] Amplifying and sharpening distinctions long made in Protestant orthodoxy between Christ's economic or donative rule and his natural or essential rule, Schleiermacher firmly demarcates Christ's kingship from the divine sovereignty of the Father, concentrates its form and scope exclusively upon the church, and furthermore within the church, upon the souls of individuals who experience "the purely spiritual lordship of His God-consciousness."[20] It is fair to say that the end point of this trajectory

---

[17] For insightful commentary on this vital passage in Luther's tract, see Eberhard Jüngel, *The Freedom of a Christian: Luther's Significance for Contemporary Theology* (trans. R. A. Harrisville; Minneapolis: Augsburg, 1988), 70–76.

[18] For recent discussion of these debates see David VanDrunen, *Natural Law and the Two Kingdoms: A Study in the Development of Reformed Social Thought* (Grand Rapids: Eerdmans, 2010), esp. 432 for summary remarks.

[19] Friedrich D. E. Schleiermacher, *The Christian Faith* (trans. H. R. Mackintosh; Edinburgh: T&T Clark, 1928), §105, here 467, 473.

[20] Schleiermacher, *The Christian Faith*, §105, here 473. On these distinctions in Reform theology of the seventeenth and eighteenth centuries, see Heppe, *Reformed Dogmatics*, 481–82. For the parallel materials from Lutheran theologians, see Schmid, *The Doctrinal Theology of the Evangelical Lutheran Church*, 370–71, especially the distinctions drawn between the Christ's *regnum potentiae*, *regnum gratiae*, and *regnum gloriae*.

is honestly and elegantly set out in a famous passage from Adolf von Harnack's *The Essence of Christianity*:

> The kingdom of God comes by coming to the individual, by entering into his soul and laying hold of it. True, the kingdom of God is the rule of God; but it is the rule of the holy God in the hearts of individuals; *it is God himself in his power*. From this point of view everything that is dramatic in the external and historical sense has vanished; and gone, too, are all the external hopes for the future. . . . It is not a question of angels and devils, thrones and principalities, but of God and the soul, the soul and its God.[21]

Shorn now of any dramatic and historical "husk," the kernel of Jesus' message regarding the reign of the God of the gospel in and by him remains as "a still and mighty power in the hearts of men."[22] In fact, to speak of Christ himself actively "reigning" is still one step too far into antique mythical discourse for the properly modern mind. Here, to affirm that the kingdom which Christ teaches is spiritual is now to characterize it essentially as something wholly inward, wholly personal, wholly immaterial, and wholly actualized by the actions of women and men. The historical, external, public, and political are, as it were, left to themselves. These developments, it must be said, helped to fertilize the soil in which were to grow up dangerously distorted accounts of the doctrine of the two kingdoms in subsequent decades.

The modest ambition of this chapter is to reflect on what a fresh hearing of the witness of Romans 8—and in particular of its closing section—offers for theology anxious to be instructed once more concerning the spiritual character of the *munus regnum* of Jesus Christ. We pursue this cognizant of the evident influence of this text and its themes in the formative accounts of Christ's royal office found already in Calvin and Luther. If Romans 8:31-39 offers not only a summary of chapter 8, or even of the argument of chapters 5–8, but in fact presents us with "the sum of Paul's theology" as might be claimed, then we have good reason to inquire as to its bearing upon this matter.[23] More particularly, I am provoked to this attempt by two observations

---

[21] Adolf von Harnack, *What Is Christianity?* (trans. T. B. Saunders; London: Williams and Norgate, 1901), 56.

[22] Von Harnack, *What Is Christianity?*, 54.

[23] So Ernst Käsemann, *Commentary on Romans* (trans. G. W. Bromiley; Grand Rapids: Eerdmans, 1980), 252.

made by the twentieth-century Reformed theologian Otto Weber in his discussion of the *munus regnum*. First, Weber remarks that Calvin's rendering of the doctrine reflects the deep logic of evangelical *promeity*. He argues that, "the emphasis on 'for us' is the central theme of all that Calvin has to say about the 'office' of Christ. Nothing happens here 'for itself' but everything is 'for us.' Soteriology is nothing other than Christology properly understood and accepted."[24] Celebration and elucidation of the theme of "God for us" is at the heart of the climax of Romans 8, and deepening our appreciation of this promises to help us win through to a proper understanding of Christ's kingship. Second and in strong reaction to the position represented by von Harnack, Weber contends for a markedly different understanding of the spiritual nature of Christ's dominion. Over against the idea of Christ's spiritual rule—here in Albrecht Ritschl's formulation—as a "divinely vouched-for highest good of the community" and an "ethical idea" for the sake of whose realization Christians "bind themselves together through their definite reciprocal action," Weber contends that Christ's dominion is spiritual precisely as it is *eschatological*.[25] As he writes:

> "Spiritual rule," a traditional term, does not mean that the kingly rule of Christ is intellectual [*geistliche*] or ethical in nature. We do not understand the Kingdom as a "religious idea" . . . but rather as the Eschaton, which we do not bring about but which we are called to accept and to expect. . . . The "reign" is "spiritual" properly understood as an eschatological reality, breaking into our world pneumatically . . . [i.e.,] that which is presently active in the Spirit, which is already being introduced. . . [but] cannot be calculated in terms of what is going on within the "history of death."[26]

This eschatological reading of the royal office sits very happily indeed with a wider hearing of Paul's own apocalyptic gospel, a gospel whose primary concern is with "the assault of grace on the world and the sphere of corporeality" and the seizure of power in and over us by the determinative onset of the Spirit of Christ, the crucified and risen

---

[24] Otto Weber, *Foundations of Dogmatics* (trans. D. L. Guder; Grand Rapids: Eerdmans, 1971), 2:174.

[25] The citation from Albrecht Ritschl comes from his *Instruction in the Christian Religion*, as found in *Three Essays* (trans. P. Hefner; Philadelphia: Fortress, 1972), 174–75.

[26] Weber, *Foundations of Dogmatics*, 2:253–54, translation altered.

Lord.²⁷ Paul's witness in Romans 8 serves to remind us that the royal office of Jesus Christ is not an idea to be implemented by our subsequent actions, but rather, the announcement to us of "the presence of the Lord who acts."²⁸ The point is that in discharging his royal office, Jesus Christ really "*makes history* for all of humankind" in virtue of his being the sovereign power and claim of the very God of love.²⁹

The Witness of Romans 8:31-39
The Dominion of the Lord of Love

The following theological observations on the form and substance of the final verses of Romans 8 aim to elucidate Weber's suggestive claim that *qua* spiritual Christ's lordship is eschatological. Alert in particular to the apocalyptic grammar of Paul's climatic conclusion to the so-called "second proof," I want to remark very briefly on three salient aspects of this witness: first, the depiction of the *agon* of the church militant; second, Christ's possession of the saints and his status as cosmocrator; and, third and finally, the mutually defining relation of divine love and divine lordship.

"We are reckoned as sheep for the slaughter"
A Church Militant

The community which acknowledges the revelation of Christ's lordship is beset in this world. These verses represent the church as a community under assault: indeed much of the passage is devoted to enumeration of the manifold threats which conspire against those Christ claims as his own. Paul distills the threats into the series of rhetorical questions which animate the passage. The Christians to whom he writes are afraid of that which stands *against* them (v. 31), which threatens to *impeach* and *condemn* them (v. 33) and so also to *separate* them from their God and Christ (vv. 35, 39). The present is a time of suffering for the community, as Paul has already said (v. 18): faith knows that the *pax romana*—and all its successors—which purportedly mark this day and age deliver no real peace at all.³⁰ The sevenfold trials of affliction,

---

²⁷ Käsemann, *Commentary on Romans*, 213, 222.
²⁸ Bosc, *The Kingly Office*, 44.
²⁹ Eberhard Jüngel, "Der königliche Mensch. Eine christologische Reflexion auf die Würde des Menschen in der Theologie Karl Barths," in *Barth Studien* (Gütersloh: Gütersloher Verlagshaus, 1982), 240 (my translation).
³⁰ See Robert Jewett, *Romans* (Minneapolis: Fortress, 2007), 508–9.

distress, persecution, hunger, nakedness, peril, and the sword—a list perhaps reflecting Paul's own experiences, perhaps recalling those of Christ himself, or else reiterating a stereotyped antique catalogue of tribulations[31]—are all too well known to the community, for they are a consequence of the violent reflexes of the age which is passing away. Whatever Christ's kingship entails, it does not insulate the community from the agonism of the clash of the ages; neither is the existence of such distress a mark of divine disfavor, as might perhaps anxiously be thought. Rather, Paul stresses that such sufferings are in fact for the sake of the God of the gospel (v. 36); they are the mark of a faith conformed to Christ who was himself delivered over to death (vv. 32-33). As Karl Barth comments, "even this tumult can only bind Christians more closely to him against whom that tumult is really aimed."[32]

It is interesting that the threat, while it has a variety of specified aims and forms, has no single evident source or definite identity here. The origin of this assault—whatever it is that brings about "all these things" (v. 37)—would seem to be the "no one" which is the implied answer to Paul's driving questions: "who is against us?," "who shall impeach us?," "who will condemn?," "who will separate?"[33] The juxtaposition of this "no one" with frank and open admission of the painful reality of the assault is jarring. Perhaps like those "gods which are no gods" but which still previously enslaved the Gentiles (Gal 4:8), so here the powers of the dying age exercise themselves impotently yet still actually upon the church even as they once did upon its Lord. "Paul has," Barth writes, "visualized a whole upsurge of spiritual realities, a whole agitated sea of hidden rebellion of which the persecution of the Christians is merely a symptom."[34] Perhaps this reality is also reflected in the singular use of the term "supervictors" or "more than conquerors" [ὑπερνικῶμεν] in verse 37—Christians do not simply prevail against such assaults because the struggle here is not being fought

---

[31] Jewett, *Romans*, 544–45; cf. Ben Witherington III, *Paul's Letter to the Romans: A Socio-Rhetorical Commentary* (Grand Rapids: Eerdmans, 2004), 233.

[32] Karl Barth, *Romans: A Shorter Commentary* (trans. D. H. van Daalen; London: SCM Press, 1963), 108.

[33] Beverly Roberts Gaventa observes that in the first instance Paul implies only that "some agent" (τίς) does in fact attempt—impossibly but really—to stand against those for whom God is; see her "Neither Height Nor Depth: Discerning the Cosmology of Romans," *SJT* 64 (2011): 273.

[34] Barth, *Romans: A Shorter Commentary*, 108.

by opponents of the same kind. Rather, Christians are themselves a stake in the contest between the powers of the fallen creation animated by the *nihil* of the passing age and Jesus Christ, "the unresting arm of God."[35] Theirs is a "triumph of the assaulted" that is owed entirely to the work of another.[36] A remark of George Fox, the early Quaker leader, expresses this salutary imbalance memorably:

> such as are more than conquerors see the end of wars, and that which causeth wars. He that is a conqueror may be in the war; but he that is more than a conqueror, is in that which takes away the occasion of wars, and is come to that which was before wars were.[37]

The painful struggle in which Christians are caught up is indeed not merely with "flesh and blood" (Eph 6:12); the conspiring powers which beset the people of God—the powers of the "old aeon, rebellious, threatening, and perverted"[38]—are themselves being overcome by "the God of peace who," Paul assures, "will soon crush Satan under [their] feet" (Rom 16:20). This is what funds the hope that all creatures may yet be drawn into that divine peace which will be just as it indeed "was before wars were." The belligerence of the passing age has been and is ever outbid by the peaceable sovereignty of the Christ of God exercised on the cross. Paul admits that faith hopes for this peace in the teeth of all appearances (vv. 24-25) in a Spirit-driven act of the "most powerful, the most paradoxical, and the most venturing faith."[39]

In sum, Christ's spiritual kingship is eschatological in that it draws the congregation into—and promises to draw it finally through—the present struggle of the old and new ages. Life animated by the hope of such a "super-victory" has already been seized by the congregation on the basis of the reality of Christ's redemption, and so it polemically "represents the earthly rule of the truth" in the present by its faith and discipleship. Käsemann was surely right to claim that "only the apocalyptic worldview can describe reality *thus*."[40]

---

[35] So Karl Barth, *Epistle to the Romans* (trans. E. Hoskyns; Oxford: Oxford University Press, 1933), 327, translation altered.

[36] Käsemann, *Commentary on Romans*, 251.

[37] George Fox, *The Great Mystery* (The Works of George Fox; State College, Pa.: New Foundation Publications, 1990), 3:160.

[38] Käsemann, *Commentary on Romans*, 247.

[39] So Paul Tillich, "The Meaning of Providence" [Romans 8:38-39], in *Shaking of the Foundations* (New York: Charles Scribner's Sons, 1953), 106.

[40] Käsemann, *Commentary on Romans*, 251.

"None can separate us"
Christ's Possession of His Church amidst the Cosmos

The second motif to be considered is closely related to the first. The great lists of threats to the Christian community which Paul enumerates here are summarily captured in a single concept: *separation*. The term used (χωρίζω) is used elsewhere in the New Testament and cognate literature to describe a movement into isolation, a distancing, and the undoing of personal relationships, including the case of divorce.[41] In this context, the separation that threatens is severance from "the love of Christ" (v. 35) or the "love of God in Christ Jesus our Lord" (v. 39). To be removed from the ambit of divine love would entail nothing less than the forfeit of salvation itself;[42] it would be synonymous with the dissolution of our being "in Christ," a soteriological motif at the heart of Paul's gospel.[43] There can of course be no thought of cool mystical ontology in connection with this motif; for as we have just observed, this passage makes plain that to be "in Christ" is to be recruited by the assault of grace and the Spirit's advent into the worship and service of the church militant. To be "in Christ" is to have been seized by grace and set within the sphere of his active domain; it is to be incorporated into the lordship of the crucified.[44] Thus, while the peril of separation Paul considers here can be thought that of personal defection, it ought more properly and basically to be understood as the threat of being repossessed by other powers and lords (cf. Gal 5:1).

We can improve our purchase on this conception by recalling that basic to Pauline anthropology is the view that to be a human being—to have life in the body as a creature of this world—is to be irrevocably knit into the fabric of "the world" and always and everywhere subject to rule. In his famous essay "On the Subject of Primitive Christian Apocalyptic," Käsemann explains:

> Man, for Paul, is never just on his own. He is always a specific piece of world and therefore becomes what in the last resort he is by determination from outside, i.e., by the power which takes possession of

---

[41] See "χωρίζω," BDAG, s.v.

[42] See Jewett, *Romans*, 543.

[43] See Douglas A. Campbell, *The Quest for Paul's Gospel: A Suggested Strategy* (London: T&T Clark/Continuum, 2005), 38–42, 110–11.

[44] See Käsemann, *Commentary on Romans*, 219, where he contends that the motif of "union with Christ" must be understood as dynamic incorporation into Christ's lordship by the power of the Spirit.

him and the lordship to which he surrenders himself. His life is from the beginning a stake in the confrontation between God and the principalities of this world. In other words, it mirrors the cosmic contention for the lordship of the world and is its concretion. As such, man's life can only be understood apocalyptically.[45]

Romans 5:12f. represents the antithesis of Adam and Christ as a global confrontation of "alternative, exclusive, and ultimate" spheres in which the "old world and a new world are at issue. . . there is no third option."[46] To be at home in the world of Adam is to be claimed, formed, and animated by its constellation of overlapping and mutual contesting sovereignties; it is to be possessed by the "ravishing and enslaving powers" of the rebellious creation.[47] As a possession of sin, women and men are bound to serve what Barth styles the "inevitable" and "monstrous" contrasts of the rebellious creation, and to be ground up in their contest.[48] On such a view, salvation must be conceived as *redemption*, a repossession of creaturely life by God out from under the catastrophic dominion of sin and so the consequent surrender and loss of a whole previously determinative world of meaning.[49] As has already been signaled, the concept of lordship proves decisive here. Käsemann again:

> Redemption means nothing else but a change of lordship—indeed, a return from slavery to supra-earthly and earthly powers to the Father who awaits his children and in promise says to each, "I am your God because I remain your Creator, and as Creator, I must be and remain *for* and *not against* humankind. . . . Transferred into the

---

[45] Ernst Käsemann, "On the Subject of Primitive Christian Apocalyptic," in *New Testament Questions of Today* (trans. W. J. Montague; London: SCM Press, 1969), 136.

[46] Käsemann, *Commentary on Romans*, 146.

[47] J. Louis Martyn, "Comment #39," in *Galatians* (New York: Doubleday, 1997), 370–71; cf. Ernst Käsemann, "On Paul's Anthropology," in *Perspectives on Paul* (trans. M. Kohl; Philadelphia: Fortress, 1971), 27–28; idem, "Healing the Possessed," in *On Being a Disciple of the Crucified Nazarene* (trans. R. A. Harrisville; Grand Rapids: Eerdmans, 2010), 198.

[48] Barth, *Epistle to the Romans*, 329.

[49] On this, see J. Louis Martyn, "The Apocalyptic Gospel in Galatians," *Interpretation* 54 (2000): 257–58. One wonders how these pairs of creaturely/cosmic realities (vv. 38–39) might be related to those other cosmic antinomies which Paul knows to have been rendered meaningless by the apocalypse of the gospel in Galatians 3. See idem, "Apocalyptic Antinomies," in *Theological Issues in the Letters of Paul* (Edinburgh: T&T Clark, 1997), 111ff.

kingdom of his beloved Son, we belong to a world that likewise has its lord and king."[50]

Paul can distill the "problem" of Romans 5–8 into a single fear of separation precisely because the positive reality of salvation is essentially that of being repossessed from the world of sin by the effective reign of the crucified and risen Christ, the Lord who gathers us into the freedom of his service, and by whom we are ever claimed. His people—chosen, called, justified, and glorified—fundamentally *belong* to Jesus Christ, in whom God's primordial purpose is publically realized and displayed.[51] By winning and holding his people "in Christ," God demonstrates a divine faithfulness to creation and covenant that surpasses any and all "human dereliction."[52] The saving action which begins with election cannot ultimately be frustrated—once again present faith and hope rest on an eschatological reality, here that of Jesus Christ as Lord *of lords*, who will not be dispossessed of all he has won for the Kingdom of God. The incarnate Son is shown to be the strong man of his own parable, "who invades the tyrant's house and by his power subdues him, binds him, and spoils him of all he has unjustly usurped."[53]

Hence, while it is undoubtedly true to affirm that Paul here teaches that "God's power to pursue is greater than our power to escape,"[54] in fact his gospel is more basically concerned to affirm that Christ *must reign* (1 Cor 15:25) amidst and over all the disordered powers of the creation. As Beverly Gaventa has observed, Paul's theology concerns "the unimaginable size of God's actions on behalf of the entire cosmos, including humanity itself."[55] Discussion of the fate of the Christian community and its assurance is here encircled and bound up with a decidedly *cosmic* discourse: it is the whole creation (and not just the Christian congregation) which longs and hopes for the eschatological

---

[50] Käsemann, "Healing the Possessed," 198. One thinks of passages like Rom 5:17, 21; 6:9, 12, 14 et al. where Paul speaks of the displacement of the reign of sin and death by the reign of Christ and grace.

[51] See Paul Ziesler, *Paul's Letter to the Romans* (London: SCM Press, 1989), 218.

[52] Ernst Käsemann, "The Righteousness of God in an Unrighteous World," in *On Being a Disciple of the Crucified Nazarene*, 183.

[53] See T. F. Torrance, *Incarnation: The Person and Life of Christ* (Downers Grove: InterVarsity, 2008), 78, 155.

[54] Francis C. Rossow, "The Hound of Heaven, A Twitch upon the Thread, and Romans 8:31-39," *Concordia Journal* 23 (1997): 93.

[55] Beverly Roberts Gaventa, "Maternal Imagery in Its Cosmic, Apocalyptic Context," in *Our Mother Saint Paul* (Louisville: Westminster John Knox, 2007), 84.

resolution of God's saving work (Rom 8:9-24), and as the final verses of chapter 8 indicate, it is the cosmos in all its dimensions which is subjected to the sovereign love of God for the sake of the realization of that very salvation. The catalogue of verses 38-39 is particularly notable on this score. For it signals that all dimensions of creaturely life are effectively superintended by the dominion of Christ's saving love: the biological (life, death), the temporal/historical (present, future), the "metaphysical" (angels, powers, and principalities) as well as the physical or possibly astrophysical (height, depth). The inclusion of *all things* in Paul's final flourish—"neither anything else in all creation"—is not hyperbole, but an "all embracing addendum" which expresses faith's acknowledgment that, having been raised to the right hand of the Father, Christ even now exercises his royal office over all things (v. 34).[56] As Edward Adams explains,

> The rhetorical effect of closing the catalogue with *tis ktisis hetera* is to qualify the preceding items in such a way that these potential threats are now brought within the compass of God's creation and the sphere of his control. . . . [A]ll possible menaces to the believer are comprehended within God's creative and providential purposes: even the hostile spiritual powers are placed within the orb of the created order.[57]

For present purposes, we note in particular the way Paul here closely associates the salutary work of the risen and ascended Christ with divine governance of creation as a whole, perhaps thereby laying open the grounds for his earlier providential claim that "in everything God works good with those who love him" (v. 28). The only world Paul knows is the one in which creaturely powers of all kinds are "being reduced" under "continued pressure from the regnant Christ."[58] In this way Paul identifies the power of Christ as the very power of the Creator, suggesting thereby that the characterization of salvation as "new creation" is no mere metaphor when understood evangelically. Moreover—and this is a theme to which we will return—if it is true

---

[56] For discussion of the details of the catalogue, see Jewett, *Romans*, 550–54; cf. Gaventa, "Neither Height nor Depth," 273–77; Edward Adams, *Constructing the World: A Study in Paul's Cosmological Language* (London: T&T Clark/Continuum, 2000), 183–86.

[57] Adams, *Constructing the World*, 185.

[58] G. B. Caird, *Principalities and Powers* (Oxford: Clarendon, 1956), 82, cf. 16.

that we may discern something of the nature of Christ's lordship from its association with the power of the Creator God here, then surely the reverse must also be the case, i.e., that the specific character of Christ's reign as it is attested in the gospel tells importantly of the nature of divine creative and providential rule *per se*.

In these ways we learn that to characterize Christ's kingship as spiritual is to acknowledge that Christ exercises a *divine* office marked by the power to redeem his beloved creatures from their captivity to false gods and lords, an act whose nature, scope, and effectiveness bespeak nothing less than the creative power of God *per se*. This kingship is *eschatological* in as much as it stakes a full and indissolubly *final* claim upon our lives, our service, and our destiny; this it can and may do because there is nothing within the sphere of the creation—heaven and earth, invisible and visible— which falls beyond the present rule of the ascended Christ.[59]

"The love of God which is in Christ Jesus our Lord"
A Lordship of Love

We come then, more briefly, to venture one further observation on the significance of Romans 8:31-39 for our understanding of the lordship of Christ. It is highly significant that in these verses Paul explicitly testifies that the royal work of Christ is the outpouring of divine *love* itself. God is "for us" (v. 31)—this stands as a title over the remainder of the chapter. And the substance and form of this *promeity* are precisely that series of events in which God did not spare his Son, but coming low, gave him up unto death, then raised and exalted him to the heavenly session for the sake of his intercession for us (vv. 32-34). The love of God is thus not represented here so much as a divine emotion or disposition, as it is identified with a divine *act*, namely, God's gracious saving action on our behalf in Jesus Christ.[60] Paul catches up the essence of this entire narrative when he refers to Christ by the epithet,

---

[59] See Oscar Cullmann, "The Kingship of Christ and the Church in the New Testament," in *The Early Church* (trans. A. J. B. Higgins; London: SCM Press, 1956), 122. It is perhaps a little misleading, therefore, when Douglas Moo asserts, in relation to this passage, that "it is not with the universe but with Christians, that Paul is concerned here," for it appears that all such concerns are thoroughly entangled within Paul's apocalyptic gospel; see Moo's *The Epistle to the Romans* (Grand Rapids: Eerdmans, 1996), 543.

[60] The point is frequently made; see e.g., Moo, *The Epistle to the Romans*, 543.

"he who loved us" (v. 37). Christ is the one who takes possession of us by a powerful work of love and thereby secures for us a place within the sphere of his own dominion. By thus identifying the love of Christ (v. 33) with the love of God itself, eternal and omnipotent (v. 39), Paul decides "the meaning for this life of calling Jesus of Nazareth, crucified and raised, 'Christ Jesus our Lord.' "[61]

It is the testimony of this tract of Romans that in Christ's person and work we are met by the "marriage of God's omnipotence to God's compassion."[62] In him the God of the gospel has come upon the world and made himself known: to claim with Paul that "God is for us" is therefore not to proffer an abstract concept of divine benevolence, but rather to fix one's eyes upon the saving act centered upon the death of Jesus wherein God concretely exegetes his own identity and purpose.[63] And in this marriage of power and *agape*, power is properly ordered to love: God's saving acts in Jesus Christ disclose that divine power is the power of gracious, divine self-giving. Revelation here is clearly less a matter of drawing back the curtain on the identity and purposes of God than it is of acknowledging, as J. Louis Martyn has put it, that "*One* who has been on the other side rips the curtain apart, steps through to our side, altering irrevocably our time and space."[64] A passage like Romans 8 is bold to characterize this movement—this divine apocalypse—as a movement of love. In the free and sovereign coming of the Son, in his self-giving unto death, and in his resurrection and ascension to the right hand of the Father, God's love has invaded and traversed the landscape of the fallen world concretely and with momentous effect. Christians can be assured that nothing can separate them from God, because the power of God which appeared

---

[61] See Paul Meyer, *The Word in the World* (Louisville: Westminster/John Knox, 2004), 193. T. F. Torrance has argued that amongst the Reformers it is Martin Bucer who wins through to this "profoundly Pauline and moving understanding of *love* as the eschatological reality that abides" and by which he is able to conceive of the *regnum Christi* extending beyond the church *per se* and pressing "externally upon the state" (*Kingdom and Church*, 89).

[62] Rossow, "The Hound of Heaven," 91.

[63] See Käsemann, *Commentary on Romans*, 247; cf. Witherington, *Paul's Letter to the Romans*, 232: "Not an abstract concept of God, but rather God with flesh on, God in Christ reconciling the world to himself, characterizes Paul's understanding of deity. Paul speaks of God only as the God who reveals himself."

[64] J. Louis Martyn, "From Paul to Flannery O'Connor with the Power of Grace," in *Theological Issues in the Letters of Paul*, 282.

in his Son is the power of love, by which power God has chosen and gathered his people to himself and holds on to them forever.[65] The kingdom of heaven is a dominion of love because its Lord is the Word of love incarnate, a Word we can and must "hear and which we have to trust and obey in life and in death," as the Barmen Theological Declaration put it. Christ's kingship is not an austere and distant sovereignty demanding our obedience alone; it is rather an eschatological gift of love which redeems women and men from the world of unlove by an irresistible divine self-giving, thereby conscripting them into his service as creaturely agents of his love and its purposes.[66]

In *Cur Deus Homo*, Anselm famously informed his interlocutor Boso, and thereby also his readers, that they had "not yet duly estimated the gravity of sin."[67] That may well be true, then as now. But Paul calls Christians to put their store in the even greater truth that nothing in all of creation is of sufficient gravity to dislodge us from the orbit of Christ's sovereign love. Hence, "in His love our love celebrates its victory."[68]

The Love of God Is a Sovereign Thing
Four Theses in Place of a Conclusion

What christological and soteriological insights are to be taken away from reflections such as those we have ventured on this particular moment in the telling forth of Paul's apocalyptic gospel? The following theses attempt to summarize in a brief span something of what might be learned of Christ's royal office from a fresh hearing of Romans 8:31-39.

1. *The royal office of Christ is exercised not only in and as a consequence of the* status exaltationis, *but also and importantly in and as a consequence of the* status *exanitionis*. Only when this is so can we grasp the contours of his dominion as a lordship of divine love, and discern that Christ's royal office consists in "the continuous work of

---

[65] See Peter Stuhlmacher, *Paul's Letter to the Roman* (trans. S. Hafemann; Louisville: Westminster John Knox, 1994), 141.

[66] Emil Brunner (*The Christian Doctrine of Creation and Redemption*, 298–300) argues down this line particularly clearly in his treatment of the royal office of Christ.

[67] Anselm, *Cur Deus Homo*, XXI (*Anselm of Canterbury: The Major Works*; ed. and trans. B. Davies and G. R. Evans; Oxford: Oxford University Press, 1998).

[68] Barth, *Epistle to the Romans*, 327.

[69] Stuhlmacher, *Paul's Letter to the Romans*, 140; cf. Helmut Thielicke, *The*

the Crucified One."[69] For it is from under the cross, in the power of the Spirit, that "full of joy and peace, Christians confess: Lord, our God, other lords indeed rule over us besides you, but we call on you alone and on your name."[70]

2. *Christ's kingship is spiritual in and because it is an eschatological reality which even now invades the world pneumatically, repossessing, sustaining, and directing his people in their corporate faith and life amidst the yet unruly powers of the age.* So, the love of God enacted in Jesus Christ is "the content of the activity of the exalted Lord, who rules the world by the word of the gospel and the power of the Spirit, creating faith in the gospel, putting all opposition to it to shame, assembling believers and in this way preparing the way for the kingdom of the Father in the world."[71]

3. *Acknowledgment of the cosmic scope of Christ's royal office requires that theology draw together very closely its understanding of the* munus regnum Christi *and its account of divine providence generally.* Similarly, theology should resist any strong separation between the "essential" and "economic" modes of Christ's royal office.[72] An evangelical doctrine of providence will look to conceive of *conservation, concursus,* and *gubernatio Dei* by way of reflection on the entailments of Christ's lordship over church *and* world.[73] This raises interesting questions for political theology, where accounts of church, state, and politics have often been framed precisely by a clear demarcation of these doctrines. But when the gospel acclaims

---

Evangelical Faith (trans. G. W. Bromiley; Edinburgh: T&T Clark, 1978), 2:421: "as the exalted one he is still he whose love impelled him to become man to enter into the solidarity of the most profound humiliation."

[70] Ernst Käsemann, "One Lord Alone," *ExpTim* 110 (1999): 251.

[71] Pannenberg, *Systematic Theology,* 2:448.

[72] Helmut Thielicke asked the pertinent question when he noted that key to any account of the *munus regnum* is "understanding how the kingdom of power and the kingdom of grace are related to one another in the lordship of Christ. What is meant by the personal union between the Lord of the world and the Lord of the community?" (*The Evangelical Faith,* 422–23). He did not answer his own question here, though he does refer his readers to related discussions of relevance of Christ's lordship for social and political ethics in his *Theological Ethics* (trans. W. H. Lazareth; Philadelphia: Fortress, 1966–69), 1:359ff. and 2:565ff.

[73] See W. Dantine, "Creation and Redemption III: Attempt at a Theological Understanding in the Light of the Contemporary Understanding of the World," *SJT* 18 (1965): 99; cf. also his essay "*Regnum Christi—Gubernatio Dei.* Dogmatische Überlegungen zum Begriff der 'Herrschaft,'" *TZ* 15 (1959): 195–208.

that Christ is for us the true Lord of the world, it acknowledges his Lordship "over body and soul, heart and mind, disciples and demons, this world and the world to come, [as] a *political fact*."[74]

4. *Faith in Christ's exercise of his royal office takes shape in lives of Christian freedom marked by joyful assurance in the midst of adversity and the perplexities of life in the not yet redeemed world.* Such was Luther's insight: as those who have a share in Christ's priestly reign, Christians are free to love and serve God and neighbor without fear or accounting, and thereby to give faithful witness to the victory Christ has won for us over the powers of the age.[75] "Even when inferno threatens the Christian on all sides," Käsemann argued, the Christian "is marked by the Lord, who is present for him, and set in παρρησία" will refuse to let discipleship be hindered.[76] By both its freedom and its cruciformity, the Christian life testifies to the world about the truth of Christ's eschatological lordship.

---

[74] Ernst Käsemann, "What I Have Unlearned in 50 Years as a German Theologian," *CurTM* 15 (1988): 334–35.

[75] Caird, *The Principalities and Powers*, 95.

[76] Käsemann, *Commentary on Romans*, 251; cf. Bosc, *The Kingly Office*, 147: The church "knows that all fatalism, whether of sin, or falsehood, or of slavery in its many forms, is conquered and that it can confront *royally*, that is without fear and in the integrity of its being, all the powers opposing it. But it is a place of liberty *in the world* and *in history*, which it knows to be in the hands of its Lord. . . . It is thus free for [the world] in being a sign that this freedom is already present, as a gift, but as a gift already given."

8
Creation, Cosmos, and Conflict in Romans 8–9

Neil Elliott

The heart of my argument is that in Paul's day, as in ours, creation is a fundamentally *political* and *ideological*, not simply a *theological* topic; that what Paul has to say about the present and future of creation in Romans 8 has everything to do with what he says about Israel in Romans 9–11; that in the larger rhetorical context of Romans, these statements constitute a polemical engagement with themes in Roman imperial ideology; and that a serious, critical engagement with those statements today requires moving beyond the customary boundaries of "theology" to a critical understanding of the ideological currents at work in our own world—and a creative opposition to them.[1]

A Note on the Present Climate

In August 2011, Hurricane Irene tore its way up the Eastern Seaboard of the country, making landfall in New Jersey on the 27th. Seven people were killed by the storm in that state alone; thousands were temporarily displaced. Damage to homes and businesses was estimated at $1 billion. President Obama declared the state a disaster area in order to authorize the expenditure of federal funds through the Federal Emergency Management Agency.

What happened next quickly became notorious. The spokesperson for House Majority Leader Eric Cantor (Republican from Virginia) declared that Congress would approve funds for disaster relief only if

---
[1] My thanks to Beverly Roberts Gaventa for the invitation to give this address as a part of Princeton Theological Seminary's bicentennial observances.

they were "offset with spending cuts" elsewhere in the federal budget.[2] The statement provoked an immediate outcry that the Republican majority was holding disaster-stricken people hostage to their political agenda of "fiscal discipline"—shrinking the federal budget while refusing to raise taxes. A few days later, Cantor backed off, insisting that he had never meant to hold up funds to disaster victims—and that the House had "found the money" after all (by making cuts in another part of the federal budget). But the political damage had been done.[3]

Those demands were part and parcel of the Republican agenda in the budget battle in the summer of 2011. More to my point, they represent a larger pattern, thoroughly documented by journalist Naomi Klein in her best-selling volume *The Shock Doctrine*.

Klein's title describes the economic policy prescriptions of Milton Friedman and the "Chicago School" of economists, who for the last four decades have advocated the enforced privatization of national economies. The preferred term for economic neoliberalism is "free-market" economics, although these are economic policies that no people would freely choose for themselves.[4] Hence the "shock" in "shock doctrine." As Klein shows, privatization policies often can be imposed

---

[2] "With Hurricane Bearing Down Cantor Says Disaster Relief Should Be Paid for with Spending Cuts," *Talking Points Memo*, 25 August 2011, reporting an e-mail from Cantor's spokesperson, Laena Fallon, n.p. [cited 17 March 2012]. Online: http://tpmdc.talkingpointsmemo.com/2011/08/cantor-spox-if-theres-hurricane-damage-costs-will-have-to-be-paid-for-with-spending-cuts.php?ref=fpa.

[3] Cantor had in fact previously made the same demand, on the record, in his own state of Virginia and regarding victims of tornado damage in Missouri, according to an earlier story on *Talking Points Memo*, n.p. [cited 17 March 2012], http://tpmdc.talkingpointsmemo.com/2011/08/eric-cantor-well-pay-for-post-quake-relief----if-we-can-find-the-cuts-video.php. A little more than a year later, Hurricane Sandy became the largest Atlantic hurricane on record before it came ashore in the northeastern United States, killing 131 people. True to the convictions Cantor had expressed earlier, in December 2012, a majority of Republicans in the House opposed a bill offering $51 billion in federal relief aid unless accompanied by across-the-board cuts to defense and domestic spending. They were defeated, early in the 2013 legislative session, by a united front of Democrats and Republican representatives from the afflicted northeastern states who, noting that most of the opposing Republicans had recently sought similar relief funds for their own states, dubbed the obstructionists the "Hypocritical Caucus" (see Jennifer Oldham and Greg Giroux, "Republicans Called Hypocrites Asking Own Aid Not Sandy's," *Bloomberg News*, 18 January 2013, www.bloomberg.com/news/2013-01-18/republicans-called-hypocrites-asking-own-aid-not-sandy-s.html).

[4] Naomi Klein observes that "the three trademark demands" of neoliberalism—"privatization, government deregulation, and deep cuts to social spending—tended to

only on a people stressed, disoriented, "shocked" by disaster—natural disaster if possible, but artificial or manufactured disaster such as war, state terrorism, or disabling "austerity" policies when more efficient.

"Shock treatment" was Friedman's phrase for the recommended imposition of sweeping, disruptive social and economic change, all at once. It refers to the genuine shock felt by whole societies when Friedman's policies have been implemented, but also, Klein shows, to CIA-funded experiments in electric shock therapy in the 1950s, applied to "unmake and erase faulty minds, then rebuild new personalities" on a "clean slate." The phrase also describes the CIA-promoted use of electricity in torture regimes to destroy dissent by attacking the bodies and minds of actual or possible dissenters.[5]

Klein writes that since the 1970s, "using moments of collective trauma to engage in radical social and economic engineering" has become "the preferred method of advancing corporate goals" in country after country, in a global regime she calls "disaster capitalism."[6] Those

---

be extremely unpopular with citizens"; *The Shock Doctrine: The Rise of Disaster Capitalism* (New York: Metropolitan Books, 2007), 9.

[5] Klein, *Shock Doctrine*, 71. On Friedman's use of "shock treatment," Klein cites Milton Friedman and Rose D. Friedman, *Two Lucky People: Memoirs* (Chicago: University of Chicago Press, 1998), 592. Klein focuses on the work of psychiatrist Ewen Cameron, who was funded by the CIA to experiment on his patients with devastating levels of electroshock and whose work became the basis for torture techniques used in U.S.-supported dictatorships throughout Latin America (Klein, *Shock Doctrine*, chap. 1). Regarding Pinochet's Chile, where Friedman's recommendations were first offered a "clean slate," and then elsewhere in Latin America, Klein writes, "these three forms of shock converged on the bodies of Latin Americans and the body politic of the region. . . . The shock of the coup prepared the ground for economic shock therapy; the shock of the torture chamber terrorized anyone thinking of standing in the way of the economic shocks" (9). In successive chapters, Klein shows that the specific combination of doctrines that constituted Friedman's shock therapy was successively applied in Russia after the fall of the Soviet Union, in Iraq after the 2003 U.S. occupation, and in Sri Lanka after the 2004 tsunami. More recently, Arun Gupta has extended Klein's analysis to describe predatory development in post-Sandy New York: "Disaster Capitalism Hits New York: The City Will Adapt to Flooding—But at the Expense of the Poor?" *In These Times* 37, no. 2 (2013): 24–27. Meanwhile, disaster capitalism is hyper-accelerated in Haiti three years after a catastrophic earthquake: Amy Wilentz, "Letter from Haiti," *The Nation* 296, no. 4 (2013): 21–26.

[6] Klein, *Shock Doctrine*, 9. We should bear in mind that as Mike Davis showed in *Late Victorian Holocausts: El Niño Famines and the Making of the Third World* (London: Verso, 2002), "disaster capitalism" is actually much older than the twentieth century—practically as old, in fact, as capitalism itself.

policies "came home," gaining traction in the United States among the new Republican congressional majority in 1995, then expanding after 9/11, as an administration stocked with Friedman's disciples and close friends "seized the moment of collective vertigo with chilling speed."[7] Klein's book culminates in flood-devastated New Orleans after Katrina in 2005; but in subsequent essays, she has tracked the expansion of shock doctrine after the economic collapse in 2008. Again and again, the pattern has been the same because, as Klein shows, so many of the policy makers have come from the same circle and been shaped by the same doctrine. As she sums up the pattern,

> The original disaster—the coup, the terrorist attack, the market meltdown, the war, the tsunami, the hurricane—puts the entire population into a state of collective shock. The falling bombs, the bursts of terror, the pounding winds serve to soften up whole societies much as the blaring music and blows in the torture cells soften up prisoners. Like the terrorized prisoner who gives up the names of comrades and renounces his faith, shocked societies often give up things they would otherwise fiercely protect.[8]

An Implicit Doctrine of Creation

I invoke Naomi Klein's analysis of our present situation for two reasons related to the topic of cosmos and conflict in Romans 8 and 9.

The first reason is a principle of theological method. The theology of liberation requires that the first step in our theological work must be a clear analysis of our present situation from the perspective of the poor.[9] Although Klein is not a theologian, the sort of analysis of the present world order that she offers is necessary for responsible theological work today. Liberation theologian Ivan Petrella makes much the same point, insisting that "the defining mark of the current global context is the spread of zones of social abandonment." The challenge facing the theologian, Petrella writes, is the abject failure of contemporary theologies—including liberation theologies—to put the material

---

[7] Klein, *Shock Doctrine*, 11. Klein writes that the Bush administration carried out a version of "shock treatment" in the U.S. "not . . . because the administration deviously plotted the crisis but because the key figures of the administration . . . were part of a movement that prays for crisis the way drought-struck farmers pray for rain" (12).

[8] Klein, *Shock Doctrine*, 17.

[9] Gustavo Gutiérrez, *A Theology of Liberation: History, Politics, and Salvation* (trans. Sister Caridad Inda and John Eagleson; Maryknoll: Orbis, 1973), 11.

poverty of the global majority at the forefront of analysis and interpretation.[10] Mark Lewis Taylor has made a similarly compelling case regarding *The Theological and the Political*.[11]

The second reason is more directly related to the theological theme of creation. Naomi Klein emphasizes that at the heart of neoliberal "shock doctrine" is *an implicit doctrine of creation*. We have heard that doctrine clearly enough when entrepreneurs have enthused that destruction in New Orleans offered a "clean sheet to start again" with "new opportunities" to "reform" the public school system; or that "the fear and disorder" in post-invasion Iraq "offered real promise" for replacing civil society with U.S. contractors; or that the tsunami that swept whole fishing villages in Sri Lanka into the sea left behind the pristine beaches of "a vacation Eden," awaiting only the developers' blueprints and bulldozers. Klein observes that "most people who survive a devastating disaster want the opposite of a clean slate; they want to salvage whatever they can and begin repairing what was not destroyed." But disaster capitalists "have no interest in repairing what was"; their agenda, rather, is "erasing what was left of the public sphere and rooted communities, then quickly moving to replace them with a kind of corporate New Jerusalem—all before the victims of war or natural disaster were able to regroup and stake their claims to what was theirs."[12]

Klein's play on biblical metaphors of creation and re-creation is not incidental. She describes the purported "science" of Friedman's closed-loop economic system as a "neoliberal creation myth," the logic of which is rooted not in empirical observation but "in biblical fantasies of great floods and great fires."[13] But in shock doctrine, it is economic engineers who assume the role of Creator: "the world as it is must be erased to make way for their purist invention."[14] "The

---

[10] Ivan Petrella, *Beyond Liberation Theology: A Polemic* (London: SCM Press, 2008).

[11] Taylor argues that for us to ignore the conflictive political fabric of our world and remain preoccupied with the business as usual of "guild theology"—seeking or asserting an "epistemic privilege," an appeal to the transcendent basis of theological discourse (alone), as a refuge from the secular or non-theological discourse of our age—is an act of bad faith; Mark Lewis Taylor, *The Theological and the Political: On the Weight of the World* (Minneapolis: Fortress, 2011).

[12] Klein, *The Shock Doctrine*, 4, 8–9.

[13] Klein begins her book with the quotation of Gen 6:11, in which God resolves to "make an end of all flesh," for the earth was "corrupt in God's sight."

[14] Klein, *Shock Doctrine*, 446, 19.

signature desire for unattainable purity" that characterizes Friedman-esque policy, the longing "for a clean slate on which to build a reengineered model society," is nothing less than a "desire for godlike powers of total creation. . . . Nonapocalyptic reality is simply not hospitable to their ambitions." Rather, the "freedom and possibility" promised by this mythology is "available only in times of cataclysmic change—when people, with their stubborn habits and insistent demands, are blasted out of the way." Only in moments of catastrophe, when the rest of us "are psychologically unmoored and physically uprooted," can these "artists of the real plunge in their hands and begin their work of remaking the world."[15]

This metaphorical play should stand as a warning regarding the real-world consequences of biblical images of creation. It would be naïve to imagine that any of us could retreat from Klein's analysis to some safely biblical "higher ground" to do our theology there. It will not suffice simply to reaffirm with Genesis that "in the beginning" it was God who created "the heavens and the earth" in order to convict the adherents of shock doctrine of bad exegesis. True, any number of biblical theologians have extolled the grandeur and dignity of the Priestly creation account in Genesis 1 and opposed it to the myths of creation through combat in surrounding ancient Near Eastern cultures. But scholars have also criticized the biblical motif, which first arose in the literature of Persian-era "colonial Israel," of the "myth of the empty land" (or in the language attributed to Ezra, the land of "pollution" and "abomination"). According to that motif, Ezra's "restoration" of Judah depended on the availability of a holy population of returning Jewish exiles—and on breaking any connection between this holy "remnant" and the "people of the land," even when the latter insisted they, too, were faithful adherents of the LORD; even when the break required sundering families, dispossessing wives and children.[16] Seen from this perspective, the Priestly creation account that opens

---

[15] Klein, *Shock Doctrine*, 20–21. Repeatedly, however, the dream turns out to be a nightmare. When "the people who live on the land refuse to abandon their past," the "dream of the clean slate morphs into its doppelgänger, the scorched earth . . . the dream of total creation morphs into a campaign of total destruction" (374).

[16] Robert Carroll, "The Myth of the Empty Land," in *Ideological Criticism of Biblical Texts* (ed. David Jobling and Tina Pippins; *Semeia* 59; Atlanta: Society of Biblical Literature, 1992), 79–93; Joseph Blenkinsopp, "The Bible, Archaeology, and Politics; or the Empty Land Revisited," *JSOT* 27 (2002): 169–87; Norman K. Gottwald, *The Politics of Ancient Israel* (Louisville: Westminster John Knox, 2001), 96–107.

the Torah—an account in which God brings order out of chaos, *tohu vabohu* (Gen 1:2)—can be read as describing a "blank slate" without parallel. We can well imagine that such a myth could have provided ideological legitimization for a fledgling colonial administration implementing its own ancient version of social shock.[17]

Creation, I conclude, is—and has long been—a *political* topic.

Creation and Conquest

What Naomi Klein describes as the neoliberal quest for a "blank slate" had ancient historical precedents in the foreign empires that cast their shadows over Jewish and Christian scriptures. In her groundbreaking study *Apocalypse against Empire*, Anathea E. Portier-Young offers a thick description of Hellenistic imperialism as the context for the invention of Jewish apocalypticism.[18] Portier-Young describes the "totalizing" imperial policy of the Seleucids as involving the systematic "*reconquest, de-creation,* and *re-creation* of Judea."[19] The systematic application of state terror to discipline the bodies of the ruled was a part of this policy; so was the ideological project of naturalizing that violent discipline as necessary for the perpetuation of a larger cosmic order.[20] Terror and ideology met in the routinized and ritualized re-enactment of conquest as one or another restive element of the subject population was represented as in revolt and then violently suppressed. Symbolically, this enacted "reconquest" enabled "the recreation of empire."[21]

---

[17] Konrad Schmid describes the Priestly document in Torah as "pacifist," "pro-Persian," a "de-eschatologization" of Israelite tradition. *The Old Testament: A Literary History* (trans. Linda M. Maloney; Minneapolis: Fortress, 2012), 147–59. See also the papers gathered in James W. Watts, ed., *Persia and Torah: The Theory of Imperial Authorization of the Pentateuch* (SBLSymS 17; Atlanta: Society of Biblical Literature, 2001).

[18] Anathea E. Portier-Young, *Apocalypse against Empire: Theologies of Resistance in Early Judaism* (Grand Rapids: Eerdmans, 2011). She relies on the categories of hegemony and domination as discussed in the Marxist tradition of ideological criticism, especially by Antonio Gramsci, *Selections from the Prison Notebooks* (ed. and trans. Quintin Hoare and Geoffrey Nowell Smith; London: Lawrence & Wishart, 1971).

[19] Portier-Young, *Apocalypse against Empire*, xxiii (emphasis added).

[20] "Hegemony asserts as normative and universal what are in fact particular and contingent ways of perceiving the world, mapping the universe and humanity's place in it, and defining poles of opposition." The logic of the hegemonic cosmology "legitimates claims about truth and morality, but this very logic can become so invisible as to resist questioning" (Portier-Young, *Apocalypse against Empire*, 12).

[21] Portier-Young, *Apocalypse against Empire*, 137–38.

Against this ritualized re-creation, Jewish apocalypticism "countered the totalizing narrative of the Seleucid empire" by narrating a larger historical context and thus "put time back together." The apocalypses portrayed imperial power "as partial, contingent, and finite";[22] through the strategy of historical review, apocalypticism "asserts the transience and finitude of temporal powers, affirms God's governance of time and the outworking of God's plan in history." Apocalypses expose "the hidden structures of false power and assert . . . a more potent invisible power."[23]

What did this look like? Recent scholarship has shifted our attention from the *literary* to the *visual environment* of early Christianity: that is, from *texts* to *images*. This shift corrects our unreflective and rather narcissistic assumption that figures like Paul were as devoted to reading and writing, to interacting verbally with "scripture," as we are.[24] If we consider not only what Paul's literate contemporaries *wrote* about creation and the establishment of the world, but also what ordinary people *saw*—if we ask about the images that filled the urban public space through which people *moved*—we discover that in the Roman Empire as much in the Hellenistic period, the cosmos was represented as having been founded through the violence of conquest.

One spectacular example from the Hellenistic era of the hegemonic power of cosmogonic symbolism[25] is the Great Altar of Pergamon, the focus of Brigitte Kahl's eye-opening study of Galatians. To approach the altar requires ascending a great staircase flanked by vivid, larger-than-life carvings of the Olympian gods' primordial combat against the Giants (see figure 1). The "message" of the carvings is clear enough: the world has been established through a decisive victory of Greece's gods over inferior chthonic forces. In one panel,

---

[22] Portier-Young, *Apocalypse against Empire*, xxiii, 7.

[23] Portier-Young, *Apocalypse against Empire*, 27, 37.

[24] Generative here is Paul Zanker, *The Power of Images in the Age of Augustus* (trans. Alan Shapiro; Ann Arbor: University of Michigan Press, 1988); with application to the New Testament, see Annette Weissenrieder, Friedrike Wendt, and Petra von Gemünden, eds., *Picturing the New Testament* (WUNT 193; Tübingen: Mohr Siebeck, 2005); Davina C. Lopez, *Apostle to the Conquered: Reimagining Paul's Mission* (Paul in Critical Contexts; Minneapolis: Fortress, 2008); Brigitte Kahl, *Galatians Re-imagined: Reading with the Eyes of the Vanquished* (Paul in Critical Contexts; Minneapolis: Fortress, 2010); Davina C. Lopez, "Visual Perspectives," in *Studying Paul's Letters: Contemporary Perspectives and Methods* (Minneapolis: Fortress, 2012), 93–116.

[25] *Cosmogonic* symbolism may be a term preferable to *creation* symbolism since the latter is too easily assimilated to the predominance of biblical motifs.

Creation, Cosmos, and Conflict in Romans 8–9

FIGURE 1
The staircase of the Great Altar of Zeus in Pergamon, now in the Pergamonmuseum, Berlin. Available on Wikimedia Commons. Photograph by Hans-Günter Quaschinsky, dated October 2, 1959, and provided by the Deutsches Bundesarchiv.

FIGURE 2
Athena (center) subdues the giant Alkyoneus and his mother Earth, Γῆ; from the Pergamonmuseum, Berlin. Available on Wikimedia Commons, photograph by Sailko.

Earth herself (Γῆ) cries out as Athena tears her son from her arms and subdues them both (see figure 2). But the medium itself is also the message. To approach the altar by climbing the great staircase is to ascend from the inferior realm of the doomed Giants—and, by clear visual implication, of the indigenous barbarians—to the lofty realm of victorious Athena, Apollo, and Zeus.[26] This monument represents

[26] Kahl, *Galatians Re-Imagined*.

FIGURE 3
Wolfram Hoepfner's model of the Great Altar as victory monument, with figures of dying Gauls placed in the inner sanctuary; photo courtesy of Jakob B. Rehmann.

the foundation of the world as conquest: the defeat and suppression of brute hordes by the disciplined violence of Greek civilization.[27]

Under the Roman Empire, the visual presentation of conquest, of the difference between conqueror and conquered, was even more direct. By Paul's time, the Great Altar of Pergamon had been adorned (on one hypothesis) with statues of defeated Gallic warriors in their death-throes (see figure 3).[28] The conquered—whether barbarian warriors vanquished in battle, destitute barbarian women and children enslaved as prisoners of war, or barbarian nations represented as enslaved or violated females—were almost indispensable visual elements in representations of Roman power.

Another difference in the Roman imperial era is the remarkable narrowing of cosmogonic rhetoric and symbolism onto the single figure

---

[27] It is probably this monument that John the Seer decried as the "throne of Satan" (Rev 2:12).

[28] Kahl, *Galatians Re-Imagined*, 116–18. On Wolfram Hoepfner's view, the top platform of the Great Altar was no longer used for sacrificial purposes but had become a victory monument to Roman power, adorned with the statues not of gods but of dying Gauls; Wolfram Hoepfner, "Modell des Pergamonaltars im Masstab 1:20," in *Der Pergamonaltar: Die neue Präsentation nach der Restaurierung des Telephosfrieses* (ed. Wolf-Dieter Heilmeyer; Tübingen: Ernst Wasmuth Verlag, 1997), 171–76.

of Augustus (and later, his descendants). The "gospel" of the Augustan age rings from the stone inscription erected by the magistrates of Priene around 6 C.E., which offers us the nearest known use of the term *euangelion* to Paul's. There, the birthday of Augustus is hailed as "the foundation of everything." Augustus appeared "when indeed there was nothing that was not crumbling and changed into ruin that he did not restore to proper form." His appearance was "a boon to all the world, though it would have blithely accepted destruction if the general blessing of all, Caesar, had not been born." Such fulsome praise (which can be reproduced from a variety of poetic and inscriptional sources) is all the more remarkable given the reality that Octavian's war of vengeance and rivalry against Antony had "exhausted Italy" and nearly bankrupted the Empire.[29]

The *Res Gestae* similarly extols the "deeds of the divine Augustus" by which he—again, single-handedly—"subjected the whole world to the rule [*imperium*] of the Roman people." Here again we see intertwined the themes of cosmogony, the establishment of a hitherto undreamt-of worldwide peace, and conquest, as Augustus rehearses how he brought nation after nation under the benevolent *imperium* of the Roman people, or into their friendship. The phrases are, in Roman imperial rhetoric, interchangeable.[30]

Two other figures bear particular notice. One is the ancestor Aeneas, immortalized in Virgil's epic poem, who gave Augustan Rome both an ancient pedigree rival to the Greek and a claim to manifest destiny. The heavenly vision given to Aeneas shows his glorious descendants, Julius Caesar and Augustus, receiving the "gifts of the nations" in triumphant splendor, for it is the right of the Roman people to require the obedience of all the world's peoples.[31] This is the visual program of the Altar of Augustan Peace, erected on the order of the Senate in 9 B.C.E. One panel depicts the impeccably pious Aeneas,

---

[29] Mark Reasoner's translation of the Priene inscription in Neil Elliott and Mark Reasoner, eds., *Documents and Images for the Study of Paul* (Minneapolis: Fortress, 2010), 126–27. See G. E. M. de Ste. Croix, *Class Struggle in the Ancient Greek World* (Ithaca, N.Y.: Cornell University Press, 1981), chap. 5, for a less flattering view of Augustus' "achievements."

[30] To these inscriptions should be added the "papyrus trail" of court poets, from Horace to Calpurnius Siculus and Calpurnius Piso, and the sweeping saga of Virgil's *Aeneid*; see Elliott and Reasoner, eds., *Documents and Images*, chap. 4.

[31] Virgil, *Aeneid* (trans. H. Rushton Fairclough; rev. G. Goold; LCL); excerpted in Elliott and Reasoner, *Documents and Images*, 122–23.

FIGURE 4 (top) Aeneas offers sacrifice. Altar of Augustan Peace, Rome. Photo by Neil Elliott.

FIGURE 5 (left) Marcus Agrippa and a procession of Roman priests. Altar of Augustan Peace, Rome. Photo by Neil Elliott.

FIGURE 6
A female figure representing the fecundity of the Earth nourishes her children. Altar of Augustan Peace, Rome. Photo by Neil Elliott.

having just landed on the shore of Italy, offering sacrifice to his ancestral gods (figure 4); another depicts Augustus and Agrippa marching in a great sacred procession of all the priests of Rome, in their sheer number revealing the abundant fulfillment of the ancestry divinely promised to pious Aeneas (figure 5).[32]

The second figure is the only female figure to appear on the surfaces of the Altar: Gaia, Earth. But this is no longer the agonized, bereft mother struggling beneath Athena's heel, reaching out for her indigenous child; she now reclines in ease and abundance, her children reaching for her nourishing breasts, surrounded by the fertility of the fields, ox and lamb at her feet (figure 6). *If this is indeed Gaia; or is she Pax, or perhaps Venus?* One characteristic of Augustan-era imagery is that female figures come to represent values, abstractions, rather than specific gods carrying the "baggage" of mythic

---

[32] This pairing of ancestor and descendant, in statue and inscription, proclamation and poem, was so routine that representations of either Aeneas or Augustus alone could serve to evoke the other within the whole mythic scheme of Roman supremacy.

backstories.³³ The story line that matters is resolutely patrilineal, stretching from Aeneas—that pious loyal son and widowed father who leaves his wife's body behind in the ruins of Troy—to Augustus and the line of adopted sons that constitute the Julio-Claudian house. Actual women, and the actual bearing of sons, hardly complicate this mythic scheme.

The contrast between the Hellenistic Great Altar of Pergamon and the Altar of Augustan Peace in Rome bears emphasis. Augustus is not represented as conquering warrior but as benevolent ruler, father of the fatherland, pious high priest. Creation is not the struggle of civilized violence against the untamable brutishness of the barbarian; that warfare was accomplished in the past.³⁴ Augustus is the bringer of peace and in the bright noonday light of his rule, the nations no longer struggle; chastened as well as vanquished, they have learned their place.

Rome, the Jews, and the Letter to the Romans

What does all of this have to do with Romans? Everything.

Elsewhere, I have argued that Paul's rhetoric in Romans is directed to a particular historical situation, as Paul construes it, and that we should understand that situation as decisively shaped by elements of Roman imperial ideology.³⁵ More narrowly, in Romans 8 and 9, we see Paul interacting with the specific elements of Roman ideology that I have just described: creation and conquest; the interwoven themes of cosmogony, the establishment of universal peace, and of the necessary and destined supremacy of the Roman people.

---

³³ Zanker discusses this "matronly deity" as "typical of the new personified deities of Augustan religion, who had no traditional mythology." *Power of Images*, 172–74.

³⁴ Indeed the poetry of the Neronian era plays on the distance from Augustus' rather more bloody achievements: on the theme of the "idle sword" in Neronian propaganda see Neil Elliott, "Romans 13:1-7 in the Context of Imperial Propaganda," in *Paul and Empire: Religion and Power in Roman Imperial Society* (ed. Richard A. Horsley; Harrisburg, Pa.: Trinity Press International, 1997), 184–204.

³⁵ A rhetorical-critical understanding of the letter's rhetorical situation has occupied much of my scholarship since my dissertation at Princeton: Neil Elliott, *The Rhetoric of Romans: Argumentative Constraint and Strategy and Paul's Debate with Judaism* (JSNTSup 45; Sheffield: JSOT Press, 1990). See also idem, *Liberating Paul: The Justice of God and the Politics of the Apostle* (Maryknoll: Orbis, 1994), 214–26; and idem, *The Arrogance of Nations: Reading Romans in the Shadow of Empire* (Paul in Critical Contexts; Minneapolis: Fortress, 2008).

If the Roman people were destined to rule the world, it naturally followed that the Jews were just one more of the many peoples who were destined to be ruled. So—a century before Paul—Cicero had described Jews as a people "born for slavery."[36] While Julius Caesar and Augustus both found it expedient to secure their power by safeguarding certain rights to Herod and to Jewish populations around the Empire, that good favor was soon relinquished by their successors. Tiberius gave wide latitude to the anti-Jewish Sejanus and expelled Jews from Rome; Gaius "Caligula" entertained even more vicious anti-Jewish propagandists in his court and notoriously ordered that his own image should adorn the holy of holies in the Jerusalem Temple, a catastrophe averted only by his assassination.[37]

When Gaius' death created a temporary power vacuum in distant Alexandria, the Greek population rose up against the city's Jews in what historians have called the first pogrom. The Emperor Claudius put down the violence but blamed the victims for having inspired their own injury through presumptuousness, ingratitude, and disloyalty. That is, the Roman Empire took this occasion to construe civil strife and violence against Jews as a grave threat to Roman order *posed by the Jews themselves*. Note that the two portions of Claudius' decree are markedly imbalanced. First he accepts divine honors from the Alexandrians, then rebukes the "foreign" Jews for their effrontery and accuses them of inspiring a "common cancer" throughout the world; that is, he both reestablishes the sacred order of the Roman world and "reconquers" the hostile barbarians, the foreign Jews. World-creation and terror, paired again, as Anathea Portier-Young identified the pattern in the Hellenistic period.[38]

Moving forward a few years, Claudius' expulsion of Jews from the imperial capital in 49 C.E. (as reported later by Suetonius) has excited a wealth of scholarship because of its proximity to Paul's letter. The connection is in fact very important but must be correctly understood.

---

[36] Cicero, *Of the Consular Provinces* 5.10. The circulation of texts like Ezra 9:9 ("we are slaves") cannot have helped the situation.

[37] See Peter Schäfer, *Judeophobia: Attitudes toward the Jews in the Ancient World* (Cambridge, Mass.: Harvard University Press, 1997); sources discussed here are conveniently gathered in Elliott and Reasoner, *Documents and Images*, chaps. 4 and 5.

[38] Claudius' decree has come down to us in two forms: Josephus, *Ant.* 19.5.2–3 and a papyrus transcription discovered in 1912 (*P. London* lines 1–109). The second is considered more reliable and is the basis of my comments here. Both are presented in Elliott and Reasoner, *Documents and Images*, 206–11.

Following H. Dixon Slingerland's analysis, I see no basis for construing the agitation in Rome as caused by "Christian" proselytizing. Rather, the emperor's action was taken at the instigation of an otherwise unidentifiable Roman official, "Chrestus," and was aimed at the Jews as the object of a prejudicial stereotype: "Chrestus caused Claudius to expel the continuously rebelling Jews."[39] Both the routinized nature of this action and the appeal to stereotype ("the continuously rebelling Jews") suggest that this was another episode in what Leonard Rutgers has described as a general Roman policy: "It was quite common for the Roman authorities to expel easily identifiable groups from Rome in times of political turmoil."[40] A semblance of Roman order was restored, perhaps accompanied by offerings to the genius of Caesar and liturgical references to Augustan peace. Again: the cosmos is reestablished through the judicious "reconquest" of the usual barbarians.

A number of interpreters are convinced that Paul wrote this letter to communities in Rome whose common life had been disrupted both by Claudius' expulsion of Jewish members in 49 C.E and by the return of some of the exiles after Claudius' death, and Nero's accession, in 54 C.E. This is usually offered as partial explanation for Paul's warning, addressed to non-Jews in 11:13-36, not to boast over a "stumbling" Israel. These non-Jewish believers in Christ were tempted to draw the wrong conclusion from the failure of the gospel among Jews.

I accept parts of that hypothesis, with two important qualifications.

First, we do not have adequate evidence that any "failure" of the gospel among Jews has become for Paul a "theological fact" (indeed he argues strenuously against such a false conclusion!). Instead, the attitude of "boasting" that Paul warns against is sufficiently explained in terms of the noxious climate of anti-Jewish propaganda among elite

---

[39] Suetonius, *Claudius* 25.4; text and translation alternatives are presented in Elliott and Reasoner, *Documents and Images*, 211–12; for the interpretation taken here, see H. Dixon Slingerland, *Claudian Policymaking and the Early Imperial Repression of Judaism at Rome* (Atlanta: Scholars Press, 1997). I am grateful to Jobjorn Boman for sharing with me a study of the manuscripts of Suetonius' *Lives* from which he concludes that the original text held a Roman name, Chrestus or even Cherestrus: "Impulsore Cherestro? Suetonius' *Divus Claudius* 25.4 in Sources and Manuscripts," *Liber Annuus* 61 (2011): 355–76.

[40] Leonard Victor Rutgers, "Roman Policy toward the Jews: Expulsions from the City of Rome during the First Century C.E.," in *Judaism and Christianity in First-Century Rome* (ed. Karl P. Donfried and Peter Richardson; Grand Rapids: Eerdmans, 1998), 93–116.

circles in Rome, the pervasive ideology of Roman supremacy throughout the Empire, and the recent, repeated, public recitals, in city after city, of the Jews' foreign and inimical character vis-à-vis Roman order. In other words, Christian propaganda was not a factor in the expulsion of Jews from Rome. That event, and the subsequent return of some Jews to the city, are episodes in *Jewish* history, not *Christian* history.[41]

Second, I argue that the crisis just described—and the temptation for non-Jewish members of the Roman assemblies to show toward returning Jewish exiles a contempt informed and fueled by Roman imperial propaganda—sufficiently explains the rhetoric of the whole letter. Here I reject the notion that Romans is a mere "sample" or specimen of Paul's teaching or preaching or an outline of his gospel *as he preaches it elsewhere*. That view has no basis in the text and persists, I believe, only because of its convenience to professors of biblical or systematic theology. Further, Paul does not mention mission goals in Spain until the very end of the letter, and so I consider those goals tangential to the purpose of Romans. The warning addressed to the ἔθνος, however, comes at the very climax of the letter and is its rhetorical burden. The letter is admonitory, exhortative. Or to paraphrase J. Louis Martyn's nice distinction, it is not a letter *about* evangelization or *about* the power of God; it *is* evangelization, intended to precipitate an event in the ongoing powerful intervention of God in a rebellious world.[42]

There are several components of my reading of Romans—relying on a great cloud of scholarly witnesses, though they are not of course responsible for the use to which I have put their observations—that bear mention, if only to show the substructure of the claims I have just advanced.

---

[41] Elliott, *Arrogance of Nations*, 107–11, following Wolfgang Wiefel, "The Jewish Community in Ancient Rome and the Origins of Roman Christianity," in *The Romans Debate* (ed. Karl P. Donfried; rev. and exp. ed.; Peabody, Mass.: Hendrickson, 1991), 85–101.

[42] This is J. Louis Martyn's characterization of Paul's rhetoric in Galatians: "Events in Galatia: Modified Covenantal Nomism versus God's Invasions of the Cosmos in the Singular Gospel," in *Pauline Theology I: Thessalonians, Philippians, Galatians, Philemon* (ed. Jouette M. Bassler; Minneapolis: Fortress, 1991), 161–63. I should clarify that I take this as characteristic of Romans as well, though Martyn in another place suggests that Romans is something of a theological "white paper" written out of Paul's determination "that the Roman church [should] have an accurate grasp of his gospel" and thereby support his mission in Spain; Martyn, *Theological Issues in the Letters of Paul* (Nashville: Abingdon, 1997), 40–41. As indicated above, I dispute this characterization of the letter.

1. Paul's claim that he has been charged by God with securing "the obedience of the nations" (1:5, 6, 13; cf. 15:14) is the underlying exigence of the whole letter. It is also an indirect, but nevertheless unmistakable, challenge to the identical (and abundantly documented) imperial claim on the obedience of nations.[43]
2. Romans 1:16-17 is not a "theme" to be "expounded" or "proven" in the letter. The announcement of the revelation of God's justice is part of a dissociative argument that distinguishes God's justice from human injustice, that is, true justice from fraudulent human claims to justice. That fundamental dissociative argumentation—reality versus false claim or false appearance—structures the whole letter. It allows Paul to pull his audience back from the claims of imperial ideology without having to become entangled in arguments over the personalities or policies of particular emperors, and so on. In this letter Paul refutes and denies the fundamental imperial claim to embody justice on earth. The signals that he has *imperial* injustice—not just human iniquity in general—in mind are clear, though subtle, in Romans 1:18-32.[44]
3. Chapters 9–11 are indeed the climax of the letter; they are *not* "backwater" or an "afterthought," nor prompted by some vestigial bit of ethnic prejudice on Paul's part.[45]
4. The connection between chapters 8 and 9 is integral; this is a single rhetorical unit, a *pathos* appeal, meant to arouse emotion. Paul does not mean as a final goal to congratulate the "Gentile" Christians that "nothing can separate them from the love of God" and then turn, in morose, ethnically tinged regret, to weep for a fallen Israel. Rather, he has been driving toward the appeal in 9:1-5 from the beginning of the letter, albeit indirectly.[46]

---

[43] Elliott, *Arrogance of Nations*, 44–57.

[44] Elliott, *Arrogance of Nations*, 65–83, recapitulating arguments first broached in *Liberating Paul*.

[45] Several observations cluster together here, including Victor Furnish's characterization of the whole letter as exhortation and Nils Dahl's observation that the usual marks of a letter body are clustered in 9:1-4 more intensely than anywhere else in the letter. See V. P. Furnish, *Theology and Ethics in Paul* (Nashville: Abingdon, 1968), 103–6; Nils Dahl, "Missionary Theology in the Epistle to the Romans," in *Studies in Paul: Theology for the Early Christian Mission* (Minneapolis: Augsburg, 1977), 70–94.

[46] On Rom 9:1-5 as an *exsuscitatio* as described in the Latin rhetorical handbooks, see Elliott, *Rhetoric of Romans*, 261–62; Robert Jewett, *Romans* (Hermeneia; Minneapolis: Fortress, 2007), 556. On Rom 1–8 as *insinuatio*, the "indirect approach"

On this last point, I take issue with the popular appropriation of Paul's declaration that "nothing can separate us from the love of God" (Rom 8:38-39), perhaps one of the most popular passages in the Bible (to judge from its ubiquity in Christian gift shops). However moving Paul's reassurances there, they are not the point of his argument. Paul's intention was to *move* his audience from confidence in the love of God, which they experience as anticipation of their adoption as children (υἱοί) of God, to share in his anguish for his own people to whom that status, υἱοθεσία, rightly belongs. *These* remarks are *not* the stuff of popular Christian devotion, but they are the climax of the apostle's emotional appeal: "I could wish that I myself were accursed and cut off from Christ for the sake of my own people" (9:3). If, in Romans 8, Paul depicts for his hearers the groaning of the Spirit within the community, in Romans 9 Paul begins himself *to groan*. I suggest that Christians are too often trained *not* to pay attention, indeed, to stop listening before we hear that groaning.

The point throughout Romans 8 is the contrast between present (and deceptive) appearances and a yet unseen, but certain, future:

the sufferings of the present age	vs.	the glory about to be revealed;
creation's present subjection to futility and corruption	vs.	creation's imminent liberation;
our possession of "first fruits"	vs.	the yearned-for redemption of our bodies;
what is seen	vs.	what is hoped for;
the potential power of hardship, distress, persecution, famine, sword, and so on—present powers arrayed against the elect	vs.	the absolute power of God to redeem the elect in the future.

Note that at the crucial juncture between what we persistently, and perversely, read as two chapters (8 and 9) or even two "sections" of the letter (1–8 and 9–11), Paul draws an implicit contrast—between

---

recommended for the rhetor presenting an argument expected to meet stiff resistance, see Ben Witherington III, *Paul's Letter to the Romans: A Socio-Rhetorical Commentary* (Grand Rapids: Eerdmans, 2004), 17–18; earlier, Elliott, *Rhetoric of Romans*, 233.

the Spirit's witness in the assembly that "we are *huioi* of God"; not a false appearance, but a "sonship" not yet manifested	vs.	the Spirit's witness in Paul's heart on behalf of those to whom "sonship" rightly, firstly, and irrevocably belongs.[47]

In chapters 9–10 as well, Paul's point is not to conduct a theological postmortem on a vanquished Israel—in Paul's own words, μὴ γένοιτο, God forbid!—but to drive a final wedge between present appearances and final, ultimate, but not yet visible reality; to contrast, that is,

The *appearance* that God's word has failed, that Israel has so stumbled as fatally to fall,	vs.	the reality that it has not, cannot.[48]

With regard to this last point let us observe that Paul is doing things very similar to what Anathea Portier-Young declares the inventors of apocalypses did: "countering the totalizing narrative" of a dominant Empire, in this case the narrative of evident and inescapable worldwide subjugation to "the *imperium* of the Roman people." Implicitly, Paul is portraying imperial power, in its attempted disposition of Israel as a lapsed people, the "conquered" (*uicti*, in Seneca's term), as only "partial, contingent, and finite."[49] The apocalyptist, Portier-Young declares, seeks to assert "the transience and finitude of temporal powers, [to affirm] God's governance of time and the outworking of God's plan in history," and to expose "the hidden structures of false power and assert . . . a more potent invisible power."[50]

But Paul does not adopt the literary stratagem of the apocalypses: he does not compose an extensive retrospective historical survey and put it into the mouth (or the pen) of an ancient worthy. Nor does Paul develop the doctrine, found among advocates of imperial power and the learned among subject peoples alike, that God causes the serial rise and fall of successive empires.[51] There is for Paul only a series of

---

[47] Elliott, *Arrogance of Nations*, 114–15.

[48] Elliott, Arrogance *of Nations*, 111–17.

[49] Portier-Young, *Apocalypse and Empire*, xxiii, 7.

[50] Portier-Young, *Apocalypse and Empire*, xxiii, 27, 37.

[51] Ekkehard W. Stegemann finds in Daniel the notions of "*translatio imperii*, which means that God is the one who has appointed kings or rulers," and that of *successio*

past precedents demonstrating that God has never abandoned Israel; the word of Scripture—God's word—that God *will* never abandon Israel; and the steadfast conviction that "the gifts and calling of God are irrevocable" (11:29). How will it come about that "all Israel shall be saved" (11:26)? Paul does not describe any specific scenario. A good apocalypse-writer would surely have supplied a timeline, a storyboard, for the dramatic countdown. Paul only announces "a mystery" (11:25), which explains not the future, but why Israel's *present* circumstances tell us nothing about it.

Imperial ideology seeks always to portray the disposition of powers between ruler and ruled as natural, predestined, inevitable; the world around us looks the way it does because we stand at "the end of history." For Paul, what is visible, the "givens" of imperial dominion, are irrelevant. Rome's power doesn't require a learned apocalyptist's explanation because, for Paul, it simply belongs to a night that is "far gone" (13:12). This is the "restoration of time" of Portier-Young's apocalyptists, but it is truncated; we might say that the apocalyptic stratagem has been field-stripped for more urgent use.

Cosmos and Conflict

With those observations in mind, I draw several conclusions about creation and cosmos in Romans 8 and 9.

First, by sketching in large strokes some lines of Roman imperial ideology, I mean to show that a powerful and ubiquitous cosmogonic doctrine was at work in Paul's environment. We might suppose that many of his readers were familiar with the Genesis creation story; but, I suggest, *none* of them would have been unaware of at least the outlines of the Augustan gospel, according to which a single divine figure had brought unprecedented peace to the whole earth. In this doctrine, the establishment of cosmos went hand in hand with conquest, whether it

---

imperii, "the speculative idea of the succession of empires"; examples are ready to hand in Josephus and Philo (see Elliott, *Arrogance of Nations*, passim). Against these notions Stegemann contrasts Paul's *dysangelion*, "an almost radical and bleak perspective" according to which "the world has arrived at a very critical stage, with an impending universal demise" facing current rulers; Stegemann, "Coexistence and Transformation: Reading the Politics of Identity in Romans in an Imperial Context," in *Reading Paul in Context: Explorations in Identity Formation: Essays in Honour of William S. Campbell* (ed. Kathy Ehrensperger and J. Brian Tucker; Library of New Testament Studies 428; London: T&T Clark, 2010), 3–23.

was depicted frankly as subjugation or euphemized as including other peoples in the "friendship" of the Roman people.

Second, Paul's argument in Romans is directed against the Roman ideological characterization of Israel as a vanquished people, a poison that (I suggest) had begun to infect the churches in Rome. I do not want to be misunderstood here; Paul is not primarily concerned to counter specific aspects of Roman ideology *as such* nor to debate doctrines of creation for their own sake. The concern at the heart of the letter—and the Spirit's witness in his own anguished heart (9:1-4)—is for the identity of Israel and, with them, the nations who obey Israel's God as the true inheritors of the world.

So why should we bring "creation" into the discussion at all? I think there are two motifs in Romans 8 that need to be set against the cosmogony motifs of Roman imperial ideology and iconography.

First is simply Paul's reference to κτίσις, "creation" (8:19, NRSV). That translation inevitably evokes for English-speaking ears the first book of the Bible, and Robert Jewett (among many interpreters) finds here "allusion to the Genesis story." But (as Jewett also points out), the term κτίσις was more current in Paul's day for the ritual founding of cities than for what *we* call "the" creation story.[52] Jewett offers as plausible a case as can be mounted that Paul means, by referring to creation's "subjection" to futility (ματαιότης) and corruption (φθορά), to evoke the "curses" that followed Adam's disobedience in Genesis 3, but the absence of any of those terms from Genesis, and the absence of Adam from Romans 8, don't help to make that case. Rather, Paul simply asserts the "subjection" of creation, without any narrative concerning *when* or *by whom* this subjection took place.[53]

Jewett is on much firmer ground when, repeatedly and compellingly, he compares Paul's depiction of a creation "subjected to futility" to the cosmogonic motif in Roman imperial propaganda. "Paul's formulation simply assumes, without arguing the point, that the Caesarean

---

[52] Jewett, *Romans*, 513. The LXX translation of the Genesis account relies on ποιεῖν, not κτίζειν.

[53] This leaves Jewett to appeal to distant and rather obscure references—a magical spell "apparently influenced by Jewish ideas" that refers to God as the "honored name to whom all creation [κτίσις] is subjugated," and a reference in *Genesis Rabbah* to created things being "corrupted" after Adam—as evidence that the language of "subjection" to "corruption" points to Gen 3. His connection of the term with "chronic frustration symbolized by the 'sweat' on the face of Adam's descendants" appears forced: Jewett, *Romans*, 513 n. 59; 514 n. 69.

view about the presence of a peaceful, magically prosperous golden age is illusory." The documentation for this "Caesarean view" is abundant, and much of it is contemporary with Paul.[54] But this means that instead of imagining Paul as primarily concerned simply to "interpret scripture," we should understand Paul to be *using* scripture *to interpret the world.*

Even if Paul had the Genesis story in mind, Jewett continues, his audience "could well have thought about how imperial ambitions, military conflicts, and economic exploitation had led to the erosion of the natural environment throughout the Mediterranean world, leaving ruined cities, depleted fields, deforested mountains, and polluted streams as evidence of this universal human vanity." If *they* could have thought of those realities, shouldn't we suppose that Paul could have *meant* for them to think of those realities? Speculation about what "must have" been the case may sound like special pleading, but surely in this case it is warranted, not least by the very "blanket" character of Paul's assertion. Instead of reciting a particular mythic narrative, Paul simply characterizes the world in terms that are the opposite of Roman claims. Jewett, for one, draws just this conclusion. Paul expected his audience to recognize that the rival claims of imperial ideology—to have ushered in the restoration of a golden age—were "utterly preposterous in the light of this critical biblical tradition."[55]

The same is true regarding a second motif, that of creation personified as yearning for deliverance—more specifically, as a woman, straining and groaning in childbirth. Here again, Jewett is exactly right to contrast this imagery with the fertile female figure seated in repose

---

[54] Jewett, *Romans*, 509, passim. Jewett cites Virgil's *Fourth Eclogue*, lines 11–41; the *Aeneid*, 6.789–94; and the *Eclogue* of Calpurnius Siculus. I used the same texts to make a similar point about "the ideological context" of Paul's apostolate in *Liberating Paul*, 184–89. Indeed, some of the (other) Jewish prophetic and apocalyptic texts to which Jewett points to show the Jewish interest in a coming "restoration of Edenic conditions" rely more on motifs common to Roman imagery than Genesis; and as Jewett also points out, the very notion that creation had been corrupted "had played a decisive role in the Roman civic cult" (*Romans*, 516)—though there, of course, the corruption and decline of creation was seen as a *past* reality now reversed in the Augustan golden age. In this regard Stanley K. Stowers discusses "myths of decline" in Roman-era philosophical and imperial propagandistic texts, though he does not exploit the comparison in the way Jewett does; see Stowers, *A Rereading of Romans: Justice, Jews, and Gentiles* (New Haven, Conn: Yale University Press, 1994), 85–92, 122–24.

[55] Jewett, *Romans*, 513.

FIGURE 7
A female figure, representing a subdued nation, sits dejected. First century. Palazzo Massimo, Rome. Photo by Neil Elliott.

on the Altar of Augustan Peace.⁵⁶ But we should also bear in mind what Brigitte Kahl and Davina Lopez have shown us, the other stock representations of female forms in Roman imperial iconography—as vanquished females; women enslaved, bereft of husbands and children, seated or lying in helpless and inconsolable dejection (figure 7). (The famous *Iudaea Capta* image used on a variety of coins after the Roman conquest of Jerusalem and destruction of the Temple in 70 was simply a variation on a much more prevalent and generic motif in imperial iconography.) Paul implicitly rejects both images—of the fertile mother reclining in splendid and abundant leisure, symbolizing the consummation of history in the *imperium* of the Roman people, and of the bereft mother whose irretrievable loss symbolizes the fate of any people who dared to resist that rule. Neither representation of present power relations was real. The *real* power, for Paul, was the *invisible* power of the God whose glory would soon be revealed; but that reality was already stirring as palpably and irresistibly as the contractions of childbirth, and toward just as bodily a consummation, the "revelation of the children of God," the "redemption of our bodies."⁵⁷

⁵⁶ Jewett, *Romans*, 511 nn. 48, 49; cf. 517.

⁵⁷ Again Jewett makes the comparison explicit: "If the groaning really lasts 'until now,' this would exclude the Augustan premise that the golden age had been

Paul relies here on metaphors not merely of perception and anticipation but of active, even strenuous participation: "not only the creation, but we ourselves, who have the first fruits of the Spirit, groan inwardly while we wait for adoption" (8:23 NRSV). For Jewett and others, the implications for contemporary Christians appear immediate and profound. "In Paul's case the avenue of divine action is the conversion of humans": those whose minds have been transformed "will be able to discern what God wills for the ecosystem."[58] But Jewett's allusion reference to Romans 12:2 ("those whose minds have been transformed") should give us pause. It may be easy enough for us (as contemporary readers of Paul's letters, participating in churches that appeal to his authority) to imagine that *we* are the modern heirs of Paul, those to whom his words are profitably addressed and in whose response those words may find their fulfillment. The new creation, we might presume, awaits only our being mobilized to take appropriate action. But is this identification premature? Are we so vain, we probably think he's talking about us?

Any adequate appropriation of Paul's message in Romans must take seriously the question whether we live in a situation genuinely analogous to his; or better (because analogy is inevitable in historical interpretation), which analogies are appropriate?[59]

Speaking of "empire" and "resistance" today is both popular and controversial, within academic circles and beyond them. On the other hand, a retreat into a comfortable biblicism or into an identity as "religious" persons, striving to be faithful to Paul's vision or to other biblical visions, can delude and betray us if we do not first do the hard work of understanding our present context. Is Naomi Klein right: Do we live within a hegemonic domain with an implicit "doctrine of creation" that capitalizes on crisis, on the collapse or destruction of whole communities? Are "zones of social abandonment" simply an unfortunate byproduct of failed development or unprepared or unworthy societies; or are such zones the inevitable result of the hegemony in which we live?

---

inaugurated by the Saecular Games of 17 B.C.E., or that Nero had ushered in a 'golden age of peace'" (*Romans*, 517).

[58] Jewett, *Romans*, 512.

[59] On the inevitability of analogical thinking in historical interpretation, I find compelling Fredric Jameson's arguments in *The Political Unconscious* (Ithaca, N.Y.: Cornell University Press, 1981).

What is our Christian responsibility in such a situation? But why should we limit the zone of participation to those who explicitly own the language of being "in Christ"? Doesn't Paul's language of a creation in labor pains, of a whole created order yearning for deliverance, necessarily drive us beyond the boundaries of church? I mean to ask not only what is our *human* responsibility in such a situation, but also whether it is our *Christian* responsibility, our theological responsibility, quite deliberately to look beyond churchly identity and what Mark Lewis Taylor calls the "Theological Guild." Are we not bound to discern, to lift up, and to form ourselves in solidarity with the connections and movements of people everywhere who are struggling daily to embody the thesis that "another world is possible"? Michael Hardt and Antonio Negri point us to the reality of "Multitude," the sheer proliferation of human labor subjected to the disciplines of late capitalism—yet generating new patterns and new potentialities that militate against its hegemony.[60] Mark Lewis Taylor proposes specific radical practices of an "anamnestic solidarity" that embodies the tortured and gives presence to the spectral.[61] These forms of solidarity seem to me the appropriate analogies for Paul's language in Romans 8 concerning participation, through the Spirit, in a creation-in-labor, a world yearning for the redemption of bodily life.

If Paul's words really have a correlate today, it is to be found in the common aspirations of the world's majority—who need no learned expositions of a 2,000-year-dead saint to find their motivation. Perhaps one point of a gathering like the Princeton conference is simply to convince ourselves to join their cause. To carry on with theological business as usual in isolation from these present potentialities would, I believe, be a grave error. If Paul's God is the God of the living, then it is among the living that we will find and realize his legacy today, and give flesh to the prayer drawn from the Psalms:

> Let not the needy, O Lord, be forgotten,
> Nor the hope of the poor be taken away.

---

[60] Michael Hardt and Antonio Negri, *Multitude: War and Democracy in the Age of Empire* (New York: Penguin, 2005).

[61] Taylor, *The Theological and the Political*, esp. chap. 5. Also noteworthy in this regard is William Cavanaugh's splendid reflection on the material practices of a tortured body of Christ in the world in *Torture and Eucharist* (Oxford: Blackwell, 1998).

Afterword
The Human Moral Drama

J. Louis Martyn

We are little more than a decade into the twenty-first century, and in this volume we have already what will surely prove to be one of our period's most significant international events in the study of the apostle Paul.[1]

Given my assignment to provide closing reflections, I could now attempt a summary. But to reread all of the contributions, honoring their rich complexity, is to realize that they do not lend themselves to such a synthetic treatment.

---

[1] The volume originated from a conference celebrating the bicentennial of Princeton Theological Seminary, altogether well planned by Professor Beverly R. Gaventa, and maturely executed under her guidance by senior scholars among whom there is great mutual respect. The conference opened with an evening worship service, engagingly focused by Luke Powery on the eighth chapter of Romans and reflecting a weighty fact. Paul knew that, in a way similar to the handling of his other letters, Romans would be initially communicated to and received by the little house churches in the capital by being read aloud in their corporate services of worship, doubtless more than once. There, as he thought of it, the letter itself would be used by God for his own redemptive purposes. The possibility that his letter would be interpreted apart from the active and celebrated presence of God never entered the apostle's mind. The conference proper was marked, then, by morning prayer each day, followed by numerous short papers and eight plenaries, any one of which could have served as the major lecture for its own conference. It is difficult to avoid the cliché about an embarrassment of riches, especially because those papers gave us clear indications about the future of Pauline studies. For the moment, readers of the present volume can accept the good offices of Carey Newman and Baylor University Press, in order to read and review the papers as printed here, and indeed to consult them as guides to Pauline research as it continues to unfold.

Four Shared Interpretive Steps

For readers of this volume a better route opens up, I think, when you, the reader, join me in taking four simple interpretive steps.

First, a Discussion Circle

Initially we draw on a close reading of the chapters in order to invite their authors—in our imagination—to take seats as major actors in a discussion circle. In our circle the conversation will find its own course, then, by drawing on the papers and by accepting the firm guidance of Paul's letters themselves. All participants share a passion to hear the strange and wondrous voice of the apostle, confident that in our disparate labors we can be of help to one another in this listening process. In that spirit we ourselves take seats in the circle,[2] the chief place belonging, of course, to the apostle himself.

Second, an Arresting Piece of Art

Continuing to give disciplined latitude to imagination, we take together a second interpretive step. We place before our group, so that all can see, an engaging painting by Renaissance master Raphael, *Paul Preaching in Athens* (figure 8).

With some imagination and an equal amount of boldness we can use this arresting painting to bring the historical Paul into sharp focus, sensing a number of the ways in which he was markedly *different* from the popular philosophers who lived lives of traveling preachers of the moral life.

Third, Paul and a Contemporary Competitor

Boldly and respectfully we take Raphael's work in hand, employing it twice, so as to have two versions of it, calling them "Today" and "Yesterday," and bearing both in mind as we proceed.

Today

In this version the commanding figure is indeed the apostle, arms raised for emphasis, speaking publicly on the day of his arrival in a sizable Hellenistic city, Thessalonica or Philippi or Corinth. On the day

---

[2] I make no attempt, of course, to be completely objective. My own debt to the contributors reaches back through the years, and, reading the present volume, I continue to be instructed, especially because taken together these pieces tell us important things, as I have said, about the future of Pauline studies.

FIGURE 8
St. Paul Preaching in Athens *(cartoon for the Sistine Chapel) (pre-restoration)*, Raphael *(Raffaello Sanzio of Urbino) (1483–1520) / Victoria & Albert Museum, London, UK / The Bridgeman Art Library*

portrayed in this edition of the painting, Paul has gone to the city's chief marketplace, where, obeying God's call to preach the good news of Jesus Christ to the Gentiles, he has gained the attention of a small group of auditors.

Yesterday

I will call the other version of the painting "Yesterday." In it we see the same marketplace the day before Paul's visit. Here the speaker with raised arms is one of the apostle's contemporaries and competitors, a Stoic "wise man" or a Cynic teacher, let us say, who, like Paul, travels and shares his wisdom in one city after another. In this version of the painting we see that this wisdom teacher has similarly gathered a small group of auditors. For convenience of reference I will call this man "Jason," and we who are convening our newly formed discussion circle will imagine inviting him to take a place among us, along with this book's contributors and, as I have said, Paul himself. At numerous points in Paul's letters we sense that he was well acquainted with the activities and teachings of such popular-level philosophical figures. We also see that he took great care to distinguish his message from theirs (e.g., 1 Cor 1:18-20). In order to deal with the real, first-century Paul, we need to have Jason in our discussion circle.

Fourth, a Closing Issue
The Identity of the Morally Competent Human Agent

I can express my appreciation to Beverly Gaventa and to the other contributors by drawing (a) on Raphael's painting, (b) on the papers, and (c) on a rereading of Paul's letters to address a single issue, one that will surely gain further attention in the unfolding of our labors on Pauline theology: the birth and the full identity of the morally competent human agent.[3]

Returning first to the two editions of Raphael's painting, we focus our attention for a moment on the right segment, the auditors of the two speakers. Where do the speakers understand their auditors to be? In what cosmos do Jason and Paul suppose their auditors to be living?

Jason

Representing Hellenistic wisdom teachers, Jason considers his auditors to be *individual human beings*, each of whom, morally competent to make his own decisions and free to do so, is *standing alone at one form after another of the parting of the Two Ways.*[4] There is the path of foolish vice,

---

[3] On the subject of Paul and agency see, first of all, John M. G. Barclay and S. Gathercole, eds., *Divine and Human Agency in Paul and His Cultural Environment* (Edinburgh: T&T Clark, 2006). The grand history of Christian doctrine includes periods marked by a tendency to accent human agency at the expense of divine agency (generally observable, I think, just now) and, of course, the opposite as well. Both tendencies call for correction. At the present juncture one notes—however paradoxical it may seem—the corrective dimensions in the recovery of the image of Paul as a thoroughly apocalyptic theologian, on which more below. In addition, and for one strand in what we may assuredly forecast about the never-ending study of Paul, see J. B. Davis and D. Harink, eds., *Apocalyptic and the Future of Theology* (Eugene, Ore.: Wipf & Stock, Cascade Books, 2012).

[4] See esp. A. A. Long, *From Epicurus to Epictetus* (Oxford: Oxford University Press, 2006) and A. J. Malherbe, *Paul and the Popular Philosophers* (Minneapolis: Fortress, 1989). Note in particular Long's chapter on "Seneca and the Self." Cf. also Ben Myers' comment in chap. 3 of this volume: "The philosophical traditions available in antiquity presupposed that the self is some manner of autonomous essence" (41).

and there is the path of wise virtue. Being possessed of competence and freedom, every individual can make his own choices;[5] he needs only some moral instruction and exhortation to take the better path.

Paul

Several of our contributors join hands, so to speak, in representing a tectonic shift presently occurring in Pauline studies, differentiating the apostle radically from Jason. In this relatively new view, spawned originally and centrally by the work of Ernst Käsemann, Paul is perceived to have been a thoroughly apocalyptic theologian (see especially the chapter in this volume by Martinus de Boer).[6] In the Adamic moral drama as it actually exists, human beings are *not alone*; they have in fact company, not least the lethal company of Sin as a *cosmic power*. In our discussion circle we are especially attentive at this point to Barclay, de Boer, and Gaventa. Barclay observes,

> When Paul pauses, midway through Romans 5, to *redraw the map of the cosmos*, he sees two, and only two, power structures at work within it (5:12-21). Viewed from the perspective of the Christ-event, all history, even Israel's history "under the law," has been subject to the power of sin and propelled toward death (5:12-14, 20). But in Christ, and because of Christ, a new reality has emerged, powerful enough to reverse the tendency to death, and to propel its recipients, contrariwise, towards "eternal life" (5:17, 19, 21).[7]

---

[5] Two matters seize one's attention here, the notion of the individual and the assumption that that individual possesses moral competence. Both matters will occupy us as we proceed: (1) On the notion of the individual, note Susan Eastman's critiques of Dale Martin and Robert Jewett, and see note 19 below. (2) Regarding moral competence, forms of autonomy were held among Hellenistic Jewish thinkers as well as among the popular pagan philosophers: e.g., "Do not say it was he [God] who led me astray [into transgression].... From the beginning he [God] created the human being, and he left him in the power of his own decision (*diaboulion*). If it is your will to do so, you will keep the commandments, and to act faithfully is a matter of your own choice (*eudokia*)" (Ben Sira 15:12-15). The Stoics were consistently challenged, of course, to show how they could reasonably affirm both the determinism of fate and the freedom of the human agent. See above all Susanne Bobzien, *Determinism and Freedom in Stoic Philosophy* (Oxford: Oxford University Press, 1998).

[6] See also note 3 above, and esp. the chapter by Philip Ziegler in Davis and Harink, *Apocalyptic and the Future of Theology*.

[7] See Barclay, chap. 4 in this volume, p. 59 (emphasis added). Regarding the *direction* of the decisive movement that is truly redemptive—namely God's movement

For Paul, the picture of the human being as a lonely and basically autonomous figure is wholly wide of the mark. In Paul's view, then, Jason is horribly misleading his auditors about the cosmos as it really exists.[8] The human agent—the Adamic agent—does not live solely in the realm of possibility, able to choose this path or that. Human beings live amidst orbs of power.

As de Boer writes,

> What is distinctive in Paul's use and application of the story of Adam in 5:12-21 is his characterization of sin and death as cosmological forces that have invaded the human cosmos as alien intruders: "Sin [capital S] came into the world, and through Sin, Death [capital D] [came into the world]." In short, Paul personifies and thereby "mythologizes" the notions of sin and death, which is to say, he talks about them as he elsewhere does about Satan (cf. Rom 16:20; 1 Cor 5:5; 7:5; 2 Cor 2:11; 11:14; 12:7; 1 Thess 2:18; cf. 2 Cor 4:4; 6:14; 1 Thess 3:5), evil angels (cf. Rom 8:38; 1 Cor 4:9; 6:3; 2 Cor 11:14; 12:7), or demons (cf. 1 Cor 10:20-21), i.e., as inimical powers or beings that victimize and enslave human beings, and that do so contrary to God's intention for the world.[9]

And Gaventa, following Paul as he speaks in Roman 7 of the Law and Sin, comments that Paul's "concern with the cosmic power of Sin . . . comes to the foreground. As Meyer argues, the problem is not with the Law itself but with Sin's overpowering even of God's holy and good and right Law."[10]

---

toward us—see Christopher L. Morse, *The Difference Heaven Makes* (Edinburgh: T&T Clark, 2010); idem, "If Johannes Weiss Is Right: A Brief Retrospective on Apocalyptic Theology," in Davis and Harink, *Apocalyptic and the Future of Theology*, 131–53. Cf. Abraham Joshua Heschel, *God in Search of Man* (New York: Farrar, Straus & Giroux, 1955).

[8] In listening to de Boer, we will see that the enmity between Paul and Jason is not simply a personal matter. It is truly seen only when it is "mythologized." When Jason misleads his auditors, he functions as a servant of Sin, the great deceiver (Rom 7:11). He is not simply Paul's enemy. Were he a false brother in the church, Paul would identify him as a cosmic enemy of the cross (Phil 3:18).

[9] See de Boer, chap. 1 in this volume, p. 13.

[10] See Gaventa, chap. 5 in this volume, p. 90; and also Gaventa, "'Neither Height Nor Depth': Cosmos and Soteriology in Paul's Letter to the Romans," in Davis and Harink, *Apocalyptic and the Future of Theology*, 183–99.

The Dark and Sinister Form of Dual Agency
Sin as Enslaving Power and Sin as a Human Act

When now we return to the letters themselves, we see that Paul emphasizes his apocalyptic view of Sin as an enslaving power without altogether eclipsing his view of sin as a human act. Not long after saying that "Jews and Greeks alike are all *under the power of Sin*" (Rom 3:9), Paul adds, ". . . all *have sinned*" (Rom 5:12).

The tension between these two texts and their equivalents is real and complex.[11] Here, having no space for extended discussion, I will say only that for Paul in his "mythologizing program" (de Boer) the view of Sin as slavemaster is *primary*, while the view of the Adamic agent as active sinner is *secondary*. As we ponder this assertion, we find interpretive help in the term "complicity."[12] In the full picture, that is, the prisoner (Rom 3:9) became—and becomes—*actively complicit* with the jailer (Rom 5:12). Held captive by the enslaving power of Sin, human beings commit sin. The result is the dark and sinister version of dual agency. Sin is *both* an active agent, an enslaving power, *and*—secondarily—a complicit act of the Adamic agent, for which he is subject to God's judgment (Rom 3:19).

As our contributors tell us, however, the Pauline form of the human moral drama does not end with God's calling the Adamic agent to judgment for the universal and complicit act of sinning. Sinful complicity cannot close the drama because by militantly invading the realm of Sin in the sending of his Son, God has in fact created a second, ultimately determinative form of dual agency. Here we return first to Barclay, accenting his comment about the "new reality" that has emerged in Christ, the reality "powerful enough to reverse the tendency to death."

Regarding this determinative form of dual agency, we remind ourselves of a simple fact about Paul's letters. All of them—and thus all of Paul's confidently composed imperatives and exhortations—are addressed to communities "in Christ," *churches in which he knows the Spirit of Christ to be active*. In his letters, that is, Paul is not speaking to the Adamic agent at all. He is addressing a different agent, the

---

[11] See Eastman, chap. 6 in this volume, p. 99.

[12] See notably Philip Ziegler's use of this term in "'Christ Must Reign': Ernst Käsemann and Soteriology in an Apocalyptic Key," in Davis and Harink, *Apocalyptic and the Future of Theology*, 200–18.

one who can be confidently exhorted because this agent is *able to obey God's command*.

If, now, he is speaking to a different agent, possessed of genuine moral competence, how are we to identify this agent fully, and what are we to say of the origin and sustaining nature of its competence?

The Redemptive Form of Dual Agency
The Gospel as God's Liberating Power and the Newly Competent Corporate Agent in Whom the Spirit of Christ Is Active

Rereading Paul's letter to his Galatian churches, we note that after referring to God's deed of sending the Spirit of Christ into the Galatians' hearts (Gal 4:6), Paul speaks of the fruit borne in the communal life of the Galatian churches by the daily activity of this Spirit (Gal 5:17-24). Love, joy, and living at peace are acts of human beings, to be sure, but they are specifically identified by Paul as acts of the newly created *corporate* agent *in whose corpus* the Spirit of Christ is active.[13]

We return yet again, then, to Barclay, de Boer, and Gaventa, adding now Eastman, with her reference to "double participation."[14] When Paul speaks in Galatians 5 of the fruit of the Spirit of Christ, he refers to nothing less than God's steadfast *participation* in the moral drama itself. He refers in short to the dual agency that is a mark of the new creation, that new creation being the newly competent agent itself.[15]

---

[13] With regard to the matter of divine *invasion*—certainly the center of Paul's understanding of agency as a whole—there is a highly illuminating theological analogue in Ezek 11:19, where the prophet hears God say, "I will give them a different heart and put a new spirit in them." Note especially the perceptive labors on Ezekiel by J. Lapsley, *Can These Bones Live?* (Berlin: De Gruyter, 2000). As for Ezekiel, so also for Paul dual agency is the creation of the invasive God.

[14] Note that in her chapter Eastman speaks of the "reconstitution of agency." The similarities and the differences between my use of the expression "dual agency" and her references to "double participation" may be a subject worth pursuing. See my earlier references to "dual agency" in "The Gospel Invades Philosophy," in *Paul, Philosophy, and the Theopolitical Vision* (ed. Douglas Harink; Eugene, Ore.: Cascade Books, 2010), 13–33, and esp. 31–33.

[15] To speak of God's steadfast participation in the moral drama is to leave behind what we might call "the two-step understanding of morality" (see Martyn, "The Gospel Invades Philosophy," 20). In the theistic form of that two-step pattern, prominent among the pagan popular philosophers, God makes the first move, *offering* to the human agent *an instructive possibility*. Then, in a second and separable step, the

The Birth of Redemptive Dual Agency in the Genesis of Faith

With the invasive event of God's sending his Son, and with the oral enactment of that event in the divine power that *is* the gospel (Rom 1:16)—the word in which God is himself active—there is the birth of redemptive dual agency in the act of faith. When a human being believes the gospel, that event is one in which God has played—and plays—an active role, establishing the redemptive dual agency with its asymmetrical form.[16]

Faith is emphatically not an autonomous, second-act move on the part of the human agent, as though (Act 1) Paul preaches and (Act 2) as a second and distinctive act a human being decides to believe. On the contrary, faith is itself *incited* by the power of the gospel (Rom 10:17).

Daily Sustenance of Dual Agency

Something similar is to be said about the sustenance of liberating dual agency. As I have said above, love, joy, and living at peace are deeds of human beings, to be sure, but specifically deeds carried out every day as the Spirit of Christ bears its fruit *in* the dual agency known in the daily life of the church, the "body of Christ" (1 Cor 11).[17]

The identity, then, of the morally competent agent is clear. That agent is itself the new creation, the new *community*, the *corpus Christi*, the body of Christ that is daily brought newly into being by God's own participation in the moral drama, as he places that drama under the liberating Lordship of Christ. Here is the sustaining dual agency in which the communal fruit of love, joy, and peace is born anew every day, causing the corporate human agent, the church, to flourish as

---

human agent responds, God looking on from afar in order to *assure the independence of the human decision*. In private communication Barclay is clear that when he speaks of a human "obligation," he is referring to a task issuing from God's completely free gift. He does not intend to refer prospectively to a human act designed to gain something from God. Here we agree enthusiastically; but can one thus use the term "obligation" and still avoid altogether the two-step understanding of morality?

[16] *Asymmetry* is characteristic of the redemptive dual agency from its inception. God's participation in human morality begins with his incitement of faith *and* with his effective demand of absolute obedience to his liberating lordship, in accordance with the first commandment.

[17] See Ernst Käsemann, "Corporality in Paul," in Käsemann, *On Being a Disciple of the Crucified Nazarene* (Grand Rapids: Eerdmans, 2010), 38–50.

a light to the whole of the world.[18] It is in this dual agency that the humanity willed by God took shape, continues to take shape, and will in the end take final shape.[19]

So it is to this *newly flourishing human agent* that Paul speaks a *hortatory* word of God's *active assurance*:

> . . . *work out your own salvation* with fear and trembling, *for God is at work in you* [a corporate plural referring to the Body of Christ], both to will and to work for his good pleasure. (Phil 2:12-13)[20]

It is in concert with the apostle that we can say, "For this hortatory assurance of our Lord's activity we give thanks to him!"

---

[18] Paul's view of the world included something *somewhat similar* to what we post-Enlightenment moderns call "individuals." See, e.g., Gal 6:3-5. Regarding individuality in Paul's time, one can make a beginning by consulting "Individuum, Individualitaet," in *Historisches Wörterbuch der Philosophie* (13 vols.; Basel: Schwabe, 1971). Concerning the individual and moral competence, note that Paul can even speak in the hortatory mood to named persons (Phil 4:2). All "individuals" addressed by him, however, existed *in* the church in which the Spirit of Christ was corporately active; and they were all addressed by him in light of that fact. A brother's "going astray," for example, was handled by Paul as a communal matter, yet another indication that the competent agent was for him the *corpus Christi*. In the case of a seriously erring brother, that is, "you who are spiritual are to restore him to his former condition in the community [thus bearing] one another's burdens" and so fulfilling the Law of Christ (Gal 6:1-2). One cannot read Paul's letters and then imagine his standing before a Roman magistrate and addressing him in either the imperative or the hortatory subjunctive (cf. Acts 18:12-14). As we have seen, being under the power of Sin, the Adamic agent is not exhortable.

[19] Rather than a sect removed from the world, the church is the beachhead the invasive and militant God is establishing in the world of humanity as he carries out his war of liberation, freeing the whole of the human race from the powers of Sin and Death (Gal 6:10; 1 Cor 15:20-28). Cf. Udo Schnelle, *The Human Condition: Anthropology in the Teachings of Jesus, Paul, and John* (Minneapolis: Fortress, 1996) 149.

[20] This passage in Philippians is only one of the Pauline sentences in which the two clauses show divine agency "trumping" human agency. In the redemptive dual agency to which Paul is a witness there is, as we have noted above, a marked asymmetry honoring the fact that God has shared his lordship with his Christ, and with none other, emphatically not with the individual "self." But his victory does not bring our eclipse, or even our diminishment. On the contrary, it issues in our dramatic *flourishing* as the liberated ones who serve him and one another in the corporate agent named *corpus Christi*. When God acts in a way that "trumps" human agency, he consistently does that to cause the human agent to thrive as the apple of his eye (note the verb "reign" in Rom 5:17).

Works Cited

Acolatse, Esther E. "Unraveling the Relational Myth in the Turn Toward Autonomy: Pastoral Care and Counseling with African Women." In *Women Out of Order: Risking Change and Creating Care in a Multicultural World*, edited by J. Stevenson-Moessner and T. Snorton. Minneapolis: Fortress, 2010.

Adams, Edward. *Constructing the World: A Study in Paul's Cosmological Language*. London: T&T Clark/Continuum, 2000.

Anselm. "Cur Deus Homo." In *Anselm of Canterbury: The Major Works*, edited and translated by B. Davies and G. R. Evans. Oxford: Oxford University Press, 1998.

Augustine. *The City of God*, translated by R. W. Dyson. Cambridge: Cambridge University Press, 1998.

———. *Confessions*, translated by Henry Chadwick. Oxford: Oxford University Press, 1991.

———. "Enarrationes in Psalmos, 37.27." In *Expositions of the Psalms*, translated by Maria Boulding. 6 vols. Hyde Park, N.Y.: New City, 2000–2004.

———. "Expositio epistulae ad Galatas liber unus." In *Augustine's Commentary on Galatians: Introduction, Text, Translation, and Notes*, translated by Eric Plumer. Oxford: Oxford University Press, 2003.

———. "Expositio quarundam propositionum ex epistula apostoli ad Romanos." In *Augustine on Romans: Proposition from the Epistle to the Romans, Unfinished Commentary on the Epistle to the Romans*, edited by Paula Fredriksen. Chico, Calif.: Scholar's Press, 1982.

Barclay, John M. G. "Believers and the 'Last Judgement' in Paul: Rethinking Grace and Recompense." In *Eschatologie-Eschatology*, edited by H.-J.

Eckstein, C. Landmesser, and H. Lichtenberger. Tübingen: Mohr Siebeck, 2011.

———. "'Do We Undermine the Law?': A Study of Romans 14:1–15:6." In *Paul and the Mosaic Law*, edited by J. D. G. Dunn. WUNT 89. Tübingen: J. C. B. Mohr, 1996. Reprint, Grand Rapids: Eerdmans, 2001.

———. "Grace within and beyond Reason: Philo and Paul in Dialogue." In *Paul, Grace and Freedom: Essays in Honour of John K. Riches*, edited by P. Middleton, A. Paddison, and K. Wenell. London: T&T Clark, 2009.

———. *Paul and the Gift*. Grand Rapids: Eerdmans, forthcoming.

———. *Pauline Churches and Diaspora Jews*. WUNT 275. Tübingen: Mohr Siebeck, 2011.

———. "Stoic Physics and the Christ-event: A Review of Troels Engberg-Pedersen, *Cosmology and Self in the Apostle Paul: The Material Spirit*." *JSNT* 33 (2012): 406–14.

Barclay, John M. G., and S. Gathercole, eds. *Divine and Human Agency in Paul and His Cultural Environment*. Edinburgh: T&T Clark, 2006.

Barth, Karl. *Church Dogmatics*, translated by G. W. Bromiley. Edinburgh: T&T Clark, 1956–1969.

———. *Epistle to the Romans*, translated by E. Hoskyns. Oxford: Oxford University Press, 1933.

———. *Romans: A Shorter Commentary*, translated by D. H. van Daalen. London: SCM Press, 1963.

Bayer, Oswald. "The Ethics of Gift." *LQ* 24 (2010): 447–68.

Benveniste, Emile. *General Linguistics*. London: Harvill Secker, 2008.

———. *Problems in General Linguistics*, translated by Mary Elizabeth Meek. Coral Gables, Fla: University of Miami Press, 1971.

Berkouwer, G. C. *The Work of Christ*, translated by C. Lambregtse. Studies in Dogmatics. Grand Rapids: Eerdmans, 1965.

Berlin, Adele. "Psalms and the Literature of Exile: Psalms 137–44, 69, and 78." In *The Book of Psalms: Composition and Reception*. VTSup 99. Leiden: Brill, 2005.

Beutler, Brian. "With Hurricane Bearing Down Cantor Spox Says Disaster Relief Should Be Paid For." *Talking Points Memo*, August 25, 2011. http://tpmdc.talkingpointsmemo.com/2011/08/cantor-spox-if-theres-hurricane-damage-costs-will-have-to-be-paid-for-with-spending-cuts.php?ref=fpa.

Blenkinsopp, Joseph. "The Bible, Archaeology, and Politics; or the Empty Land Revisited." *JSOT* 27 (2002): 169–87.

Bobzien, Susanne. *Determinism and Freedom in Stoic Philosophy*. Oxford: Oxford University Press, 1998.

Works Cited

Boman, Jobjorn. "Impulsore Cherestro? Suetonius' *Divus Claudius* 25.4 in Sources and Manuscripts." *Liber Annuus* 61 (2011): 355–76.
Boring, M. Eugene. "The Language of Universal Salvation in Paul." *JBL* 105 (1986): 269–92.
Bornkamm, Karin. "Amt Christi." In *Religions in Geschichte und Gegenwart 4*, edited by Hans D. Betz et al. Band 1. Tübingen: Mohr Siebeck, 2007.
———. *Christus-König und Priester: Das Amt Christi bei Luther im Verhältnis zur Vor- und Nachgeschicte*. Tübingen: Mohr Siebeck, 1998.
Bosc, Jean. *The Kingly Office of the Lord Jesus Christ*, translated by A. K. S. Reid. Edinburgh: Oliver and Boyd, 1959.
Bourdieu, Pierre. *The Logic of Practice*, translated by R. Nice. Stanford: Stanford University Press, 1980.
———. *Outline of a Theory of Practice*, translated by R. Nice. Cambridge: Cambridge University Press, 1977.
Bråten, Stein, ed. *On Being Moved: From Mirror Neurons to Empathy*. Amsterdam: John Benjamins, 2007.
Briones, David E. "Paul's Financial Policy: A Socio-Theological Approach." Ph.D. diss., Durham, 2011.
Brown, Peter. *Augustine of Hippo: A Biography*. 2nd ed. Berkeley: University of California Press, 2000.
Brown, William P. *Psalms*. IBT. Nashville: Abingdon, 2010.
Brunner, Emil. *The Christian Doctrine of Creation and Redemption*, translated by O. Wyon. London: Lutterworth, 1952.
Bultmann, Rudolf. "Adam and Christ According to Romans 5." In *Current Issues in New Testament Interpretation: Essays in Honor of Otto A. Piper*, edited by W. Klassen and G. F. Snyder. New York: Harper & Brothers, 1962.
———. "New Testament and Mythology: The Problem of Demythologizing the New Testament Proclamation." In *New Testament and Mythology and Other Basic Writings*, edited by S. M. Ogden. Philadelphia: Fortress, 1984.
———. *Theology of the New Testament*. 2 vols. New York: Scribner, 1951; London: SCM Press, 1952.
Burns, J. Patout, trans. and ed. *Romans Interpreted by Early Christian Commentators*. The Church's Bible. Grand Rapids: Eerdmans, 2012.
Caird, G. B. *Principalities and Powers*. Oxford: Clarendon, 1956.
Calvin, John. *Institutes of the Christian Religion*. Edited by J. T. McNeil, translated by Ford Lewis Battles. Library of Christian Classics. Philadelphia: Westminster, 1960.

Cameron, Michael. *Christ Meets Me Everywhere: Augustine's Early Figurative Exegesis*. Oxford: Oxford University Press, 2012.
Campbell, Douglas A. *The Quest for Paul's Gospel: A Suggested Strategy*. London: T&T Clark/Continuum, 2005.
Carroll, Robert. "The Myth of the Empty Land." In *Ideological Criticism of Biblical Texts*, edited by David Jobling and Tina Pippins. Semeia 59. Atlanta: Society of Biblical Literature, 1992.
Cavanaugh, William. *Torture and Eucharist*. Oxford: Blackwell, 1998.
Chadwick, Henry. *Augustine of Hippo: A Life*. Oxford: Oxford University Press, 2009.
Clark, Andy. *Supersizing the Mind: Embodiment, Action, and Cognitive Extension*. Oxford: Oxford University Press, 2011.
Cottrill, Amy. *Language, Power, and Identity*. Edinburgh: T&T Clark, 2008.
Cranfield, C. E. B. *The Epistle to the Romans*. 2 vols. ICC. Edinburgh: T&T Clark, 1975, 1979.
———. *Romans 1–8*. ICC. Edinburgh: T&T Clark, 1975.
Cullmann. Oscar. "The Kingship of Christ and the Church in the New Testament." In *The Early Church*, translated by A. J. B. Higgins. London: SCM Press, 1956.
Dahl, Nils. "Missionary Theology in the Epistle to the Romans." In *Studies in Paul: Theology for the Early Christian Mission*. Minneapolis: Augsburg, 1977.
Danker, F. W. *Benefactor: Epigraphic Study of a Graeco-Roman Semantic Field*. St. Louis: Clayton, 1982.
Dantine, W. "Creation and Redemption III: Attempt at a Theological Understanding in the Light of the Contemporary Understanding of the World." *SJT* 18 (1965): 99.
———. "Regnum Christi—Gubernatio Dei. Dogmatische Überlegungen zum Begriff der 'Herrschaft.'" *TZ* 15 (1959): 195–208.
Davis, J. B., and D. Harink, eds. *Apocalyptic and the Future of Theology*. Eugene, Ore.: Wipf & Stock, Cascade Books, 2012.
Davis, Mike. *Late Victorian Holocausts: El Niño Famines and the Making of the Third World*. London: Verso, 2002.
de Boer, Martinus C. "The Defeat of Death: Apocalyptic Eschatology in 1 Corinthians 15 and Romans 5." JSNTSup 22. Sheffield: Sheffield Academic, 1988.
———. *Galatians*. Louisville: Westminster John Knox, 2011.
———. "Paul and Jewish Apocalyptic Eschatology." In *The Defeat of Death: Apocalyptic Eschatology in 1 Corinthians 15 and Romans 5*. JSNTSup 22. Sheffield: Sheffield Academic, 1988.

Works Cited

de Ste. Croix, G. E. M. *Class Struggle in the Ancient Greek World*. Ithaca, N.Y.: Cornell University Press, 1981.

Division of Studies of the World Council of Churches. "The Lordship of Christ over the Church and the World." *Ecumenical Review* 11 (1959): 437–49.

Dunn, James D. G. *Romans 1–8*. WBC 38a. Waco, Tex.: Word, 1988.

———. *Romans 9–16*. WBC 38b. Dallas: Word, 1988.

———. *Theology of Paul the Apostle*. Edinburgh: T&T Clark, 1998.

Elliott, Neil. *The Arrogance of Nations: Reading Romans in the Shadow of Empire*. Paul in Critical Contexts. Minneapolis: Fortress, 2008.

———. *Liberating Paul: The Justice of God and the Politics of the Apostle*. Maryknoll: Orbis, 1994.

———. *The Rhetoric of Romans: Argumentative Constraint and Strategy and Paul's Debate with Judaism*. JSNTSup 45. Sheffield: JSOT Press, 1990.

———. "Romans 13:1-7 in the Context of Imperial Propaganda." In *Paul and Empire: Religion and Power in Roman Imperial Society*, edited by Richard A. Horsley. Harrisburg, Pa.: Trinity Press International, 1997.

Elliott, Neil, and Mark Reasoner, ed. *Documents and Images for the Study of Paul*. Minneapolis: Fortress, 2010.

Engberg-Pedersen, Troels. *Cosmology and the Self in the Apostle Paul*. Oxford: Oxford University Press, 2010.

———. *Paul and the Stoics*. Edinburgh: T&T Clark, 2000.

Fox, George. *The Great Mystery*. The Works of George Fox. State College, Pa.: New Foundation Publications, 1990.

Fredriksen, Paula. *Augustine and the Jews: A Christian Defense of Jews and Judaism*. New Haven, Conn.: Yale University Press, 2010.

Friedman, Milton and Rose D. Friedman. *Two Lucky People: Memoirs*. Chicago: University of Chicago Press, 1998.

Furnish, V. P. *Theology and Ethics in Paul*. Nashville: Abingdon, 1968.

Gathercole, Simon J. "Sin in God's Economy: Agencies in Romans 1 and 7." In *Divine and Human Agency in Paul and His Cultural Environment*, edited by John M. G. Barclay and Simon J. Gathercole. London: T&T Clark, 2001.

Gaventa, Beverly Roberts. "The Cosmic Power of Sin in Paul's Letter to the Romans." In *Our Mother Saint Paul*. Louisville: Westminster John Knox, 2007.

———. "Maternal Imagery in Its Cosmic, Apocalyptic Context." In *Our Mother Saint Paul*. Louisville: Westminster John Knox, 2007.

———. "'Neither Height Nor Depth': Cosmos and Soteriology in Paul's Letter to the Romans." In Davis and Harink, *Apocalyptic and the Future of Theology*, 183–99.

———. "Neither Height nor Depth: Discerning the Cosmology of Romans." *SJT* 64 (2011): 265–78.

Giroux, Greg, and Jennifer Oldham. "Republicans Called Hypocrites Asking Own Aid Not Sandy's." *Bloomberg News* (18 January 2013). http://www.bloomberg.com/news/2013-01-18/republicans-called-hypocrites-asking-own-aid-not-sandy-s.html.

Godelier, Maurice. *The Enigma of the Gift*, translated by N. Scott. Chicago: University of Chicago Press, 1999.

Gottwald, Norman K. *The Politics of Ancient Israel*. Louisville: Westminster John Knox, 2001.

Gramsci, Antonio. *Selections from the Prison Notebooks*, edited and translated by Quintin Hoare and Geoffrey Nowell Smith. London: Lawrence & Wishart, 1971.

Gundry, Robert H. *Sôma in Biblical Theology, with emphasis on Pauline Anthropology*. Cambridge: Cambridge University Press, 1976.

Gupta, Arun. "Disaster Capitalism Hits New York: The City Will Adapt to Flooding—But at the Expense of the Poor?" *In These Times* 37 (2013): 24–27.

Gutiérrez, Gustavo. *A Theology of Liberation: History, Politics, and Salvation*, translated by Sister Caridad Inda and John Eagleson. Maryknoll: Orbis, 1973.

Hardt, Michael, and Antonio Negri. *Multitude: War and Democracy in the Age of Empire*. New York: Penguin, 2005.

Harnisch, Wolfgang. *Verhängnis und Verheissung der Geschichte. Untersuchung zum Zeit- und Geschichtsverständnis im 4. Buch Esra und syr. Baruchapokalypse*. FRLANT. Göttingen: Vandenhoeck & Ruprecht, 1969.

Harrison, Carol. *Rethinking Augustine's Early Theology*. Oxford: Oxford University Press, 2006.

Harrison, James R. *Paul's Language of Grace in its Graeco-Roman Context*. WUNT 2.172. Tübingen: Mohr Siebeck, 2003.

Hasselmann, Niels. "The Lordship of Christ in Ecumenical Discussion." *Lutheran Forum* 14 (1967): 93–101.

Haugeland, John. "Mind Embodied and Embedded." In *Having Thought; Essays in the Metaphysics of Mind*, edited by J. Haugeland. Cambridge, Mass.: Harvard University Press, 2000.

Henze, Matthias. "4 Ezra and 2 Baruch: Literary Composition and Oral Performance in First-Century Apocalyptic Literature." *JBL* 131 (2012): 181–200.

Heppe, Heinrich. *Reformed Dogmatics*, translated by G. T. Thompson. London: George Allen & Unwin, 1950.

Works Cited

Heschel, Abraham Joshua. *God in Search of Man*. New York: Farrar, Straus & Giroux, 1955.
Hillert, Sven. *Limited and Universal Salvation: A Text-Oriented and Hermeneutical Study of Two Perspectives in Paul*. Stockholm: Almqvist & Wiksell, 1999.
Hoepfner, Wolfram. "Modell des Pergamonaltars im Masstab 1:20." In *Der Pergamonaltar: Die neue Präsentation nach der Restaurierung des Telephosfrieses*, edited by Wolf-Dieter Heilmeyer. Tübingen: Ernst Wasmuth Verlag, 1997.
Hooft, W. A. Visser't. *The Kingship of Christ*. London: SCM Press, 1948.
Horrell, David G. *Solidarity and Difference: A Contemporary Reading of Paul's Ethics*. New York: Continuum, 2005.
Hultgren, Arland J. *Paul's Letter to the Romans: A Commentary*. Grand Rapids: Eerdmans, 2011.
Hurley, Susan, and Nick Chater, eds. *Perspectives on Imitation: From Neuroscience to Social Science*. Vol. 2. Cambridge, Mass.: MIT Press, 2005.
Jameson, Fredric. *The Political Unconscious*. Ithaca, N.Y.: Cornell University Press, 1981.
Janzen, J. Gerald. "Sin and the Deception of Devout Desire: Paul and the Commandment in Romans 7." *Encounter* 70 (2009): 29–61.
Jenkins, Richard. *Pierre Bourdieu*. London: Routledge, 1993.
Jervis, Ann. "Reading Romans 7 in Conversation with Post-colonial Theory: Paul's Struggle Toward a Christian Identity of Hybridity." *Theoforum* 35 (2004): 173–93.
Jewett, Robert. *Romans*. Minneapolis: Fortress, 2006.
Jüngel, Eberhard. "Der *königliche Mensch*. Eine christologische Reflexion auf die Würde des *Menschen* in der Theologie Karl Barths." In *Barth Studien*. Gütersloh: Gütersloher Verlaghaus, 1982.
Kahl, Brigitte. *Galatians Re-imagined: Reading with the Eyes of the Vanquished*. Paul in Critical Contexts. Minneapolis: Fortress, 2010.
Käsemann, Ernst. *An die Römer*. HNT. Tübingen: Mohr Siebeck, 1980.
———. *Commentary on Romans*, translated by G. W. Bromiley. Grand Rapids: Eerdmans, 1980.
———. "Healing the Possessed." In *On Being a Disciple of the Crucified Nazarene*, translated by R. A. Harrisville. Grand Rapids: Eerdmans, 2010.
———. *On Being a Disciple of the Crucified Nazarene*. Grand Rapids: Eerdmans, 2010.
———. "On Paul's Anthropology." In *Perspectives on Paul*, translated by M. Kohl. London: SCM Press, 1971; Philadelphia: Fortress, 1969.
———. "On the Subject of Primitive Christian Apocalyptic." In *New*

Testament Questions of Today, translated by W. J. Montague. London: SCM Press, 1969.

———. "One Lord Alone." *ExpTim* 110 (1999): 251.

———. *Perspectives on Paul*. Tübingen: J. C. B. Mohr, 1969. Reprint, translated by M. Kohl, Mifflintown, Pa.: Sigler, 1996.

———. "The Righteousness of God in Paul." In *New Testament Questions of Today*. London: SCM Press, 1969.

———. "What I Have Unlearned in 50 Years as a German Theologian." *CurTM* 15 (1988): 334–35.

Keck, Leander E. "The Absent Good: The Significance of Rom 7:18a." In *Text und Geschichte: Facetten theologischen Arbeitens aus dem Freundes und Schülerkreis, Dieter Lührmann zum 60 Geburtstag*, edited by Stefan Maser and Egbert Schlarb. Marburger Theologische Studien 50. Marburg: Elwert, 1999.

———. "*Pathos* in Romans? Mostly Preliminary Remarks." In *Paul and Pathos*, edited by Thomas H. Olbricht and Jerry L. Sumney. SBLSymS 16. Atlanta: Society of Biblical Literature, 2001.

———. *Romans*. ANTC. Nashville: Abingdon, 2005.

———. "What Makes Romans Tick?" In *Pauline Theology, vol. 3: Romans*, edited by David M. Hay and E. Elizabeth Johnson. Minneapolis: Fortress, 1995.

Keesmaat, Sylvia C. "The Psalms in Romans and Galatians." In *The Psalms in the New Testament*, edited by Steve Moyise and Maarten J. J. Menken. London: T&T Clark, 2004.

King, Anthony. "Thinking with Bourdieu against Bourdieu: A 'Practical' Critique of the Habitus." *ST* 18 (2000): 417–33.

Klein, Naomi. *The Shock Doctrine: The Rise of Disaster Capitalism*. New York: Metropolitan Books, 2007.

Klijn, A. F. J. "2 (Syriac Apocalypse of) Baruch." In *Apocalyptic Literature and Testaments*, vol. 1 of *The Old Testament Pseudepigrapha*, edited by J. H. Charlesworth. Garden City, N.Y.: Doubleday, 1983.

Lapsley, Jacqueline. *Can These Bones Live?* Berlin: De Gruyter, 2000.

Long, A. A. *From Epicurus to Epictetus*. Oxford: Oxford University Press, 2006.

Lopez, Davina C. *Apostle to the Conquered: Reimagining Paul's Mission*. Paul in Critical Contexts. Minneapolis: Fortress, 2008.

———. "Visual Perspectives." In *Studying Paul's Letters: Contemporary Perspectives and Methods*. Minneapolis: Fortress, 2012.

Luther, Martin. *Dr Martin Luthers Werke* [WA]. 69 vols. Weimar: Böhlau, 1883–1993.

Works Cited

———. "Freedom of a Christian." In *Martin Luther: Selections from His Work*, edited by J. Dillenberger. New York: Anchor, 1961.

———. *The Freedom of a Christian: Luther's Significance for Contemporary Theology*, translated by R. A. Harrisville. Minneapolis: Augsburg, 1988.

———. *Luther's Works* [LW]. 55 vols. St Louis: Concordia Publishing House; Philadelphia: Fortress, 1955–1986.

———. "Treatise on Good Works." In *Luther's Works*, edited by Jaroslav Pelikan. Philadelphia: Fortress, 1966.

Malherbe, A. J. *Paul and the Popular Philosophers*. Minneapolis: Fortress, 1989.

Martin, Dale B. *The Corinthian Body*. New Haven, Conn.: Yale University Press, 1995.

Martyn, J. Louis. "Apocalyptic Antinomies." In *Theological Issues in the Letters of Paul*. Edinburgh: T&T Clark, 1997.

———. "The Apocalyptic Gospel in Galatians." *Int* 54 (2000): 257–58.

———. "Comment #39." In *Galatians*. New York: Doubleday, 1997.

———. "Events in Galatia: Modified Covenantal Nomism versus God's Invasions of the Cosmos in the Singular Gospel." In *Pauline Theology I: Thessalonians, Philippians, Galatians, Philemon*, edited by Jouette M. Bassler. Minneapolis: Fortress, 1991.

———. "The Gospel Invades Philosophy." In *Paul, Philosophy, and the Theopolitical Vision*, ed. Douglas Harink, 13–33. Eugene, Ore.: Cascade Books, 2010.

———. *Theological Issues in the Letters of Paul*. Nashville: Abingdon, 1997.

Mauss, Marcel. *The Gift*, translated by W. D. Halls. London: Routledge, 1990.

Mays, James Luther. *Psalms*. Interpretation. Louisville: John Knox, 1994.

McMorris-Santoro, Evan. "Eric Cantor: We'll Pay For Post-Quake Relief—If We Can Find The Cuts." *Talking Points Memo*. August 25, 2011. http://tpmdc.talkingpointsmemo.com/2011/08/eric-cantor-well-pay-for-post-quake-relief----if-we-can-find-the-cuts-video.php.

Metzger, Bruce M. "The Fourth Book of Ezra." In *Apocalyptic Literature and Testaments*. Vol. 1 of *The Old Testament Pseudepigrapha*, edited by J. H. Charlesworth. Garden City, N.Y.: Doubleday, 1983.

———. "Paul and Jewish Apocalyptic Eschatology." In *Apocalyptic and the New Testament: Essays in Honor of J. Louis Martyn*, edited by Joel Marcus and Marion L. Soards. JSNTSup 24. Sheffield: Sheffield Academic, 1989.

———. *A Textual Commentary on the Greek New Testament*. 2nd ed. Stuttgart: German Bible Society, 1994.

Meyer, Paul. *The Word in the World*. Louisville: Westminster/John Knox, 2004.

———. "The Worm at the Core of the Apple: Exegetical Reflections on

Romans 7." In *The Conversation Continues: Studies in Paul and John in Honor of J. Louis Martyn*, edited by Robert T. Fortna and Beverly R. Gaventa. Nashville: Abingdon, 1990. Also included in *The Word in This World: Essays in New Testament Exegesis and Theology*, edited by John T. Carroll. Louisville: Westminster John Knox, 2004.

Miller, Patrick D. *The Ten Commandments*. Louisville: Westminster John Knox, 2009.

———. *They Cried to the Lord: The Form and Theology of Biblical Prayer*. Minneapolis: Fortress, 1994.

Montefiore, Claude G. *Judaism and St. Paul*. London: Max Goschen, 1914.

Moo, Douglas. *The Epistle to the Romans*. Grand Rapids: Eerdmans, 1996.

Morse, Christopher L. *The Difference Heaven Makes*. Edinburgh: T&T Clark, 2010.

———. "If Johannes Weiss Is Right: A Brief Retrospective on Apocalyptic Theology," in Davis and Harink, *Apocalyptic and the Future of Theology*, 131–53.

Müller, E. F. Karl. "Jesus Christ, Threefold Office of." In *New Schaff-Herzog Encyclopedia of Religious Knowledge*, edited by S. Macauley Jackson. Vol. 6. Reprint, Grand Rapids: Baker, 1953.

Newsom, Carol. "The Self as Symbolic Space: Constructing Identity and Community at Qumran." *STDJ* 52 (2004): 200.

O'Donnell, James J. *Augustine: Confessions*. 3 vols. Oxford: Clarendon, 1992.

Pannenberg, Wolfhart. *Jesus-God-Man*, translated by L. L. Wilkins and D. A. Priebe. Philadelphia: Westminster, 1976.

———. *Systematic Theology*, translated by G. W. Bromiley. London: T&T Clark/Continuum, 2004.

Patte, Daniel, and Eugene TeSelle, ed. *Engaging Augustine on Romans: Self, Context, and Theology in Interpretation*. London: T&T Clark, 2002.

Petrella, Ivan. *Beyond Liberation Theology: A Polemic*. London: SCM Press, 2008.

Portier-Young, Anathea E. *Apocalypse against Empire: Theologies of Resistance in Early Judaism*. Grand Rapids: Eerdmans, 2011.

Raisanen, Heikki. "A Controversial Jew and His Conflicting Convictions: Paul, the Law, and the Jewish People Twenty Years After." In *Redefining First-Century Jewish and Christian Identities: Essays in Honor of Ed Parish Sanders*, edited by Fabian E. Udoh, with Susannah Heschel, Mark Chancey, and Gregory Tatum. Notre Dame, Ind.: University of Notre Dame Press, 2008.

Ramsey, Boniface, trans. *Revisions*. Hyde Park, N.Y.: New City Press, 2010.

Works Cited

Reynolds, Kent Aaron. *Torah as Teacher: The Exemplary Torah Student in Psalm 119*. VTSup 137. Leiden: Brill, 2010.

Ritschl, Albrecht. *The Christian Doctrine of Justification and Reconciliation*, translated by H. R. Mackintosh. Edinburgh: T&T Clark, 1902.

———. "Instruction in the Christian Religion." In *Three Essays*, translated by P. Hefner. Philadelphia: Fortress, 1972.

Ritter, Joachim, Karlfried Gründer, and Gottfried Gabriel. *Historisches Wörterbuch der Philosophie*. 13 vols. Basel: Schwabe, 1971–2007.

Rossow, Francis C. "The Hound of Heaven, A Twitch upon the Thread, and Romans 8:31-39." *CJ* 23 (1997): 93.

Russell, D. S. *The Method and Message of Jewish Apocalyptic*. OTL. Philadelphia: Westminster, 1964.

Rutgers, Leonard Victor. "Roman Policy toward the Jews: Expulsions from the City of Rome during the First Century C.E." In *Judaism and Christianity in First-Century Rome*, edited by Karl P. Donfried and Peter Richardson. Grand Rapids: Eerdmans, 1998.

Sanders, E. P. *Paul and Palestinian Judaism*. Philadelphia: Fortress, 1977.

Schäfer, Peter. *Judeophobia: Attitudes toward the Jews in the Ancient World*. Cambridge, Mass.: Harvard University Press, 1997.

Schleiermacher, Friedrich D. E. *The Christian Faith*, translated by H. R. Mackintosh. Edinburgh: T&T Clark, 1928.

Schmid, Heinrich. *The Doctrinal Theology of the Evangelical Lutheran Church*, translated by C. A. Hay and H. E. Jacobs. 3rd ed. Minneapolis: Augsburg, 1961.

Schmid, Konrad. *The Old Testament: A Literary History*, translated by Linda A. Maloney. Minneapolis: Fortress, 2012.

Schnelle, Udo. *The Human Condition: Anthropology in the Teachings of Jesus, Paul, and John*. Minneapolis: Fortress, 1996.

Schweitzer, Albert. *The Mysticism of Paul the Apostle*. New York: Seabury, 1931.

Seifrid, Mark A. "Righteousness Language in the Hebrew Scriptures and Early Judaism." In *Justification and Variegated Nomism*, edited by D. A. Carson, Peter T. O'Brien, and Mark A. Seifrid. Tübingen: Mohr Siebeck, 2001.

———. "The Subject of Rom 7:14-25." *NovT* 34 (1992): 322–33.

Sherman, Robert J. *King, Priest and Prophet: A Trinitarian Theology of Atonement*. London: T&T Clark, 2004.

Silva, Moisés. "The Greek Psalter in Paul's Letters: A Textual Study." In *The Old Greek Psalter: Studies in Honour of Albert Pietersma*, edited by

Robert J. V. Hiebert, Claude E. Cox, and Peter J. Gentry. *JSOTSup* 332 (2001): 277–88.

Silverman, Kaja. *The Subject of Semiotics*. New York: Oxford University Press, 1984.

Slingerland, H. Dixon. *Claudian Policymaking and the Early Imperial Repression of Judaism at Rome*. Atlanta: Scholars Press, 1997.

Southall, David J. *Rediscovering Righteousness in Romans*. Tübingen: Mohr Siebeck, 2008.

Stegemann, Ekkehard W. "Coexistence and Transformation: Reading the Politics of Identity in Romans in an Imperial Context." In *Reading Paul in Context: Explorations in Identity Formation: Essays in Honour of William S. Campbell*, edited by Kathy Ehrensperger and J. Brian Tucker. Library of New Testament Studies 428. London: T&T Clark, 2010.

Stendahl, Krister. "The Apostle Paul and the Introspective Conscience of the West." *HTR* 56 (1963): 199–215 [a revision and translation of "Paulus och Samvetet." *Svensk exegetisk arsbok* 25 (1960): 62–77]. Reprinted in "The Apostle Paul and the Introspective Conscience of the West." In *Paul among Jews and Gentiles*, 78–96. Minneapolis: Fortress, 1976.

———. *Paul among Jews and Gentiles and Other Essays*. Philadelphia: Fortress, 1983.

Stock, Brian. *Augustine the Reader: Meditation, Self-Knowledge, and the Ethics of Interpretation*. Cambridge: Belknap, 1996.

———. *Augustine's Inner Dialogue: The Philosophical Soliloquy in Late Antiquity*. Cambridge: Cambridge University Press, 2010.

Stowers, Stanley K. *Cosmology and Self in the Apostle Paul: The Material Spirit*. New York: Oxford University Press, 2010.

———. *A Rereading of Romans: Justice, Jews, and Gentiles*. New Haven, Conn.: Yale University Press, 1994.

———. "Romans 7.7-25 as a Speech in Character (προσωποιία)." In *Paul in His Hellenistic Context*, edited by Troels Engberg-Pedersen. Minneapolis: Fortress, 1995.

Stuhlmacher, Peter. *Paul's Letter to the Romans: A Commentary*, translated by Scott J. Hafemann. Louisville: Westminster John Knox, 1994.

Tannehill, Robert C. *Dying and Rising with Christ: A Study in Pauline Theology*. Berlin: Töpelmann, 1967. Reprint, Eugene, Ore.: Wipf & Stock, 2006.

Taylor, Mark Lewis. *The Theological and the Political: On the Weight of the World*. Minneapolis: Fortress, 2011.

Thielicke, Helmut. *The Evangelical Faith*, translated by G. W. Bromiley. Edinburgh: T&T Clark, 1978.

Works Cited

———. *Theological Ethics*, translated by W. H. Lazareth. Philadelphia: Fortress, 1966–1969.

Thielman, Frank. *From Plight to Solution: A Jewish Framework for Understanding Paul's View of the Law in Galatians and Romans.* Leiden: Brill, 1989.

Tillich, Paul. "The Meaning of Providence [Romans 8:38-39]." In *Shaking of the Foundations.* New York: Charles Scribner's Sons, 1953.

Tobin, Thomas H., S. J. *Paul's Rhetoric in Its Contexts: The Argument of Romans.* Peabody, Mass.: Hendrickson, 2004.

Torrance, T. F. "The Eschatology of Hope: John Calvin." In *Kingdom and Church: A Study in the Theology of the Reformation.* Edinburgh: Oliver & Boyd, 1956.

———. *Incarnation: The Person and Life of Christ.* Downers Grove: InterVarsity, 2008.

VanDrunen, David. *Natural Law and the Two Kingdoms: A Study in the Development of Reformed Social Thought.* Grand Rapids: Eerdmans, 2010.

von Harnack, Adolf. *What Is Christianity?*, translated by T. B. Saunders. London: Williams and Norgate, 1901.

Wagner, J. Ross. "Paul and Scripture." In *The Blackwell Companion to Paul*, edited by Stephen Westerholm. Chichester: Blackwell, 2011.

Wainwright, Geoffrey. *For Our Salvation: Two Approaches to the Work of Christ.* Grand Rapids: Eerdmans, 1997.

Watts, James W., ed. *Persia and Torah: The Theory of Imperial Authorization of the Pentateuch.* SBLSymS 17. Atlanta: Society of Biblical Literature, 2001.

Weber, Otto. *Foundations of Dogmatics*, translated by D. L. Guder. Grand Rapids: Eerdmans, 1971.

Webster, John. *Barth's Ethics of Reconciliation.* Cambridge: Cambridge University Press, 1995.

Weiner, Annette B. *Inalienable Possessions: The Paradox of Keeping while Giving.* Berkeley: University of California Press, 1992.

Weissenrieder, Annette, Friedrike Wendt, and Petra von Gemünden, ed. *Picturing the New Testament.* WUNT 193. Tübingen: Mohr Siebeck, 2005.

Westerholm, Stephen. "Paul's Anthropological 'Pessimism' in Its Jewish Context." In *Divine and Human Agency in Paul and His Cultural Environment*, edited by John M. G. Barclay and Simon J. Gathercole. London: T&T Clark, 2006.

———. *Perspectives Old and New on Paul: The "Lutheran" Paul and His Critics.* Grand Rapids: Eerdmans, 2004.

Wetzel, James. "Predestination, Pelagianism, and Foreknowledge." In *The*

Cambridge Companion to Augustine, edited by Eleonore Stump and Norman Kretzmann. Cambridge: Cambridge University Press, 2001.

Wiefel, Wolfgang. "The Jewish Community in Ancient Rome and the Origins of Roman Christianity." In *The Romans Debate*, edited by Karl P. Donfried, rev. and exp. ed. Peabody, Mass.: Hendrickson, 1991.

Wilentz, Amy. "Letter from Haiti." *The Nation* 296 (2013): 21–26.

Williams, Sam K. "The 'Righteousness of God' in Romans." *JBL* 99 (1980): 241–90.

Winger, Michael. "From Grace to Sin: Names and Abstractions in Paul's Letter." *NovT* 41 (1999): 145–75.

Winninge, Mikael. *Sinners and the Righteous: A Comparative Study of the Psalms of Solomon and Paul's Letters*. Stockholm: Almqvist & Wiksell, 1995.

Witherington III, Ben. *Paul's Letter to the Romans: A Socio-Rhetorical Commentary*. Grand Rapids: Eerdmans, 2004.

Wright, N. T. *Justification: God's Plan and Paul's Vision*. Downers Grove, Ill.: IVP Academic, 2009.

———. "Paul in Current Anglophone Scholarship." *ExpT* 123 (2012): 367–81.

Zanker, Paul. *The Power of Images in the Age of Augustus*, translated by Alan Shapiro. Ann Arbor: University of Michigan Press, 1988.

Ziegler, Philip. "'Christ Must Reign': Ernst Käsemann and Soteriology in an Apocalyptic Key." In Davis and Harink, *Apocalyptic and the Future of Theology*, 200–18.

Ziesler, Paul. *Paul's Letter to the Romans*. London: SCM Press, 1989.

List of Contributors

JOHN M. G. BARCLAY
Lightfoot Professor of Divinity, Durham University

MARTINUS C. DE BOER
Professor of New Testament, Vrije Universiteit Amsterdam

SUSAN EASTMAN
Associate Professor of the Practice of Bible and Christian Formation, Duke Divinity School

NEIL ELLIOTT
Acquisitions Editor in Biblical Studies, Fortress Press
Adjunct Professor, United Theological Seminary of the Twin Cities
Adjunct Instructor, Metropolitan State University

BEVERLY ROBERTS GAVENTA
Helen H. P. Manson Professor of New Testament Literature and Exegesis Emerita, Princeton Theological Seminary
Distinguished Professor of New Testament Interpretation, Baylor University

J. LOUIS MARTYN
Edward Robinson Professor Emeritus of Biblical Theology
Union Theological Seminary

BENJAMIN MYERS
Lecturer in Systematic Theology, Charles Sturt University

STEPHEN WESTERHOLM
Professor of Early Christianity, Department of Religious Studies, McMaster University

PHILIP G. ZIEGLER
Senior Lecturer in Systematic Theology, University of Aberdeen

Index of Ancient Sources

I: Greek and Latin Sources		
Cicero		
Of the Consular Provinces		
5:10	145n36	
Josephus		
Against Apion		
1.246	63n11	
Jewish Antiquities		
19.5.2-3	145n38	
Suetonius		
Divus Claudius		
25.4	146n39	
Virgil		
Aeneid		
6.789–94	153n54	
Fourth Eclogue		
11–41	153n54	
II: Jewish Sources		
Dead Sea Scrolls		
CD		
III, 20	9	
1QH		
XVII, 15	9	
1QS		
IV, 23	9	
Old Testament Pseudepigrapha		
Apocalypse of Moses		
20:2	9	
21:6	9	
39:2-3	9	
2 Baruch		
14:15-19	12	
15:8	16	
19:1	15	
23:4	12	
38:1	10	
42:7-8	15	
44:3, 7-15	15	
46:3	15	
48:38-40	15	
48:46	12	
48:47, 50	15	
51:3	9, 15	
51:7-8, 16	15	
54:15	9, 12	
54:15-16	15	
54:18	12–13	
54:19	12	
54:21	9	
56:6	12	
84:2	15	
2 Esdras		
3–14	3n4	
4 Ezra		
3:7	12	
3:20, 21-22, 26	15	
4:4	15	

7:13, 17, 21, 45	16	Job	
7:48	15–16	4:17-19	29
7:50, 77, 89, 92, 97	16	12:4	27
7:113	16	15:14-16	29
7:118-20	12	22:19	27
7:122-25	9	25:4-6	29
7:127-29	16	Psalms	
8:33, 36	16	1:6	27
8:60	12	2:6, 7	81n14
9:36	15–16	5:8 (LXX)	82n18
14:30	10, 16	12:6 (LXX)	82n18
Sirach		16:4, 6 (LXX)	82n17
15:12-15	161n5	16:15 (LXX)	82n17, 82n18
17:11	10	17	82–84
45:5	10	17:6	82
Wisdom of Solomon		17:9	83
10:1	17	17:13	83
		19	81n12
III: Biblical Sources		21:7 (LXX)	82n18
Old Testament		22	86n27
Genesis		22:1	55
1	136	23:3	29n8
1:2	137	25:1 (LXX)	82n17
2:17	12	25:11 (LXX)	82n17, 82n18
3	11, 49–50, 152, 152n53	30:7, 15, 23 (LXX)	82n17, 82n18
3:7	53	32:11	27
3:19	12	34:13 (LXX)	82n18
6:9	27–28	35:3	81n14
7:1	28	37:14 (LXX)	82n17, 82n18
15:6	23, 26	37:18, 19 (LXX)	82n17
18:24	29	38:5, 11, 13 (LXX)	82n17
18:25	27	39:18 (LXX)	82n18
Exodus		46:10	81n14
23:7	30	50:7	81n14
Leviticus		51	86n27
19:35-36	29n8	54:17, 24 (LXX)	82n17, 82n18
Numbers		55:4 (LXX)	82n18
15:30-31	32	58:17 (LXX)	82n18
Deuteronomy		64:10	27
4:6-8	29	68:14 (LXX)	82n17, 82n18
25:1	30	68:15, 21 (LXX)	84
30:19	15–16	68:24 (LXX)	83
1 Kings		68:30 (LXX)	82n17
21:1-19	30	69	82–84, 86n27
Ezra		69:5	83
9:9	145n36	69:6 (LXX)	82n18

69:9	84	25:21-22	105
69:13	83	28:6	28
69:22	84	29:7	28
69:29	83–84	30:12	28
70:14 (LXX)	82n17, 82n18	Isaiah	
70:22 (LXX)	82n17	5:23	30
75:2, 3	81n14	26:13	111
81:10	81n14	Ezekiel	
94:21	27	11:19	164n13
97:11	27	18:5-9	27
108:4 (LXX)	82n17, 82n18		
108:22, 25 (LXX)	82n17	**New Testament**	
118 (LXX)	82n17, 84	Matthew	
118:19, 63, 67 (LXX)	82n17	5:20	21n1
118:69, 70, 78, 87 (LXX)	82n17, 82n18	7:13-14	21n1, 22
		7:21	21n1
118:94, 125, 141, 162 (LXX)	82n17	10:34-35	22
119	81n12, 82, 84, 84n24, 87n30	10:36	25
119:19, 42, 61	84	10:37-39	22
119:63	85, 87	11:2-6, 28	21
119:67, 69, 70	85	12:30	21–22
119:78	84–85	16:24-25	22
119:82-84, 86	84	19:16-26	22
119:87	85, 87	19:21	54
119:94	85	Mark	
119:95, 125	84	1:14-15, 16-20	21
119:141, 162	85	9:43-48	21n1
130:3-4	29	10:15, 23-27	21n1
143:2	29	Luke	
Proverbs		12:9	54
1:7	28	13:23-24	22
3:7, 19	28	John	
8:12-36	28	18:36	115
10:3, 24, 27	28	Acts	
11:8, 31	28	18:12-14	166n18
12:1	29	Romans	
12:10	27–28	1	101n17
12:15, 21	28	1–3	13, 33n14, 64, 101
13:5	28	1–4	2, 7
13:18	29	1–8	100n16, 148n46, 149
13:25	28	1:1	62
15:5	29	1:5	24, 148
15:17	30	1:6	148
16:2	28	1:7	43
19:22	28	1:8	8
21:2, 26	28	1:8-15	78n2, 98

1:8-16	97n8	3:21	6, 17		
1:13	148	3:22	6		
1:14	63	3:23	9, 14		
1:16	165	3:24	59		
1:16-17	19, 148	3:24-26	33, 36		
1:17	2, 6, 34n15	3:25	32		
1:18	9, 14n37, 31, 99	3:28	17		
1:18-32	88, 148	3:29	24		
1:18-3:20	88	4	23, 64, 88		
1:18-5:21	99	4:1-25	1–2		
1:21	51	4:3	23		
1:22	51–52	4:4	59		
1:24, 26	99	4:5	23, 34		
1:28	17, 99	4:9-12	24		
1:28-32	13	4:11	23		
1:30	101	4:11-12	23		
1:32	14, 14n37	4:13	8, 23		
2:1	88, 99, 106	4:15	14n37		
2:1-11	97n8, 99	4:16	59		
2:2	88	4:17	51		
2:5	14n37, 99	4:18	23		
2:5-8	16	4:19	24		
2:7-10	31	4:23-24	23		
2:8	14n37	4:25	17		
2:11	31	5	2, 7, 10-11, 22-23, 37, 40–41, 46–47, 55, 57, 59, 88–89, 161		
2:12	2				
2:12-17	1	5–6	63, 77, 102		
2:13	16, 31	5–8	1–2, 93, 96–98, 117, 124		
2:16	99	5:1	8n27, 22–23, 27, 34, 36		
2:17-22	31	5:1-2	7, 20, 34		
2:17-23	98n8	5:1-2a	7		
2:17-24	88	5:1-11	8		
2:17-27	99	5:1-21	2		
3	88	5:1–7:7	107		
3–5	33	5:5	8		
3:4-30	2	5:5-8	59		
3:5	6, 88	5:6-10	31n11		
3:5-7	99	5:8	33		
3:7	78	5:8-10	8		
3:9	14, 19, 99, 163	5:8-11	89		
3:10	30, 32	5:9	7, 14n37, 33, 99		
3:12	31	5:10	7–8, 14n37, 32		
3:15	14n37	5:11	7, 36		
3:19	8, 16–17, 88, 163	5:11-21	66n16		
3:19-31	1	5:12	8, 11–12, 14, 35, 163		
3:20	17, 32	5:12-14	59, 161		

5:12-19	35, 99	6:12-14	100
5:12-21	8–9, 13–14, 14n37, 17, 19, 55, 59, 65, 99, 161–62	6:12-21	69
		6:13	68, 71–72, 103, 107
5:12–7:6	99–100	6:13-20	2
5:12–8:3	19	6:14	2, 10, 60, 100, 103, 124n50
5:12–8:39	65	6:14-15	1, 14
5:12f.	122	6:15	2
5:12a	8, 11–12	6:15-23	60
5:12b	11–12	6:16	37
5:12d	14	6:16b	14
5:13	1, 10, 14, 17	6:17	62
5:13-14	35	6:17-19	100
5:14	9, 17, 100	6:18	31, 60, 62
5:14-21	59	6:19	31, 61–62, 66n16, 67–68, 73
5:15	9, 17, 59	6:21b	14
5:15-19	36	6:22	60, 62
5:16	35, 59	6:23	37, 73
5:17	10, 17, 35-36, 59, 100, 124n50, 161, 166n20	6:23a	14
		7	50–52, 55, 57, 67, 77–78, 79n4, 81–82, 81n12, 84, 84n24, 86–91, 98, 100, 101n17, 107–9, 162
5:18	10, 17, 35		
5:18-19	9		
5:19	9, 22, 27, 35, 59, 76, 161		
5:20	1, 10, 14, 17, 59, 161	7–8	65-66, 107
5:20-21	20, 60	7:1-4	72
5:21	8, 10, 17, 20, 59–60, 100, 124n50, 161	7:1–8:4	1
		7:4	65, 89
5:21a	14	7:5	66–67, 66n15, 66n16, 71, 102
5:21b	8, 8n27	7:5b	14
6	8, 37, 60–61, 70n24, 71n27, 72, 75, 100, 103	7.5-6	66n15
		7:6	65, 100
6–8	7, 65-66, 69, 109	7:7	89, 89n32
6:1	89	7:7-11	66n16
6:1-11	65	7:7-13	32, 90, 90n33
6:2-3	103	7:7-25	66, 66n15, 66n16, 93, 97n8, 98n8, 100, 102, 102n21, 104–5, 104n23, 107
6:4	60, 65, 75, 89		
6:5	65		
6:6	56, 60, 66–67, 71	7:7–8:8	19
6:6-7	103	7:7–8:11	104n23
6:7	2	7:9	86, 90n33
6:8	65	7:10	90n33
6:9	65, 124n50	7:11	101, 105, 109, 162n8
6:11	65, 66n16, 67, 103–4	7:12	71, 86
6:11-13	69	7:12-14	18
6:11-23	62	7:13	43, 101
6:12	60, 65, 124n50	7:14	66n15, 87, 90n33
6:12-13	67	7:14-15	90n33

Index of Ancient Sources — 187

7:14-20	101	8:20b	17
7:14-25	90, 90n34	8:23	66n15, 69, 155
7:15	101	8:24-25	121
7:15-17	93–94	8:28	115–16, 125
7:16	101	8:30	2
7:16-17	51	8:31	119, 126
7:17	14, 51, 71, 90n33, 109	8:31-39	117, 126, 128
7:18	32, 101	8:32	73
7:19	78n3, 101	8:32-33	120
7:19-20	94	8:32-34	126
7:19-21	101, 105	8:33	2, 119, 127
7:20	51, 71, 90n33, 101, 104n23, 109	8:34	125
		8:35	119, 122
7:20a	78n2	8:36	120
7:21	101	8:37	120, 127
7:22	51–52, 86, 101	8:38	13, 162
7:22-25	101	8:38-39	123n49, 125, 149
7:23	67, 71, 101	8:39	119, 122, 127
7:24	65, 66n15, 69, 71, 83, 87, 90n33, 98–99	9	2, 134, 144, 148–49, 151
		9–10	2, 150
7:24-25	51–52	9–11	2, 64, 131, 148–49
7:25	67, 90n33	9:1-3	97n8
7:25a	87, 107	9:1-4	148n45, 152
7:25b	77, 107	9:1-5	148, 148n46
8	6n21, 37, 102, 104, 115, 117–19, 125, 127, 131, 134, 144, 148–49, 151–52, 156	9:3	149
		9:24	42
		9:27-29	35
8:1	93, 98, 106–7	9:30-10:10	2
8:1-2	93, 103	9:31-10:5	1
8:1-4	87, 104	10	2
8:1ff.	66n15	10:1-2	97n8
8:2	18, 77, 98–101, 98n8, 104–5	10:4-5	98n8
8:3	17, 35, 66n16, 107	10:5-10	26
8:4	104	10:6	24
8:6-8	69	10:8-13	98n8
8:7-8	32	10:10	24
8:9-11	74	10:17	25, 165
8:9-24	124–25	11:1	97n8, 98n8
8:10	2, 65–66	11:11	17, 97n8
8:11	53, 65–66, 68–69, 104	11:13-36	146
8:12-13	69	11:14	35
8:13	38, 69, 75	11:17-22	98n8
8:13-14	74	11:19-10	84
8:15	36, 61–62	11:22	17
8:18	119	11:25	97n8, 151
8:19	152	11:26	151

Index of Ancient Sources

11:29	151	15:14-32	97n8		
11:32	37	15:20, 23-33, 24-25	1		
12–14	105	15:27	63		
12–15	69, 72	15:28	1		
12:1	68, 71, 97n8	15:31	1, 2		
12:1-2	69, 96	16:1	97n8		
12:2	68, 72, 155	16:1-16	98		
12:3	62, 97n8	16:17, 19	97n8		
12:3-8	98n8, 105	16:20	13, 121, 162		
12:4	106	1 Corinthians			
12:6-7	72	1	33		
12:7	106	1:18	36–37		
12:9-13	105	1:18-20	160		
12:10	72	1:21	25n2		
12:11	62	1:27	33		
12:12	72, 106	2:12	36		
12:14-21	72, 105	4:9	13, 162		
12:15	72	5:5	13, 162		
12:20	105	6:3	13, 162		
12:21	98n8, 105, 106n25	6:6	24		
13:1, 3, 4	98n8	7:5	13, 162		
13:8-10	1	7:12-13, 21	25		
13:12	151	9:19-22	35		
13:13	71	10:20-21	13, 162		
13:13-14	51, 53, 72	10:27	24		
13:14	68	11	165		
14	106	12:12-26	67n17		
14–15	1	14:22-24	24		
14:1	51	15	9-11, 19		
14:1-12	98n8	15:13, 17	11		
14:3	99	15:20-28	166n19		
14:4	62, 99, 106	15:21	10		
14:5	99	15:21-22	9		
14:6-8	72	15:22	10, 37		
14:10	99, 106	15:25	124		
14:12	106	15:25-26	19		
14:13	99	15:42-44	68		
14:14	72	2 Corinthians			
14:15-16	98n8	2:11	13, 162		
14:17	2, 72	2:15	37		
14:20	72	2:15-16	24		
14:20-22	98n8	3:7, 9	32		
14:22	99, 106n26	4:3	37		
15:1-5	72	4:4	13, 162		
15:3	84	4:10-11	68		
15:14	148	5:14-15	25		

5:17	36, 37	3:6	87n29
5:19	8	3:9	26
5:19-20	22	3:18	162n8
5:20	34	4:2	166n18
5:21	6	Colossians	
6:1	36	1:5-6	25
6:1-2	37	1:20	37
6:14	13, 31, 162	2:17	32
11:4	26	3:6	38
11:14	13, 162	1 Thessalonians	
12:7	13, 162	1:6	36
Galatians		1:7	24
1:23	24	1:10	31
2:20	25, 25n3, 94	2:10	24
2:21	19, 26, 33	2:12	73
3	123n49	2:13	22, 24–25, 36
3:2	36	2:18	13, 162
3:6-7	23	3:5	13, 162
3:6-9, 11-12	26	3:13	73
3:13	45	5:3	31
3:14	36	5:9	22
3:21	19	2 Thessalonians	
4:4	35	1:8	24
4:6	45, 164	2:14	25
4:8	120	3:1	25
4:12	62n6	Philemon	
5	6n21, 164	10-11	25
5:1	122	Hebrews	
5:4	26	10:1	32
5:16	5n15	10:4	32
5:17-24	164	Revelation	
5:20	53	2:12	140
6:1-2, 3-5	166n18		
6:4-5	106n27	**IV: Non-Canonical Early**	
6:8	32, 75	**Christian Writings**	
6:10	166n19	Augustine	
6:16	36	*Confessions*	
Ephesians		2.1.1	49
1:10	37	2.2.3	49
5:5-6	38	2.2.4	49
5:14	53	2.3.5	49
6:12	121	2.3.6	49
Philippians		2.4.9	49-50
1:29	25	2.5.11	50
2:8	35	2.6.12	50
2:12-13	166	2.6.14	50

2.8.16	50, 54	22.16	45
2.10.18	50	25.10	46
8.2.4	54	24.6	46
8.4.9	55	31.2	45
8.5.10	52	*Exp. Prop. Rom.*	
8.5.12	52–53	29.6	43
8.6.14	54	32–34.3	43
8.6.15	54	35.2	43
8.8.19	52–53	36.5	43
8.8.19-20	52	43.2-3	43
8.10.22	52	44.3	42
8.11.25	53	46.7	43
8.11.27	55	47.2	42
8.12.19	54	48.4	43
8.12.28	53	58.4	43
8.12.29	54	64.2	42
Enarrations in Psalmos		64.3	42
37.27	56	66.1	42
58.10	58	66.2	42
Ep. Rom. inch.		68.3	42
1.1	43	82.1	42
1.4	44	82.4	42
4.3	44	*Retractions*	
6.4	44	1.25	43
Exp. Gal.			
1.5	45		

Index of Authors

Acolatse, Esther E., 97n7
Adams, Edward, 125, 125n56
Aernie, Jeff, 39n*
Ambrosiaster, 86
Anselm, 128

Barclay, John M. G., 61n4, 64n13, 72n28, 73n30, 104n23, 106n26, 160n3, 161, 162n7, 163–64
Barth, Karl, 76n32, 112, 119n29, 120, 121n35, 123, 128n68
Belichick, Bill, 30
Benveniste, Emile, 79–80, 79n7, 81n15
Berkouwer, G. C., 112n4

Berlin, Adele, 83n20
Blenkinsopp, Joseph, 136n16
Bobzein, Susanne, 161n5
Boman, Jobjorn, 146n39
Borden, Ali, 107–10
Boring, M. Eugene, 38n18
Bornkamm, Karin, 111n1
Bosc, Jean, 113n6, 113n7, 119n28, 130n76
Bourdieu, Pierre, 69–71, 70n24
Briones, David E., 63n10
Brown, Peter, 47
Brown, William P., 84, 86, 86n25
Brunner, Emil, 114n8, 128n66
Bultmann, Rudolf, 1, 3–7, 3n7, 4n12,

4n14, 5n15, 11n32, 18n40, 30n10, 62, 67–68, 71, 94
Burns, J. Patout, 86n26

Caird, G. B., 125n58, 130n75
Calvin, John, 111n1, 113–18, 114n8, 114n10
Cameron, Michael, 40n7
Campbell, Douglas A., 122n43
Carroll, Robert, 136n16
Cavanaugh, William, 156n61
Chadwick, Henry, 49n49, 58n87
Clark, Andy, 95n4
Cottrill, Amy, 86n25
Cranfield, C. E. B., 62n5, 66n16, 67n17, 79n4
Cullmann, Oscar, 126n59

Dahl, Nils, 148n45
Danker, F. W., 63n9
Dantine, W., 129n73
David, J. B., 160n3
Davis, Mike, 133n6, 161n6
de Boer, Martinus, 3n5, 6n20, 8n28, 10n31, 18n40, 161–64, 162n8
de Ste. Croix, G. E. M., 141n29
Dickens, Charles, 80
Dunn, James D. G., 18, 66n16, 96n5, 106n25

Eastman, Susan, 161n5, 163n11, 164, 164n14
Elliott, Neil, 141n29, 141n30, 141n31, 142–43, 144n34, 144n35, 145n37, 145n38, 146n39, 147n41, 148n43, 148n44, 148n46, 150n47, 150n48, 150n51, 153n54, 154
Engberg-Pedersen, Troels, 62n5, 71n27, 102, 102n21, 104n23
Epston, David, 107–10

Fox, George, 121
Fredriksen, Paula, 44n34
Friedman, Milton, 132–34, 133n5
Furnish, Victor, 148n45

Gathercole, Simon J., 101n17, 160n3
Gaventa, Beverly, 3n5, 13n34, 19n42, 19n43, 20n46, 39n*, 80, 91n35, 120n33, 124, 125n56, 131n1, 157n1, 160–64
Godelier, Maurice, 64n12
Gottwald, Norman K., 136n16
Gramsci, Antonio, 137n18
Gundry, Robert H., 68n19
Gutiérrez, Gustavo, 134n9

Hardt, Michael, 156
Harink, D., 160n3, 161n6
Harnisch, Wolfgang, 16n38
Harrison, Carol, 40n7
Harrison, James R., 63n9
Hasselmann, Niels, 113n5
Hauerwas, Stanley, 103
Haugeland, John, 95n4
Henze, Matthias, 11n33
Heppe, Heinrich, 111n1, 116n20
Herschel, Abraham Joshua, 161n7
Hillert, Sven, 38n18
Hoepfner, Wolfram, 140n28
Hooft, W. A. Visser't, 113n6
Horrell, David G., 105n24
Hultgren, Arland, J., 37n17, 79n4

Jameson, Fredric, 155n59
Janzen, J. Gerald, 81n12, 84n24
Jenkins, Richard, 70n22
Jervis, Ann, 88n31
Jewett, Robert, 40, 67n17, 78n3, 96, 99, 106n25, 106n26, 119n30, 120n31, 122n42, 125n56, 148n46, 152–55, 152n53, 153n54, 154n57, 161n5
Joyce, James, 48
Jüngel, Eberhard, 116n17, 119n29

Kahl, Brigitte, 138–40, 138n24, 154
Käsemann, Ernst, 5–7, 6n20, 6n21, 14, 18n40, 19, 62–64, 62n6, 62n7, 67–68, 94–95, 106n25, 117n23, 119n27, 121–23, 122n44, 124n50,

Index of Authors

124n52, 127n63, 129n70, 130, 130n74, 161, 165n17
Keck, Leander E., 100n15, 100n16, 102n19, 106n25
Keesmaat, Sylvia C., 81n13
King, Anthony, 70n22
Klein, Naomi, 132–37, 132n4, 133n5, 133n6, 134n7, 135n13, 136n15, 155
Klijn, Albertus F. J., 3n4

Lapsley, J., 164n13
Lodge, David, 79n7
Long, A. A., 160n4
Lopez, Davina C., 138n24, 154
Luther, Martin, 25, 25n3, 39, 60–61, 61n3, 65–66, 111n1, 115–17, 130

Maisel, Richard, 107–10
Malherbe, A. J., 160n4
Martin, Dale, 95–96, 95n4, 161n5
Martyn, J. Louis, 73n29, 123n47, 123n49, 127, 147, 147n42, 164n15
Mauss, Marcel, 63n9
Mays, James Luther, 84
Metzger, Bruce M., 3n4, 98n9
Meyer, Paul W., 77–78, 77n1, 81n12, 87n28, 90, 101n18, 106n25, 127n61, 162
Miller, Patrick D., 84n24, 89n32
Montefiore, Claude G., 32n12
Moo, Douglas, 126n59, 126n60
Morse, Christopher L., 161n7
Müller, E. F. Karl, 113
Myers, Ben, 160n4

Negri, Antonio, 156
Newsom, Carol, 80n9, 81n11
Newton, John, 80

O'Donnell, James, 51

Pannenberg, Wolfhart, 112n2, 129n71
Petrella, Ivan, 134–35
Plumer, Eric, 47

Portier-Young, Anathea E., 137–38, 137n18, 137n20, 145, 150–51
Powery, Emerson, 62n6
Powery, Luke, 157n1

Räisänen, Heikki, 37n16
Reasoner, Mark, 141n29, 141n30, 141n31, 145n37, 145n38, 146n39
Reynolds, Kent Aaron, 84n24, 87n30
Ritschl, Albrecht, 112n2, 118
Rossow, Francis C., 124n54, 127n62
Rutgers, Leonard, 146

Sanders, E. P., 32n12, 32n13, 43
Schäfer, Peter, 145n37
Schleiermacher, Friedrich D. E., 116, 116n20
Schmid, Heinrich, 111n1, 116n20
Schmid, Konrad, 137n17
Schmitt, Mary, 39n*
Schnelle, Udo, 166n19
Schweitzer, Albert, 26, 113
Seifrid, Mark A., 29n9, 81n12
Sherman, Robert J., 112n4
Silva, Moisés, 81n13
Silverman, Kaja, 79, 80
Slingerland, H. Dixon, 146
Southhall, David J., 26n5
Stegemann, Ekkehard W., 150n51
Stendahl, Krister, 32n12, 39–40
Stock, Brian, 41n8, 48n48, 55n84, 55n85
Stowers, Stanley K., 79n5, 98–99, 102n20, 102n21, 104n23, 106n25, 153n54
Stuhlmacher, Peter, 81n12, 86n27, 90n34, 128n65, 128n69

Tannehill, Robert, 99, 100n14
Taylor, Mark Lewis, 135, 135n11, 156
Thielicke, Helmut, 128n69, 129n72
Thielman, Frank, 33n14
Tillich, Paul, 121n39
Tobin, Thomas H., 79n5, 89n32

Torrance, T. F., 114n10, 114n12, 124n53, 127n61

VanDrunen, David, 116n18
von Harnack, Adolf, 117, 118
von Gemünden, Petra, 138n24

Wagner, Ross, 81n13
Wainwright, Geoffrey, 112n4
Watts, James W., 137n17
Weber, Otto, 118–19
Webster, John, 76n32
Weiner, Annette B., 64n12
Weiss, Bernhard, 113
Weissenrieder, Annette, 138n24
Wendt, Friedrike, 138n24

Westerholm, Stephen, 26n5, 31n11, 33n14, 40
Wetzel, James, 46n42
Wiefel, Wolfgang, 147n41
Williams, Sam K., 34n15
Winger, Michael, 20n45
Winninge, Mikael, 31n11
Witherington III, Ben, 120n31, 127n63, 148n46
Wright, N. T., 18n41, 27n6, 30n10
Wright, Steve, 39n*

Zanker, Paul, 138n24, 144n33
Ziegler, Philip, 161n6, 163n12
Ziesler, Paul, 124n51

Subject Index

Abraham, 23–26, 27n6, 38, 64, 88
Adam–Christ typology, 8–15, 17–19, 19n42, 35–37, 40–41, 43, 46, 48–50, 52–58, 60, 65–66, 66n16, 89, 99, 100n16, 123, 152, 152n53, 161–63, 166
Aeneas, 141–44, 143n32
Altar of Augustan Peace, 141–44, 154
anthropology, 3, 3n7, 5–6, 11, 14, 24, 32, 63, 65, 67–69, 94–95, 122, 166
apocalypse, 2–3, 11, 18, 123n49, 127, 137–38, 150–51
apocalyptic, 4–7, 6n20, 9, 11–12, 13n35, 14, 17–18, 18n40, 18n41, 22, 91, 113, 115–16, 118–19, 121–23, 123n49, 126n59, 128, 136–38, 151, 153n54, 160n3, 161, 163
Augustus, 140–41, 141n29, 143–46, 143n32, 144n33, 144n34, 151, 153n54, 154n57

baptism, 41, 60, 66n16, 67, 71, 73–74, 103

body (σῶμα), 5, 23, 52, 60, 65–73, 70n24, 71n27, 75, 87, 94–96, 95n4, 99, 102–3, 105, 109, 116, 122, 130

Christ, crucifixion and death of, 7–8, 14n37, 19–20, 25n3, 33, 35, 37–38, 56, 60, 94, 98, 103, 118–19, 122, 124, 127; 129; kingship and royal office of, 111, 113–19, 120–21, 125–26, 128–30; reign of, 114n10, 117, 124, 124n50
Claudius, 145–46, 145n38
conversion, 56, 155; of Augustine, 40–41, 48, 51–55; of Paul, 33n14, 79, 81n12, 84n24
corporate, collective, communal humanity, 11–12, 25, 41, 43, 46–50, 53–58, 72, 93–96, 97n7, 98–107, 106n25, 109–10, 118–19, 122, 124, 129, 133–34, 149, 164–66, 166n18, 166n20
cosmic, 4n14, 6–12, 15–17, 21–22, 34, 48–49, 81, 90–91, 95, 102–103,

124, 129, 137, 162n8; battle and warfare, 5–6, 63, 91, 103–4, 109, 123, 123n49
creation, 5, 31, 33, 124–26, 128, 131, 135–38, 144–45, 149, 138n25, 151–53, 152n53, 153n54, 155; fallen, 35, 121, 123, 152, 156; new, 27n6, 36–38, 65, 125, 155, 164–65; of the world, 136, 151–52

demythologization, 1, 4–5, 5n15

economics, 70, 70n24, 132–35, 133n5, 153
eschatology, 4–5, 6n20, 11, 18n40, 27n6; de-eschatologization, 137n17; eschatological, 6n21, 14n37, 15, 34n15, 68, 73, 113n7, 115, 118–119, 121, 124, 126, 127n61, 128–30
ethics, 27, 30, 69–70, 72, 118, 129n72
evil, 13, 15–16, 34, 50, 94, 99, 101–2, 104n23, 105, 107, 109, 162; present age of, 16, 34
existentialism and existence, 3–5, 3n7, 5n15, 6n20, 22–25, 38, 62, 66, 68, 93–96, 95n4, 104–5, 107

faith, 4, 5n15, 7–8, 8n27, 17, 23–27, 25n3, 29, 31n11, 34, 34n15, 36, 38, 42, 44–45, 51, 76, 106n26, 115, 119–21, 124–25, 129–30, 134, 135n11, 165, 165n16
faithfulness of Christ, 23; of God, 124; of humans, 31n11, 86, 91, 130, 136, 161n5
flesh, 2, 6n21, 32, 34–35, 38, 44, 53, 56, 61–62, 66, 66n15, 69, 75, 87, 89, 102, 107, 115, 121, 127n63, 135n13
freedom, 4, 43, 48, 51, 60, 66n16, 74, 76, 98, 100, 103–4, 107, 115, 124, 130, 130n76, 136, 161, 161n5, 166n19

grace, 2, 7–8, 10, 14, 20, 25n3, 34, 36–38, 42–44, 47, 49, 52, 59–66, 73–74, 76, 80, 88, 93, 96, 99–100,

102–4, 106–7, 118, 122, 124n50, 129n72
Great Altar of Pergamum, 138–40, 140n28, 144
Greco-Roman imperial ideology, 131, 137–38, 140–41, 144–48, 150–54, 153n54

habitus, 69–72, 75, 70n24, 71n27
hope, 7–8, 15, 18, 23, 34–35, 65, 89, 121, 124, 149, 156
human condition, 9, 13–14, 19, 33, 100n16
human response and obligation, 4, 11–12, 21–25, 31, 34, 36, 47, 60–65, 62n5, 63n9, 70, 73–74, 73n29, 76, 93–96, 99, 101, 105–7, 110, 156, 164n15; agency, 10, 70, 73–76, 93–94, 96, 100, 101n17, 102, 105, 107, 109, 160n3, 163–66, 164n13, 164n14, 165n16, 166n20; obedience and disobedience, 9–10, 15–16, 22, 35–38, 60–61, 65, 68–69, 73–76, 86, 87n30, 89–90, 128, 141, 148, 152, 164, 165n16

individualism and individual humans, 4–7, 11–13, 14–17, 21–22, 24–26, 32–33, 39–40, 42–44, 47–48, 54–55, 57–58, 68, 72, 91, 93–97, 95n4, 97n7, 100–1, 105–6, 106n26, 116–17, 160–61, 161n5, 166n18, 166n20
Israel, 2, 15, 27–30, 28n7, 35, 46, 56, 59, 64, 88, 91, 97n8, 112, 131, 136, 137n17, 146, 148, 150–52, 161

Jew-gentile relationship, 19, 24, 27, 27n6, 31, 31n11, 34, 39, 42–45, 58, 64, 72, 89, 99, 144–47, 163
Judaism, 2, 31n11
judge, judgment, 4, 15, 16, 28–31, 60, 88, 99–100, 103, 106–8, 106n27, 110, 163; forensic, 7, 14n37, 36; God as, 4, 15, 30–31, 106n27, 163

justification, 2, 3n5, 6–10, 8n27, 18, 26–27, 27n6, 34; justify, 7–8, 8n27, 20, 27, 34, 64

Kingdom of God, 21–22, 34, 38, 72–73, 113–15, 117–18, 124, 129, 129n72; of heaven, 128

law, 1–2, 2n2, 3n5, 7, 12, 14–17, 19n42, 26, 29, 31–32, 35, 39, 42, 44, 52, 59–61, 67, 72, 77–78, 81, 84–90, 87n29, 93, 98–105, 100n17, 109–110, 161–62; insufficiency of, 1, 17–20, 32, 67, 71, 77, 86–87, 90, 98–100, 162; of life, 10, 16; observance of, 14–16, 29, 31, 58, 85–87, 90; role of, 2, 10, 14–15, 18–19; of the Spirit, 98, 100, 103, 110; works of, 17, 19, 45
liberation, 7, 18, 34, 45, 49, 57, 60, 98–100, 104–5, 107, 109–10, 115, 130n76, 134, 149, 166, 166n20
life, new, 43, 51, 60, 62, 65–66, 69, 71, 73–75, 100
love, divine, 8, 25, 25n3, 33, 111, 119, 122, 125–29, 127n61, 128n69, 148–49; human, 26, 50, 125, 127n61, 130, 164–65

mythology, 136, 144n33; mythological, 3, 19, 41; mythologize, 1, 13–14, 162, 162n8

narrative therapy, 107–10

participationism, 68, 93, 101–2, 104, 107, 155–56, 164, 164n14; in Adam, 9–10, 35, 37, 52, 54–57; in Christ, 9–10, 36–37, 44, 54–58, 60, 67, 75, 93, 103–5, 107, 122, 124, 130, 156, 161, 163; in the new age, 16, 38; in sin and death, 93, 101–2, 105
personal accountability, 12, 14, 17–18; culpability, 11–14, 18, 35, 99
plight, 13, 33, 33n14, 43, 98, 102

political philosophy and theology, 70, 113, 117, 129–32, 129n72, 134–35, 135n11, 137, 146

powers, cosmic and supernatural, 4–6, 6n21, 7, 13, 18–19, 21, 32, 43, 55, 59–60, 63, 68, 91, 95, 102, 117, 120–25, 129–30, 130n76, 161–62; of Death, 11, 13–14, 16–20, 19n42, 89, 91, 93, 98–102, 104, 107, 124n50, 162, 166n19; of Flesh, 6n21, 69, 75; of grace, 60, 62, 100, 127; of Holy Spirit, 114, 122n44, 129; of Sin, 13–14, 17–20, 19n42, 19n44, 32, 42–43, 45, 57, 59, 67, 77–78, 81, 86–91, 99–100, 103, 105, 107, 161–62, 163–65, 166n19
Priene inscription, 141
Psalms of lament, 81–88, 81n12, 82n17, 86n25, 86n27

Raphael, *Paul Preaching in Athens*, 158–60
redemption, 4, 26, 34, 46, 48, 56, 69, 104–7, 121, 123, 149, 154, 156, 157n1, 161n7, 164–65, 165n16, 166n20
Res Gestae, 141
resurrection of Christ, 9, 37–38, 60, 65–66, 68, 73–74, 127; of the body, 68–69; of the dead, 9–10, 27n6, 60, 66, 68, 73–74
revelation, 34n15, 46, 119, 127, 148, 154
righteousness, 2, 6, 8n27, 18, 21–24, 26–31, 29n8, 33–37, 59–60, 62, 67–69, 71–76, 83, 89, 100, 103, 105, 107, 115; of God, 2, 6–7, 17, 19, 29, 33–34, 34n15, 38; of Christ, 35–36
Romans: audience of, 80–81, 88, 90, 99–100, 102–4, 148–49, 153; occasions and aims of, 1–2, 147

salvation, 4–5, 7, 15–16, 22, 25n2, 26, 34–35, 37, 40, 44–45, 47, 50, 61–62,

73, 77, 80, 84–85, 89, 112, 115, 122–25, 151, 166; history, 39
shock doctrine, 132–37, 133n5

sin, 2, 3n5, 4n14, 9, 11–14, 17–20, 19n43, 19n44, 22, 27, 30–38, 31n11, 40, 43, 45, 47–49, 52–54, 56–57, 59–60, 64–65, 66n15, 66n16, 67–69, 71, 75–76, 77–78, 81, 86–91, 93–94, 96–105, 100n16, 104n23, 107, 109–10, 123–24, 124n50, 128, 130n76, 161–63, 162n8, 166n18; through Adam, 8, 11–15, 19n42, 35–37, 40, 43, 50, 52, 77, 100, 162, 166n18; power of, see "powers"; slavery to, see "slavery and captivity"
slavery and captivity, 7, 13, 40, 52, 60, 62–63, 62n5, 67–68, 73n29, 84, 99, 120, 123, 130n76, 140, 145, 154, 162; to God, 22, 62, 66n16, 75; to righteousness, 60–62, 67–68, 73, 75–76, 89; to Sin, 19n42, 32, 35, 37, 60, 66n15, 77–78, 81, 86–87, 89–90, 99–100, 103–4, 163
solution, 14, 18–19, 33, 33n14, 43, 104n23
Spirit, 5n15, 6n21, 27, 27n6, 45, 65–66, 69, 74, 87, 98, 100, 103–4, 106, 110, 114, 118, 121–22, 122n44, 129, 149–50, 152, 155–56, 164; of Christ, 118, 163–65, 166n18
suffering, 16, 23–26, 102, 108–10, 115, 119–20, 149

transgress, 12, 15, 17, 31, 35; transgression, 12, 17, 35, 43, 59, 100n16, 161n5
tsaddiq, tzedeqah, hitzdiq, 27–29

wickedness, 13, 16, 27–28, 30–31, 50, 82
wrath, 7, 9, 14n37, 16, 22, 31, 37–38, 82–83, 99

www.ingramcontent.com/pod-product-compliance
Lightning Source LLC
Chambersburg PA
CBHW021141240426
43661CB00075B/1732